SOCIAL CHANGE
in Urban America

SOCIAL CHANGE
in Urban America

Max Birnbaum and John Mogey
Boston University

with the assistance of
Mary Donahue   and   **James L. Spates**
Boston University   Hobart and William Smith Colleges

Harper & Row, Publishers
New York, Evanston, San Francisco, London

SOCIAL CHANGE IN URBAN AMERICA

Copyright © 1972 by Max Birnbaum and John Mogey

Standard Book Number: 06-040701-8

Library of Congress Catalog Card Number: 72-86365

To Morris Green and
the Joseph Fels Foundation

Contents

Preface

College teaching has long suffered from too great a reliance on the lecture and discussion method. The recent demands of students for "relevance" in method/content, however off-target they may have been at times, nevertheless have been largely justified. What has been most lacking in college teaching, especially, is some effort to combine knowledge, skill, and first-hand experience with the teaching-learning transaction. This collection of readings reflects a pioneer classroom effort by the authors to achieve precisely such a synthesis. The seminar, which the authors taught experimentally for six years at Boston University, provided an excellent laboratory to test in a reality context the appropriateness of the materials. This experimental seminar was supported in part by the Joseph Fels Foundation.

This volume is published simultaneously with a handbook compiled under the authors' direction by two former Boston University graduate students, Dr. James Spates and Mary Donahue of Hobart College and Boston University, respectively.

M. B.
J. M.

Preface

SOCIAL CHANGE
in Urban America

Introduction

This book proposes to advance an understanding of the dynamic and dramatic social changes that continue to transform the modern American city. Since the thirteenth century the city has been synonymous with freedom, culture, and much of what we deem civilization. When conservative spokesmen today seriously speak of the decline of large metropolitan units in the immediate future, it is thus not fantasy to foresee catastrophic consequences for the society as a whole.

It is difficult to ensure that any classroom reading matter on the city would have meaning and utility both for those who by residence or social class have not been part of the inner city and for those who have seen at first hand the realities of city life. The authors have kept this dilemma in mind and hope that this awareness is reflected in both the preparatory and the explanatory notes and also in the selections. They are aware, however, that those unfamiliar with city life may be shocked, while those from the inner city may consider the selections far from "telling it the way it is." This is one consequence of attempting a balance; such a two-fold objection may perhaps be the best testimonial to the fairness of this presentation.

The book assumes that its use will be within the context of a class that stresses experience-based learning, including the full involvement of all classroom resources, that of the instructors as well as the members. When any of these members has lived for a significant period of time in the inner city, his first-hand account, screened for bias, can be as meaningful as those produced by writers with second-hand knowledge of the condition described. Field experiences, whenever possible, should be a basic input to individual, small-group, and classroom learning. By field experiences we mean the preparation of a project to discover something about the inner city followed by the data collection, data analysis, and report writing stages that complete the experience. We do not claim that this field experience is research, although the procedures obviously derive from the standards and methods of professional researchers. In order, however, to free the students from being constrained by a finite set of ideas arising out of professional research, the student is provided with a handbook of suggestions for field experiences and not with a set of research propositions. Finally, field projects can become a shared group experience with practice in collaborative learning.

THE STRUCTURE OF THE BOOK

This work includes introductory material on the community with emphasis on the inner city, prefaces to each group of readings, the readings themselves, and bibliographies.[1] A separate handbook contains suggestions for library and field investigation, supplementary bibliography, and some frequently used data-gathering and evaluation procedures based on research models. The inner city is the type of community where changes have the most drastic consequences and also where the actions of the agents of social control are most visible. The social control agencies here emphasized are public, tax-supported bureaucracies of local, state, and federal governments. The quality of the relationships between these bureaucracies and their clients in the inner city community is the central focus of attention.

In this book, we point to concepts and show them in use. We believe the search for verbal definitions to be sadly unproductive. In a complex and changing social world, definition would be useful only if the terms used in the definition were exactly and precisely employed in all relevant contexts. Because the authors of the readings in this book are typical of the current babel of intellectual interests and social thought, they employ words and concepts in a wide variety of meanings. Thus, in place of solid single definitions of concepts, we are forced to favor a cafeteria of concepts used by the several authors.

The readings have been chosen in order to direct attention to urban social problems in all their complexity, rather than to focus on those problems that fit well-defined traditional, psychological, or sociological solution. The readings use a variety of social science concepts. These concepts cannot now be integrated into theories, for, to repeat, none of the social sciences has either a theory or a set of theories that can explain the phenomena of the current inner city. Because of this variety of concepts, the readings require careful attention; often the same word used by two authors can have very different meanings. This mixture mirrors the real world of political and intellectual debate rather than the simplified world of most textbooks.

Although we have not selected along the cleavages of disciplines, we have used two principles to reduce the potential material to order. First, within the vast field of metropolitan dynamics, this book concentrates on the inner city. Second, within the inner city, preference has been given to the major public agencies of social control and service, education, police, and welfare institutions and their inner-city clients.

To elaborate on the first principle, in the inner city are the major social tensions of American society most clearly seen. Signs of tension such as crime, drugs, disease, desertion of wife and children, delinquency, poverty, pollution, prostitution, shoddy goods, slum housing, unemployment, and vermin are par-

---

[1] A combined bibliography for the Introduction and Chapter 1 is included at the end of Chapter 1.

ticularly relevant to the inner city. Further, every substantial population center has its own inner city. The common pathology of social tensions at "the bottom" can be found even in small-town and semirural communities. Deviant behavior, although concentrated in some measure in the inner city, is not found there exclusively, nor, by the same token, is all inner-city behavior deviant.

The second principle of selection rests on the belief that if continuing action is to take place in our society, after community decision, one must depend on an official, permanently staffed bureaucracy. Actions against crime, child neglect, poverty, or ignorance must be continuous if they are to be effective. Consequently, we concentrate attention not on the problems as such but rather on the bureaucratic organizations responsible for executing decisions regarding social problems. Each tax-supported bureaucracy, however, not only tackles social problems but develops its own vested interests in them. This career interest of the bureaucrat adds a new dimension to complicate the solution of most social problems. For these reasons we have chosen to concentrate on three publically supported service bureaucracies that operate in all urban areas of the United States—education, police, and welfare.

Education, police, and welfare are not the only universal institutions; law courts, business, and the voluntary sector can all be found in every city. But most conflicts arise from the demands for social change served on the three public bureaucracies chosen for treatment in this volume.

CITIES IN CONTEMPORARY SOCIETY

A brief introduction to the contemporary city focuses on the most salient facts. Books in the bibliography and the readings give more detail.

Contemporary ways of life are now synonymous with urbanism. In 1910 the farm population of the United States was 35 percent of the total; by 1950 it was only 16 percent of a much larger population. By 1950 more than half of the population, 64 percent, lived in metropolitan areas with 50,000 or more people. In fact, one out of every dozen United States residents lived in the New York City metropolitan area. In 1960, 70 percent of the national population lived in metropolitan areas and by 1970 this figure reached 73.5 percent.[2]

There has been a large growth in the number of metropolitan areas in the United States, from 44 in 1900 with 30 percent of the population, to 216 in 1960 with 63 percent of the population, to 243 in 1970 with 69 percent of the total population.[3] The largest metropolitan area is New York-northeastern New Jersey, which had a population of 16,206,841 in 1970. The Los Angeles-Long

[2]United States Bureau of the Census, *Statistical Abstract of the United States: 1971*, 92 ed. Washington, D.C., 1971, p. 17.

[3]United States Bureau of the Census, *Statistical Abstract of the United States: 1971*, 92 ed. Washington, D.C., 1971, p. 18.

Beach area is the second largest with 8,351,266, and Chicago is in third place with 6,714,578. There are now 25 metropolitan areas with populations of one million or more people.[4]

Because cities set the pace for the generation of new ideas and the adoption of new life styles, they are the places where social changes, stresses, and strains acting on millions of individuals and families become visible through confrontations, strikes, demonstrations, vote upsets, and riots.

Since the establishment of the United States migrants have poured into the country. From 1820 to 1920 nearly 45 million immigrants came here. Most arrived at a city on the eastern seaboard, and many stayed in that city. Between 1820 and 1966, nine countries (Austria, Canada, England, Germany, Ireland, Italy, Mexico, Russia, Sweden) had each contributed more than 1 million immigrants. In 1950 the concentration of foreign-born whites was 16 percent in cities of 3 million and over. As the size of the city declined, so did the proportion of foreign-born, until it reached only 2 percent among the rural-farm population.

In 1950 the highest concentration of Negroes was in the rural-farm areas, principally in the Southern states. Since the arrest of foreign immigration by the laws of the 1920s, the greatest population change in America has been the movement of Negroes from the South to the cities. This movement began after 1945 but reached its peak after 1950. Between 1940 and 1949 about 30,000 a year moved north; between 1950 and 1959 about 100,000 a year moved from the South and the rate continued at 85,000 a year until 1966. These individuals abandoning the South came mainly to cities and added to the black population already there. Between 1950 and 1966, 98 percent of the Negro population growth took place in the metropolitan cities; today more than two-thirds of all Negroes living outside the South live in the 12 largest metropolitan centers (New York, Chicago, Los Angeles, Philadelphia, Detroit, Baltimore, Houston, Cleveland, Washington, D.C., St. Louis, Milwaukee, and San Francisco). In 1969 seven of these central cities were 30 percent black. The eighth, Washington, D.C., was 66 percent black. Each central city is surrounded by suburban cities that are almost exclusively white. The other 30- to 60-percent segment of the inner-city population consists largely of blue-collar workers, the sons and daughters of immigrants, together with their aged foreign-born parents and some downward mobile and unsuccessful groups of the native-born white population.

In 1966 a section of Boston was to be cleared for an Inner Belt roadway. These figures that follow are not for the city as a whole, but they do tell us what a swath cut across the inner section of a major metropolitan area met in the way of inhabitants. The roadway route cut across three subareas: (1) a high-density, middle-income zone of apartments (these are mostly white, either

[4]Alexander Uhl, "A Census Portrait of the 70s," *AFL-CIO American Federationist*, November 1971, p. 7. Metropolitan areas include at minimum a central city of 50,000 inhabitants and the dependent, immediately adjacent area; county lines define metropolitan areas or Standard Metropolitan Statistical Areas, as the Census refers to them, everywhere except in New England.

students or old people); (2) a high-density, lower-income mixed zone of tenements, with industrial, commercial, and hospital usage (these are black with significant numbers of Puerto Rican, Chinese, Syrian, Portuguese, and other recent immigrant groups); (3) a low-density, low-income zone of decaying frame houses mixed with stores, warehouses, and small craft shops (these households are mostly Irish, Italian, and Polish families that have remained as more affluent families moved to the suburbs). Just under 30 percent of the population of all three areas is nonwhite, as compared with about 5 percent for Boston as a whole. Some 17 percent of all dwellings are vacant, mostly because they are unfit for habitation. Of the householders, 91 percent rent their dwelling; 50 percent of them spend less than $100 a month for both rent and all utilities. Of the nonwhite households, two-thirds earn less than $100 a week; 38 percent of the white householders earn $100 a week or less. Despite these low incomes, only 6 percent of white and 22 percent of nonwhite householders receive money from public welfare.[5]

To this explosive ecology discerned from the patterns of residence, the pattern of occupation adds a potent force. Earlier immigrants entered a society changing rapidly from a farm-based economy to a factory-based one. Numerous jobs were available for unskilled and semiskilled workers in building factories, houses, railroads, and roads. The unskilled, rural blacks from the South poured into a postindustrial society that required many workers with skills demanding education and specialized training. Now, automation in factories and offices has reduced the number of openings available to black job seekers. The fact that education in their place of origin does not prepare them for work in an advanced industrial system creates a singular type of career disadvantage for Negroes. Another type of career disadvantage is racism.

> Negroes are handicapped by having poorer parents, less education, and inferior early career experience than whites. Yet, even if these handicaps are statistically controlled by asking, in effect, what the achievement on nonwhites would be if they had the same origins, the same education, and the same first jobs as whites, their occupational chances are still consistently inferior to those of whites. Thus being a Negro in the United States had independent disadvantageous consequences for several of the factors that directly affect occupational success. The cumulation of these distinct, though not unrelated, disadvantages created profound inequalities of occupational opportunities for the Negro American.[6]

This polite language about disadvantageous consequences means that blacks in the inner city are poor; many black children grow up lacking the bare essentials in food, clothes, and housing that go to satisfy an American.

[5]Commonwealth of Massachusetts, Department of Public Works, *Summary Relocation Report*, January 1967.

[6]P. M. Blau and O.D. Duncan, *The American Occupational Structure*, N.Y., Wiley, 1967, p. 209.

Over one-half of the 4.4 million nonwhites living in poverty in central cities in 1964 were children under 16.

One consequence of the disparity in the economic chances of Negro men and women is that men find it impossible to live up to either their own ideal image, or that of their partner, of what a husband and father should be as a provider and a steady presence around the home. So, many men leave home. The rate at which they leave their wives is directly related to the unemployment rate. From 1948 to 1962, as the black unemployment rate rose, so did the number of father-absent homes. A major reason for black mother-headed households may be not the seeking of welfare payments but the lack of employment that pays adequately for the man of the home to meet his expectations as a husband and father.

The disruption of the black family as a residential unit is further complicated by the social tensions of the inner-city community. Unemployment, together with family disorganization, creates a world of frightened, anxious, unhappy, frustrated, and aggressive individuals. Thus, the inner city is a "jungle" in which the inhabitants live in the world of social networks that often hurt rather than reward them. Because they lack power, they have no control over their areas and thus have no choice but to share their neighborhoods with prostitutes, alcoholics, dope addicts, and other undesirables. The table below gives a good measure of what it is like to live in such an area. From it the problems of social control encountered by policemen, schoolteachers, and welfare workers in the inner city can be imagined. The figures in the table below give evidence of social tensions and social change.

Measures of Social Disorganization*

	Juvenile Delinquency	Venereal Disease	A.D.C. Welfare	Public Welfare
New York	52	27	121	61
Inner-city neighborhoods				
Brownsville	125	61	459	266
East New York	99	21	149	72
Bedford Stuyvesant	115	77	337	197
Harlem	111	160	266	138
South Bronx	84	31	279	166

*Figures are rates per 1000 population in each area. Source: *U.S. Riot Commission Report*, p. 263.

"DIRTY WORKERS," SOCIAL CONTROL, AND SOCIAL CHANGE

Societies change when occupations change their meanings and begin to differentiate more sharply from each other. This tendency is known as professionalization—groups of workers in a specialized area organize to regulate training, to increase skills, and to control the license to practice. Before 1800, for example, the surgeon and the barber were looked upon as having the same level of skill. As a sense of profession grew, the barbers were firmly excluded from the practice of surgery. Similarly as industry grew, the new profession of engineering arose and divided into specialist groups such as civil engineering, mechanical engineering, chemical engineering, and production engineering.

Each society and each professional group develops ideas of prestige. In the legal profession, the Justice of the Supreme Court has reached the top of the scale. Now, if jobs are thought of as falling along a ladderlike scale, there must necessarily be jobs at the bottom of the ladder as well as jobs at the top. Both occupations perform essential services for their clients, but those at the bottom are considered as doing the "dirty work" of the profession. If a Supreme Court Judge is the top of the ladder, then a lawyer who guides and advises gamblers and racketeers is near the bottom.

The concept of "dirty work" applies within the three bureaucracies that operate in the inner city. The policeman with a beat in the ghetto has the least desirable job on the police force; the schoolteacher in a ghetto is not thought of as being at the top of her profession. "Dirty work" is a matter of the way a profession looks at the situations in which its personnel are operating.

Formerly, the "dirty workers" were physical laborers, as, for example, unskilled laborers who dug and shovelled in construction work, or garbage collectors. Today most of these unpleasant physical jobs have been mechanized. The new "dirty workers" now stand guard against that part of the population on the fringe of "respectable society." The old style "dirty worker" prevented society from being overwhelmed by the undesirable materials of mud, dirt, and garbage. In the modern inner city the policeman, the schoolteacher, and the welfare worker often exercise social control over those citizens who are the least desirable in the eyes of the society. Being placed in such a position, members of the three bureaucracies are self-conscious about their roles and their statuses. Beyond the status issue are the opportunities that abound for use or misuse of bureaucratic power. On the other hand, the spokesmen for the poor and the militant organizations that have arisen in the inner city now make the lives of these "dirty workers" very difficult. The professional bureaucrats bear the brunt of the rising expectations and dissatisfactions of the poor. This conflict between the "dirty workers" and their clients has changed the nature of bureaucratic power in the inner city drastically.

ORGANIZATION OF THE READINGS

The book presents readings on the topics that are central to an understanding of social change in the inner city. The first section, on the city as community and as bureaucracy, provides background to the other three, on education, police, and welfare. Each segment of readings includes three types of literature:

(1) a descriptive selection, using traditional concepts; (2) an article about an issue, or a case study; (3) a conceptual article, mainly theoretical. Thus in Chapter 1, the readings on the inner city run from *description*, "Anatomy of a Chicago Slum"; by way of issue, the Watts "Manifesto"; to a short *theory* of metropolitan structure, in "Urbanism as a Way of Life." To clarify our intent, we will indicate into which category the readings fall, bearing in mind that such categorization is necessarily arbitrary. For example, "The 'Rotten Apple' View of Man," which falls within the context of a series of descriptive excerpts about the police, is a definitely theoretical vignette.

The order we have chosen is deliberate and fits with our conception that experience is essential to learning. Thus, the description of an issue or problem begins with widely held assumptions; then, learning requires a discussion of these issues from a novel point of view. Finally, one task of the theorist is to take the concepts that delimit an aspect of the real world and to show that another set of concepts can lay bare the skeleton to reveal a familiar problem to be quite different when the rhetoric and assumptions of familiarity are removed.

1

The Community and Bureaucracy

COMMUNITY CONCEPTS

Most human interaction occurs in the arena of the community. Communities vary from one region to another and range widely in size within any one region. For a dynamic understanding of the explosive episodes that continue to surprise us, certain key concepts from social science lay a good foundation. "Anatomy of a Chicago Slum" describes one inner-city area. The concepts of locality, or territoriality, or neighborhood, together with ethnicity, provide a framework around which a pattern of meaning can be woven. In this way the random, unpredictable, and apparently threatening behavior of masses of unknown individuals comes to have some semblance of order, and the feeling of stability, that events are under a sort of control, is reasonable. With these social science concepts, some behavior in one Chicago slum becomes predictable.

The second selection, "The Watts 'Manifesto' and the McCone Report," warns that behavior may not always be predictable. This angry discussion of the report of an official inquiry shows the limitations of social science concepts. The black inhabitants of the inner cities have first-hand experience of these conditions, *but experience is not to be confused with understanding.* If experience always led to understanding, older people would always be wiser and better judges of events than younger people.

Louis Wirth in the third selection, "Urbanism as a Way of Life," stands well back from current events and tries to see the city as a whole, not simply at the inner city. His remarkably prophetic analysis rests on two basic concepts: (1) numbers of population with high density of settlement; and (2) heterogeneity of inhabitants. Using these broad concepts, he shows that impersonality, a sense of impotence or alienation, and the need for voluntary groups to express a point of view, can all be deduced as essential social elements of city life styles. The city gives rise to the need for formal organizations to exercise social control, since the density and various interests of its inhabitants rule out the possibility of person-to-person action in the defense of social goals of civility and order.

BUREAUCRACY CONCEPTS

Two descriptive pieces continue to give new detail of conditions of life, attitudes of residents, and the practices by which social control is maintained in the inner-city areas of the United States. The concepts of heterogeneity and density used by Louis Wirth become vividly extended in "Human Relations Among the Culturally Deprived." The second selection, "White Institutions and Black Rage," outlines the attitudes and images of discrimination in the means of access to jobs, housing, food, health, and social well-being. Three major channels for mobility—employers, storekeepers, and political workers—give their views of the inner-city client. The three major agencies of social control—the teachers, the policemen, and the public welfare workers—move cautiously in a world where neither their concepts nor their experience gives them the power to predict with certainty. These elements all move against a wider background of major changes in the power structure of the metropolis and the society.

To better understand the forces that shape the behavior of agents of social control and their clients, we reprint part of Max Weber's classic paper on the structures of modern bureaucratic agencies. The six rules for the organization of the agency are necessary, but to understand the varieties of response, additional rules that deal with agency dynamics are needed. The official, whether teacher, policeman, or social worker, is not a machine part, but moves within a web of social and human relationships. The dynamic aspects of each of these rules are taken up in later selections. The last selection for this chapter, "Social Control of Riots," applies concepts from social sciences to a critical understanding of modern riots to the problems faced by city government, and to agencies of social control in preventing these outbreaks in the coming decade.

Gerald D. Suttles

Anatomy of a Chicago slum

In its heyday, the Near West Side of Chicago was the stronghold of such men as Al (Scarface) Capone and Frank (The Enforcer) Nitti, and served as the kindergarten for several figures still active in the underworld. For convenience, I will call this part of Chicago the Addams area—after Jane Addams, who founded Hull House there. The name is artificial, since it is never used by the local residents.

The Addams area is one of the oldest slums in Chicago, and researchers have invaded it almost as often as new minority groups have. Like most slums, it remains something of a mystery. In some ways it is easiest to describe the neighborhood by describing how its residents deviate from the public standards of the wider community. The area has, for example, a high delinquency rate, numerous unwed mothers, and several adolescent "gangs." It is tempting to think that the residents are simply people suffering from cultural deprivation, unemployment, and a number of other urban ills. And if the residents insist upon the irrelevance of the standards of the wider community and the primacy of their own, this can be dismissed as sour grapes or an attempt to make of necessity a virtue.

Seen from the inside, however, Addams area residents require discipline and self-restraint in the same way as the wider community does. Conventional norms are not rejected but emphasized differently, or suspended for established reasons. The vast majority of the residents are quite conventional people. At the same time, those who remain in good standing are often exceptionally tolerant of and even encouraging to those who are "deviant."

Certainly the social practices of the residents are not just an inversion of those of the wider society, and the inhabitants would be outraged to hear as much. Nor is the neighborhood a cultural island with its own distinct and imported traditions. The area's internal structure features such commonplace distinctions as age, sex, territoriality, ethnicity, and personal identity. Taken out of context, many of the social arrangements of the Addams area may seem an illusory denial of the beliefs and values of the wider society. But actually

Reprinted in abridged form with permission from *Trans*-action, 1969, 4:16-25.

11

the residents are bent on ordering local relations because the beliefs and evaluations of the wider society do not provide adequate guidelines for conduct.

In anthropology, territorial grouping has been a subject of continued interest.
Most anthropological studies begin by focusing upon social groupings that can be
defined by their areal distribution. In turn, many of the social units singled out
for particular attention—the domestic unit, the homestead, the tribe, and so
forth—frequently have locality as one of their principles of organization. And
where locality and structural forms do not coincide, anthropologists have
regarded this discrepancy as a distinct problem that raises a number of theoretical and methodological issues.

The most obvious reason for focusing on locality groups is that their members
cannot simply ignore one another. People who routinely occupy the same place
must either develop a moral order that includes all those present or fall into conflict. And because almost all societies create a public morality that exceeds the
capabilities of some of its members, territorial groups are always faced with the
prospect of people whose public character does not warrant trust. In the United
States a very large percentage of our population fails to meet the public standards we set for measuring someone's merit, trustworthiness, and respectability.

Many groups have avoided compromising these ideals of public morality by
territorial segregation. More exactly, they have simply retreated and left valuable
portions of the inner city to those they distrust. Obviously, this practice has its
limits—it tends to aggregate those who are poor, unsuccessful, and disreputable
in the same slum neighborhoods. These people must compromise the ideals of
public morality or remain permanently estranged from one another.

In slum neighborhoods, territorial aggregation usually comes before any common social framework for assuring orderly relations. After all, ethnic invasion,
the encroachment of industry, and economic conditions constantly reshuffle
slum residents and relocate them around new neighbors. Since the residents lack
obvious grounds for assuming mutual trust, a combination of alternatives seems
to offer the most promising course.

Social relations can be restricted to only the safest ones. Families can withdraw to their households, where they see only close relatives. Segregation by age,
sex, and ethnicity are maneuvers that will prevent at least the most unfair and
most likely forms of conflict and exploitation. Remaining close to the household
cuts down on the range of anonymity and reduces the number of social relations. The general pattern, then, should be a fan-shaped spatial arrangement,
with women and children remaining close by the house while males move progressively outwards, depending on their age.

Slum residents can assuage at least some of their apprehensions by a close
inquiry into one another's personal character and past history. Communication,
then, should be of an intimate character and aimed toward producing personal
rather than formal relations. In turn, social relations will represent a sort of private compact in which particular loyalties replace impersonal standards of worth.

Neither of these patterns will immediately produce a comprehensive framework within which a large number of slum residents can safely negotiate with one another. The segregation by age, sex, and territorial groups, however, does provide a starting point from which face-to-face relations can grow and reach beyond each small territorial aggregation. The development of personal relations furnishes both a moral formula and a structural bridge between groups. Within each small, localized peer group, continuing face-to-face relations can eventually provide a personalistic order. Once these groups are established, a single personal relation between them can extend the range of such an order. Thus, with the acceptance of age-grading and territorial segregation, it becomes possible for slum neighborhoods to work out a moral order that includes most of their residents.

The Addams area actually consists of four different sections, each occupied predominantly by Negroes, Italians, Puerto Ricans, and Mexicans. And each of these sections falls into a somewhat different stage in its development of a provincial order.

Despite this difference and others, all four ethnic sections share many characteristics and seem headed along the same social progression. The overall pattern is one in which age, sex, ethnic, and territorial units are fitted together like building blocks to create a larger structure. I have termed this pattern "ordered segmentation" to indicate two related features: (1) the orderly relationship between groups; and (2) the order in which groups combine in instances of conflict and opposition. This ordered segmentation is not equally developed in all ethnic sections but, in skeletal outline, it is the common framework within which groups are being formed and social relations are being cultivated.

My own experiences within the Addams area and the presentation of this volume are heavily influenced by the ordered segmentation of the neighborhood. I took up residence in the area in the summer of 1963 and left a little fewer than three years later.

As I acquired friends and close informants, my own ethnicity became a serious problem. A few people worked over my genealogy trying to find some trace that would allot me to a known ethnic group. After close inquiry, one old Italian lady announced with peals of laughter, "Geraldo, you're just an American." She did not mean it as a compliment, and I remember being depressed. In the Addams area, being without ethnicity means there is no one you can appeal to or claim as your own.

Only after a year or more in the Addams area was I able to penetrate the private world of its families, street-corner groups, and insular establishments. These are the groupings within which Addams area residents are least cautious and most likely to expose themselves. In large part my experience with these groups is limited to many adolescent male street-corner groups and my own adult friends, who formed a group of this type.

By far the most striking contrast is between the Negro and the Italian sections.

For instance, almost all the Negroes live in public housing; the Italians usually control both their households and commercial establishments. The Negroes have very similar incomes and almost no political power; among the Italians, there *is* some internal differentiation of income and political power. Such differences draw the Italians and Negroes apart and generate radically different styles of life.

In most ways, the Puerto Rican section is the least complex of those in the Addams area. There are no more than 1100 Puerto Ricans in the section and, within broad age ranges, most of them know one another. Until 1965, no named groups had emerged among the Puerto Ricans.

The Mexicans are more numerous, and several named groups have developed among the teenagers. Unlike the Italians, however, the Mexican groups have not survived into adulthood. The Mexicans seem to have much in common with the Italians, and frequently their relationships are congenial. What gives the Mexicans pause is the occasional necessity to divide their loyalties between the Italians and the Negroes.

Although one must not overemphasize the extent of differences between all thse ethnic sections, such differences as do occur loom large in the Addams area. The residents are actively looking for differences among themselves. The ethnic sections in the area constitute basic guidelines from which the residents of each section can expect certain forms of reciprocity, and anticipate the dangers that may be in store elsewhere.

The portion of the Addams area now controlled by the Italians is only a residue from the encroachments of the three other ethnic groups. But in total land space, it is the largest of any controlled by a single ethnic group. In population, it is not exceptionally big, though, and throughout the section an unusually high percentage of Mexicans have been accepted by the Italians as neighbors.

What the Italians lack in numbers, they often make up for by their reputation for using sheer force and for easy access to "influence" or "connections." It is said, for example, that many of the Italians are "Outfit people," and that many more could rely on mobsters if they needed help. Also, it is the general view that the Italians control both the vice and patronage of the First Ward, a political unit that includes the spoils of the Loop—downtown Chicago.

There are some very famous Italians in the Addams area, and they frequently get a spread in the city newspapers. There are many others not nearly so prominent but whose personal histories are still known in the neighborhood. At least five Italian policemen live in the area, and a few more who grew up there are assigned to the local district. The other ethnic groups have not a single resident or ex-resident policeman among them. Most of the precinct captains are also Italian; and, outside the projects, the Italians dominate those jobs provided by public funds. There are a number of Italian businessmen, each of whom controls a few jobs. It is also widely believed that they can "sponsor" a person into many of the industries of the city—the newsstands in the Loop, the city parks, the beauty-culture industry, a large printing company, and a number of clothing firms.

While there is some substance to this belief in Italian power and influence, it is actually quite exaggerated. Many of the Italian political figures seem to have little more than the privilege of announcing decisions that have been made by others. In most of the recent political actions that have affected the area, they have remained mute and docile. When the Medical Center was built and then extended, they said nothing. The Congress and the Dan Ryan Expressways were constructed with the local politicians hardly taking notice. Finally, when the University of Illinois was located at Congress Circle, the politicians, mobsters, and—indeed—all the male residents accepted it without even a show of resistance. In fact, only a group of Italian and Mexican housewives took up arms and sought to save some remnant of the neighborhood.

The Italians' notoriety for being in the rackets and having recourse to strong-arm methods is also a considerable exaggeration, or at least a misinterpretation. The majority of the local Italians are perfectly respectable people and gain nothing from organized crime. Yet, many of the common family names of the area have been sullied by some flagrant past episode by a relative. And in the area, family histories remain a basis for judging individual members and are extended to include all persons who share the same name. In another neighborhood, this information might be lost or ignored as improper; in the Addams area, it is almost impossible to keep family secrets, and they are kept alive in the constant round of rumor and gossip.

The local Italians themselves contribute to their reputation—because on many occasions they find it advantageous to intimate that they have connections with the Outfit. For example, outsiders are often flattered to think they are in the confidence of someone who knows the underworld. Also, it is far more prestigious to have other people believe that one's background is buried in crime and violence than in public welfare. In America, organized crime has always received a certain respect, even when this respect had to be coerced. A recipient of public welfare is simply dismissed as unimportant. And during the Depression many of the Italians went on welfare.

"RIGHT PEOPLE" CAN PROTECT THEM

In addition, some of the Italians feel that a reputation of being in with the "right people" can in some circumstances ensure them against victimization. They often hint about their connections with the Outfit when facing the members of another ethnic group under uncertain odds, or when in an argument among themselves. Yet with friends and relatives, the Italians often complain bitterly of how they are maligned by the press and their neighbors.

Ironically, the Italians are cautious in their dealings with one another; more than any other group, they are intimidated by the half-myth that is partly of their own creation. And indirectly this myth gives them considerable cohesion, and a certain freedom from the judgments and actions of the wider society. It is almost impossible to persuade one of them to make a complaint to the police, for instance, because of their fear of the Outfit; indeed, they shun all public sources of social control. They handle grievances, contracts, and exchanges in a very informal manner, usually limited to the immediate parties. If in need, they exact aid in the form of favors and generally ignore sources available to the general public. As a result, the Italians have been able to sustain among themselves the image of an independent, powerful, and self-confident people.

BEHIND THE SCENES BARGAINING

Yet the cohesion and solidarity of the Italians are very limited. They are based primarily on the suspicion that social arrangements are best made by private settlements. This suspicion, in turn, is based on the assumption that recourse to public means can do little more than excite retaliation and vengeance. These same suspicions and doubts undermine the possibilities of a unified and explicit stance by the Italians toward the wider community and political organization. First, very few of them believe that the others will cooperate in joint efforts unless it is to their personal advantage or they are under some dire threat. Second, the Italians simply fear that a united public stand will elicit a similar posture on the part of their adversaries and eliminate the opportunity for private negotiations. Accordingly, the Italians either shun public confrontations or slowly draw away, once so engaged. In retrospect, the spirit of *omerta* seems ineffectual when it confronts the explicit efforts of the wider community. (Literally, *omerta* means a conspiracy between thieves. The Italians use it to mean any private agreement that cannot be safely broached before the general public.)

The inability of the Italians to accept or engage in public appeals leaves them somewhat bewildered by the Negroes' civil-rights movement. By the Italians' standards, the Negroes are "making a federal case" out of something that should be handled by private agreement. Indeed, even those who accept the justice of the Negroes' cause remain perplexed by the Negroes' failure to approach *them* in some informal manner. Throughout the summer of 1964, when demonstrators were most active, the Italians always seemed aggrieved and surprised that the Negroes would "pull such a trick" without warning. The Negroes took this view as a "sham" and felt that the Italians had ample reason to anticipate their demands. To the Italians this was not the point. Of course, they knew that the Negroes had many long-standing demands and desires. What struck the Italians as unfair about the Negroes' demonstrations was their tactics: sudden public confrontations, without any chance for either side to retreat or compromise with grace.

Ultimately, both the Italians and Negroes did take their differences behind closed doors, and each settled for something less than their public demands. The main bone of contention was a local swimming pool dominated by the Italians and their Mexican guests.

In the background, of course, was the oppressive belief that the benefits of social life make up a fixed quantity and are already being used to the maximum. Thus, even the most liberal Italians assume that any gain to the Negroes must be their loss. On their own part, the Negroes make the same assumption and see no reason why the Italians should give way without a fight. Thus, whatever good intentions exist on either side are overruled by the seeming impracticality or lack of realism.

The Italians' career in the Addams area has been shaped by a traditional world view that relies heavily on a belief in "natural man." For example, it is felt to be "natural" for men to be sexual predators; for mothers to love their children, regardless of what their children do; for girls to connive at marriage; for boys to hate school; for a businessman to cheat strangers; and for anyone to choose pleasure in preference to discipline and duty. Implicit in the concept of natural man is the conviction that moral restraints have little real power in a situation in which they contradict man's natural impulses. Civilization is a mere gloss to hide man's true nature.

Often, although not always, man's natural impulses are at odds with his moral standards. Indeed, otherwise there would be no need for the church, the police, the government, and all other bodies of social control. But it is not always possible for these external bodies of social control to keep track of what people are doing. Inevitably, then, there will be occasions when people are free to choose between acting naturally and acting morally. For their own part, the Italians may have considerable conviction of their personal preferences for morality. In their dealings with other people, however, they have little faith in this thin thread of individual morality. Correspondingly, to them their own personal morality becomes utterly impractical and must be replaced by whatever amoral expedient seems necessary for self-defense.

The general outcome seems to be an overwhelming distrust of impersonal or "voluntary" relationships. The other side of the coin is an equally strong tendency to fall back on those relationships and identities where one's own welfare is guaranteed by "natural inclinations." For the most part these are kin relations, close friendship, common regional origins *(paesani)*, joint residential unity, and sacred pledges like marriage, God, parenthood, etc. Thus, the Italians in the Addams area have tended to turn in upon themselves and become a provincial moral world.

Actually, many of the Italians are quite "Americanized." Frequently, though, these people lead something of a double life. During the daytime they leave the neighborhood and do their work without much thought of their ethnicity. When they come home in the evening, they are obliged to reassume their old world identity. This need not be so much a matter of taste as necessity. Other people are likely to already know their ethnicity, and evasions are likely to be interpreted as acts of snobbery or attempts at deception. Moreover, members of the other three ethnic groups refuse to accept such a person's Americanization, no matter how much it is stressed. To others, an attempt to minimize one's ethnicity is only a sly maneuver to escape responsibility for past wrongs or to gain admission into their confidence.

• • •

Finally, there are still many old-timers in the neighborhood, and it would be very ill-mannered to parade one's Americanism before them. Thus, within the bounds of the local neighborhood, an Italian who plays at being an "American" runs the risk of being taken as a snob, phony, opportunist, coward, or fink.

Among the Italians themselves, notions of ethnicity are particularly well-elaborated. For the most part, these internal subdivisions are based on regional origins in Italy. By contrast, the other ethnic groups have very little internal differentiation. The Negroes make only a vague distinction between those raised in the South and those raised in the North. Among the former, Mississippians are sometimes singled out for special contempt. However, none of these divisions leads to cohesive social unities. But among the Italians their *paesani* (regional origins) take on great importance, and it remains the first perimeter beyond the family within which they look for aid or feel themselves in safe hands. Most *paesani* continue to hold their annual summer picnics and winter dance. Some have grown into full-scale organizations with elected officers, insurance plans, burial funds, and regular poker sessions.

Of all the ethnic groups in the Addams area, the Italians still have the richest ceremonial life. Aside from the annual *paesani* dances and picnics, there are parades, *feste*, and several other occasions. In the summer, their church holds a carnival that duplicates much of the Italian *feste*. On Columbus Day there is a great parade in the Loop, exceeded in grandeur only by the one held by the Irish on St. Patrick's Day. During Lent there are several special religious events and afterwards a round of dances, parties, and feasts. Throughout the summer a local brass band periodically marches through the streets playing arias from Puccini and Verdi. Sidewalk vendors sell Italian lemonade, sausages, and beef sandwiches. Horsedrawn carts go about selling grapes during the fall winemaking season, tomatoes when they are ready to be turned to paste, and fruit and vegetables at almost any time of the year.

COMMUNAL CEREMONIES AND FESTIVITIES

Even weddings, communions, funerals, and wakes maintain some of their communal nature. Weddings are usually known of beforehand and often attract a number of onlookers as well as those invited. Afterwards the couple and their friends drive around the neighborhood in decorated cars, honking their horns at one another and whoever they recognize on the streets. Parochial-school children usually receive first communion as a group and attract a good deal of attention. Wakes are also open to almost anyone, and funeral processions often tour a portion of the neighborhood. On this sort of occasion, the Mexicans follow much the same practice, although they lack full control of a local church where they can carry out these affairs to the same extent as the Italians. Among the Negroes and Puerto Ricans, weddings, funerals, and religious events tend to be quite private affairs open through invitation alone.

The Italians are also favored by the relatively long period over which many of them have been able to know one another and to decide upon whom they can or cannot trust. Over time, a considerable amount of information has been accumulated on many people, and this circulates in such a way as to be available to even a fairly recent resident. Moreover, the intertwining of social relations has become so extensive that contact with one person often opens passage to many others. In this sense, "getting acquainted" is almost unavoidable for a new resident.

The forms of social organization in the Italian section are far more extensive and complicated than those of the other ethnic groups. At the top are two groups, the "West Side Bloc" and the "Outfit," which share membership and whose participants are not all from the Addams area. The West Side Bloc is a group of Italian politicians whose constituency is much larger than the Addams area but which includes a definite wing in the area. Generally its members are assumed to belong to or to have connections with the Outfit. A good deal of power is attributed to them within the local neighborhood, city, state, and nation. The Outfit, more widely known as the Syndicate, includes many more people, but it is also assumed to reach beyond the Addams area. Locally, it is usually taken to include almost anyone who runs a tavern or a liquor store, or who relies on state licensing or city employment. A few other businessmen and local toughs are accredited with membership because of their notorious immunity to law enforcement or their reputed control of "favors."

Indirectly, the Outfit extends to a number of adult social-athletic clubs (s.a.c.'s). These clubs invariably have a storefront where the members spend their time in casual conversation or drink, or play cards. A few of their members belong to the Outfit, and a couple of these clubs are said to have a "regular game" for big stakes. Each group is fairly homogeneous in age, but collectively the groups range between the late 20's up to the late 60's.

Below these adult s.a.c.'s are a number of other s.a.c.'s that also have a clubhouse, but whose members are much younger. As a rule, they are somewhat beyond school age, but only a few are married, and practically none have children. To some degree, they are still involved in the extrafamilial life that occupies teenagers. Occasionally they have dances, socials, and impromptu parties. On weekends they still roam around together, attending "socials" sponsored by other groups, looking for girls or for some kind of "action." Within each young man's s.a.c., the members' ages cover a narrow range. Together, all the groups range between about 19 and the late 20's. They form a distinct and well-recognized age grade in the neighborhood because of their continuing involvement in those cross-sexual and recreational activities open to unmarried males.

Nevertheless, these young men's s.a.c.'s are somewhat outside the full round of activities that throw teenagers together. A good portion of their time is spent inside their clubhouse out of sight of their rivals or most bodies of social control. Most members are in their 20's and are able to openly enjoy routine forms of entertainment or excitement that the wider community provides and accepts. When they have a dance or party, it is usually restricted to those whom they invite. Being out of school, they are not forced each day to confront persons from beyond their neighborhood. Since many of them have cars, they need not trespass too much on someone else's domain.

These s.a.c.'s are not assumed to have any active role in the Outfit. At most, it is expected that they might be able to gain a few exemptions from law enforcement and an occasional "favor," e.g., a job, a chance to run an illegal errand, a small loan, someone to sign for their clubhouse charter (required by law), and the purchase of stolen goods or of anything else the boys happen to have on hand. It is assumed that they could solicit help from the Outfit if they got into trouble with another group, but very rarely are they drawn into this type of conflict. Almost invariably the opponent is a much younger "street group" that has encroached on what the s.a.c. considers its "rights"—e.g., tried to "crash" one of their parties, insulted them on the streets, made noise nearby, or marked up their clubhouse. Even at these times, their actions seem designed to do little more than rid themselves of a temporary nuisance. Once rid of their tormentors, they usually do not pursue the issue further, and for good reason. To charter such a club requires three cosigners, and these people may withdraw their support if the group becomes too rowdy. Also, they have a landlord to contend with, and he can throw them out for the same reason. Finally, they cannot afford to make too many enemies; they have a piece of property, and it would be only too easy for their adversaries to get back at them. Unlike all the groups described in the other three sections. they have a stake in maintaining something like law and order.

All the remaining Italian groups include members who are of high-school age. While they too call themselves s.a.c.'s, none of them has a storefront. All of them do have an established "hangout," and they correspond to the usual image of a street-corner group.

While the street groups in this section of the area often express admiration for the adult s.a.c.'s, they seldom develop in an unbroken sequence into a full-fledged adult s.a.c. Usually when they grow old enough to rent a storefront they change their name, acquire new members from groups that have been their rivals, and lose a few of their long-term members. Some groups disband entirely, and their members are redistributed among the newly formed s.a.c.'s. Of the 12 young men's and adult s.a.c.'s, only one is said to have maintained the same name from the time it was a street-corner group. Even in this case some members have been added and others lost. Together, then, the Italian street-corner groups make up the population from which future young men's s.a.c.'s are drawn, but only a few street-corner groups form the nucleus of an s.a.c.

Conceptually, the Italian street groups and the older s.a.c.'s form a single unity. In the eyes of the boys, they are somewhat like the steps between grammar school and college. While there may be dropouts, breaks, and amalgamations, they still make up a series of steps through which one can advance with increasing age. Thus, each street group tends to see the adult s.a.c.'s as essentially an older and more perfect version of itself. What may be just as important is their equally strong sense of history. Locally, many of the members in the street groups can trace their group's genealogy back through the Taylor Dukes, the 40 game, the Genna Brothers, and the Capone mob. Actually, there is no clear idea of the exact order of this descent line; some people include groups that others leave out. Moreover, there is no widespread agreement on which specific group is the current successor to this lineage. Nonetheless, there is agreement that the groups on Taylor Street have illustrious progenitors. On some occasions this heritage may be something of a burden, and on others a source of pride. In any case, it is unavoidable, and usually the Italian street group prefaces its own name with the term "Taylor". Among the younger groups this is omitted only when their name is an amalgam made up from a specific street corner or block. Only the adult s.a.c.'s regularly fail to acknowledge in their name the immediate territory within which they are situated.

DIRECT LINE OF SUCCESSION FROM THE OUTFIT

Since they see themselves in a direct line of succession to groups reputed to be associated with the Outfit, these street-corner groups might be expected to have a strong criminal orientation. In the Addams area, however, the Italian groups are best known for their fighting prowess, and their official police records show no concentration on the more utilitarian forms of crime. The fact is that, like the other adolescent groups in the area, the Italian boys are not really free to choose their own goals and identities. Territorial arrangements juxtapose them against similar groups manned by Negro and Mexican boys. If the Italian street-corner groups fail to define themselves as fighting groups, their peers in the other ethnic groups are certainly going to assume as much.

There is also considerable rivalry between Italian street-corner groups of roughly the same age. Commonly they suspect each other of using force to establish their precedence. In turn, each group seems to think it must at least put on a tough exterior to avoid being "pushed around." Privately there is a great deal of talk among them about the Outfit and about criminal activities, but it is academic in the sense that there is no strong evidence that their behavior follows suit.

It is interesting that the adult s.a.c.'s that actually have members in the rackets avoid any conspicuous claims about their criminal activities or fighting abilities. Their names, for example, are quite tame, while those of the street groups tend to be rather menacing. And their dances, leisuretime activities, and interrelationships are quite private and unpretentious. Unlike the street groups, they never wear clothing that identifies their group membership. The older men in the s.a.c.'s make no apparent attempt to establish a publicly-known hierarchy among themselves. Other people occasionally attribute more respect to one than another of them, but there seems to be little consensus on this. On their own part, the older groups seem to pay little attention to their relative standing and to be on fairly good terms. During my three years in the area, I never heard of them fighting among themselves.

Unlike the Negro and Mexican ethnic sections, there are no female counter-parts to the named Italian street-corner groups. A very few Italian girls belong to two Mexican girls' groups that "hung" in the Mexican section. This, in itself, was exceptional; almost always the minority members in a street group are from a lower-ranking ethnic group. The Italian girls, however, are under certain con-straints that may be lacking for those in the other ethnic groups. Naturally, their parents disapprove of such a blatant display of feminine unity. The Italian par-ents may gain stature by their power and precedence in comparison to the Negro and Mexican adults. Yet what seems far more significant is the general form that boy-girl relationships take among the Italians. On either side, the slightest hint of interest in the other sex is likely to be taken in the most serious way; as either a rank insult or a final commitment. Thus, any explicit alliance between a boys' and girls' group can be interpreted in only one of two ways: (1) all the girls are "laying" for the boys, or (2) they are seriously attached to each other. Neither side seems quite willing to betray so much and, thus, they avoid such explicit alliances.

This dilemma was quite evident on many occasions while I was observing the Italian boys and girls. The girls seemed extraordinarily coy when they were in a "safe" position—with their parents, in church, etc. When alone and on their own they became equally cautious and noncommittal. On public occasions, the boys seemed almost to ignore the girls and even to snub them. On Taylor Street, for instance, an Italian boys' group and an Italian girls' group used to hang about 10 feet from each other. Almost invariably they would stand with their backs to each other, although there were many furtive glances back and forth. During almost two years of observation, I never saw them talk. Later, I was surprised to learn that everyone in each group was quite well-known to the other. For either of them to have acknowledged the other's presence openly, however, would have been too forward. The boys are quite aware of this dilemma and complain that the girls are not free enough to be convenient companions. This, they say, is one reason why they have to go elsewhere to date someone. At the same time, they perpetuate the old system by automatically assuming that the slightest sign of interest by a girl makes her fair game. Out of self-defense, the girls are compelled to keep their distance. On private occasions, of couse, there are many Italian boys and girls who sneak off to enjoy what others might consider an entirely conventional boy-girl relationship (petting, necking). In public, though, they studiously ignore each other. Throughout my time in the area I never saw a young Italian couple hold hands or walk together on the sidewalk.

The Barracudas were the first Mexican street-corner group to emerge in the Italian section. They first became a named group in the spring of 1964, and all members were Mexican.

Once established, the Barracudas installed themselves in the northwest corner of Sheridan Park. Virtually every Italian street group in the area makes use of this park, and several have their hangout there. Other people in turn refer to the Italian groups collectively as "the guys from the Park." The park itself is partitioned into a finely graduated series of more or less private enclosures, with the most private hangout going to the reigning group and the least private to the weakest group. The northwest corner of the park is the most exposed of any portion, and this is where the Barracudas installed themselves. Even in this lowly spot, they were much resented by the other groups. To the Italians the Park was almost a sacred charge, and the Mexicans' intrusion was a ritual pollution. The Barracudas were harassed, ridiculed, and insulted. On their own part, they became belligerent and vaunted all sorts of outrageous claims about themselves. Soon the situation deteriorated and the Italian groups became extremely harsh with the Barracudas. Since the Barracudas were no match for even some of the younger Italian groups, they removed themselves to one member's house.

Their new hangout placed them in an anomalous position. Ethnically they were identified as a Mexican group. Yet they were located in a part of the area that had been conceded to the Puerto Ricans. And individually most of them continued to reside in the Italian section. The general result seems to have been that the Barracudas were isolated from any of the other group hierarchies and placed in opposition to every group in the area. Within a year every white group was their enemy, and the Negroes were not their friends. The Barracudas responded in kind and became even more truculent and boastful. More than any group in the area, they openly embraced the stance of a fighting group. They wrote their name all over the neighborhood and even on some of the other groups' hangouts. In the meantime, they made a clubhouse out of a lean-to adjacent to a building on Harrison Street. Inside they installed a shield on which they wrote "hate," "kill," and other violent words. Carrying a weapon became almost routine with them, and eventually they collected a small arsenal. In time they had several small-scale fights with both the Italians from the Park and the Mexicans around Polk and Laflin. In due course, they acquired so many enemies that they could hardly risk leaving the immediate area of their hangout. At the same time, some of them began to go to Eighteenth Street, where they had "connections"—relatives. This only brought them into conflict with other groups in this neighborhood. By the summer of 1965, the Barracudas were as isolated and resentful as ever.

"INCOGNITOS" AND THE "PICA PEOPLE"

There are two other groups in the Italian section, the Pica People and the Incognitos. The groups' names are themselves an expression of their isolation.

The Incognitos self-consciously avoided comparison with the other groups: They did not hang in the Park, hold socials, or become involved in any of the local sidewalk confrontations. About the same age as the Contenders, the Incognitos were notably different in their exclusion from the local round of praise and recriminations.

"Pica People" is a derisive name meant as an insult for five young men about 19 to 25 years of age. Although these five individuals associate regularly, they claim no group identity and become angry when called the Pica People. Unlike the Incognitos, the Pica People are well-known and often accused of some predatory display. They do not fight for group honor, but there is friction between them and all the other street-corner groups in the Addams area.

It was impossible to determine how these two groups came into existence. (I talked only twice with the Incognitos, who simply said they "grew up together." Local people started calling the Pica People by that name after a movie in which the "Pica People" were sub-humans. I knew some of the members of this group, but they became so angry at any mention of the name that I could not discuss it with them.) What is known of their composition may throw some light on why they were excluded from the structure of the other groups. All informants described the Incognitos as "good guys," still in school and no trouble to anyone. They were not considered college boys but, if asked, most informants said they thought some of them might go to college. Local youth agencies made no attempt to work with them, and the entire neighborhood seemed to feel they were not dangerous. Other street-corner groups in the Italian section did not look down on them, but they did exempt them from the ambitions that brought other groups into opposition.

The Pica People were just the opposite. All members were boastful of their alleged Outfit connections and their ability to intimidate other people. But the Pica People possessed so many personal flaws that they were rather useless to the Outfit. One member was slightly claustrophobic. Another was so weak that even much younger boys pushed him around. A third had an exceedingly unfortunate appearance. Under the circumstances, their pretensions became laughable.

EXTREMES OF STREET-CORNER GROUPS

The Incognitos and the Pica People seem to represent the extremes of a range in which the street-corner group is considered the normal adolescent gathering. Modest and well-behaved youngsters are excluded as exceptions, as are criminally inclined but unsuccessful young men. Both of these groups fell outside the range considered normal by the local residents and were thereby dissociated from the total group heirarchy.

The social context of the Italian street groups is somewhat different from that of the street groups in the other three ethnic sections. Among the Italians, the major share of coercive power still remains in adult hands. The wider community may not be very pleased with the form *their* power takes, but it is the only case where the corporate power of the adolescents is tempered by that of the adults. Also, since many of the same adults have an active role in distributing some of the benefits that are held in store by the wider community, their power is augmented. Perhaps the most obvious result of the adults' ascendency is that the adolescents do not simply dismiss them or adulthood as unimportant. A more immediate consequence is to give many of the adults the prerogative of exacting considerable obedience from the local adolescents. It is not all uncommon to see an Italian adult upbraid and humble one of the local youths. Not all adults have this privilege; but many do, and their example provides a distinct contrast to the other ethnic groups where similar efforts would be futile.

In the long run, the effectiveness of these coercive controls among the Italians may do little more than confirm their convictions that, outside of natural tendencies, there is no guarantee to moral conduct except economic and numerical strength. Within their own little world, however, such coercive measures constitute a fairly effective system of social control. Personal privacy and anonymity are almost impossible. In turn, each person's known or assumed connections dampen most chances at exploitation because of the fear of unknown consequences. Thus, the opportunities for immorality presented by transient relations and "fair game" are fairly rare. Within these limits, such an authoritarian system of social control will work. Outside their own section, of course, these conditions do not hold; and the Italian boys find themselves free to seize whatever advantages or opportunities present themselves. Among themselves, they are usually only a rowdy and boisterous crowd. With strangers or in other parts of the Addams area, they become particularly arrogant and unscrupulous.

With these qualifications, it appears that well-established adolescent street-corner groups are quite compatible with strong adult authority and influence. In fact, judging from the Italian section, these adolescent street-corner groups seem to be the building blocks out of which the older and more powerful groups have originated. The younger groups continue to replenish the older ones and help maintain the structure within which adults are shown deference.

Moreover, the total age-graded structure of groups in the Italian section relates youngsters to the wider society both instrumentally and conceptually. The Italian street groups see themselves as replacements in an age structure that becomes progressively less provincial. At the upper age level, groups even stop prefacing their name with the term "Taylor"; and a few of their members have a place in the wider society through the Outfit and West Side Bloc. The relationship between these age grades also provides a ladder down which favors and opportunities are distributed. The wider community may hesitate at accepting the legitimacy of these transactions, but they are mostly of a conventional form. The "Outfit" and the "West Side Bloc" have a strong interest in maintaining a degree of social order, and the sorts of wanton violence associated with gangs do not at all fit their taste.

IN CONCLUSION

The Addams area is probably a more orderly slum than many others, and it departs sharply from the common image of an atomized and unruly urban rabble. For all its historical uniqueness, the neighborhood does establish the possibility of a moral order within its population. The recurrence of the circumstances that led to its organization is as uncertain as the future of the Addams area itself. In spite of all these uncertainties, the Addams area shows that slum residents are intent upon finding a moral order and are sometimes successful in doing so.

Bayard Rustin

The Watts "Manifesto"
and the McCone Report

The riots in the Watts section of Los Angeles last August continued for six days, during which 34 persons were killed, 1,032 were injured, and some 3,952 were arrested. Viewed by many of the rioters themselves as their "manifesto," the uprising of the Watts Negroes brought out in the open, as no other aspect of the Negro protest has done, the despair and hatred that continue to brew in the Northern ghettoes depsite the civil-rights legislation of recent years and the advent of "the war on poverty." With national attention focused on Los Angeles, Governor Edward P. Brown created a commission of prominent local citizens, headed by John A. McCone, to investigate the causes of the riots and to prescribe remedies against any such outbreaks in the future. Just as the violent confrontation on the burning streets of Watts told us much about the underlying realities of race and class relations in America—summed up best, perhaps, by the words of Los Angeles Police Chief William Parker, "We're on top and they're on the bottom"—so does the McCone Report, published under the title *Violence in the City—An End or a Beginning?*, tell us much about the response of our political and economic institutions to the Watts "manifesto."

Like the much-discussed Moynihan Report, the McCone Report is a bold departure from the standard government paper on social problems. It goes beyond the mere recital of statistics to discuss, somewhat sympathetically, the real problems of the Watts community—problems like unemployment, inadequate schools, dilapidated housing—and it seems at first glance to be leading toward constructive programs. It never reaches them, however, for, again like the Monynihan Report, it is ambivalent about the basic reforms that are needed to solve these problems and therefore shies away from spelling them out too explicitly. Thus, while it calls for the creation of 50,000 new jobs to compensate for the "spiral of failure" that it finds among the Watts Negroes, the McCone Report does not tell us how these jobs are to be created or obtained and instead recommends existing programs which have already shown themselves to be inadequate.

Reprinted with permission from *Commentary*, March 1966: 29-35.

27

The Moynihan Report, similarly, by emphasizing the breakdown of the Negro family, also steers clear of confronting the thorny issues of Negro unemployment as such.

By appearing to provide new viewpoints and fresh initiatives while at the same time repeating, if in more sophisticated and compassionate terms, the standard white stereotypes and shibboleths about Negroes, the two reports have become controversial on both sides of the Negro question. On the one hand, civil-rights leaders can point to the recognition in these reports of the need for jobs and training, and for other economic and social programs to aid the Negro family, while conservatives can find confirmed in their pages the Negro penchant for violence, the excessive agitation against law and order by the civil-rights movement, or the high rates of crime and illegitimacy in the Negro community; on the other hand, both sides have criticized the reports for feeding ammunition to the opposition. Unfortunately, but inevitably, the emphasis on *Negro* behavior in both reports has stirred up an abstract debate over the interpretation of data rather than suggesting programs for dealing with the existing and very concrete situation in which American Negroes find themselves. For example, neither report is concerned about segregation and both tacitly assume that the Civil Rights Acts of 1964 and 1965 are already destroying this system. In the case of the McCone Report, this leaves the writers free to discuss the problems of Negro housing, education, and unemployment in great detail without attacking the conditions of de facto segregation that underly them.

The errors and misconceptions of the McCone Report are particularly revealing because it purports to deal with the realities of the Watts riots rather than with the abstractions of the Negro family. The first distortion of these realities occurs in the opening chapter—"The Crisis: An Overview"—where after briefly discussing the looting and beatings, the writers conclude that "The rioters seem to have been caught up in an insensate rage of destruction." Such an image may reflect the fear of the white community that Watts had run amok during six days in August, but it does not accurately describe the major motive and mood of the riots, as subsequent data in the report itself indicate. While it is true that Negroes in the past have often turned the violence inflicted on them by society in upon themselves—"insensate rage" would perhaps have been an appropriate phrase for the third day of the 1964 Harlem riots—the whole point of the outbreak in Watts was that it marked the first major rebellion of Negroes against their own masochism and was carried on with the express purpose of asserting that they would no longer quietly submit to the deprivation of slum life.

This message came home to me over and over again when I talked with the young people in Watts during and after the riots, as it will have come home to those who watched the various television documentaries in which the Negroes of the community were permitted to speak for themselves. At a street-corner meeting in Watts when the riots were over, an unemployed youth of about twenty said to me, "We won." I asked him: "How have you won? Homes have been destroyed, Negroes are lying dead in the streets, the stores from which you buy food and clothes are destroyed, and people are bringing you relief." His reply was significant: "We won because we made the whole world pay attention to us. The police chief never came here before; the mayor always stayed uptown. We made them come." Clearly it was no accident that the riots proceeded along an almost direct path to City Hall.

Nor was the violence along the way random and "insensate." Wherever a store-owner identified himself as a "poor working Negro trying to make a business" or as a "Blood Brother," the mob passed the store by. It even spared a few white businesses that allowed credit or time purchases, and it made a point of looting and destroying stores that were notorious for their high prices and hostile manners. The McCone Report itself observes that "the rioters concentrated on food markets, liquor stores, clothing stores, department stores, and pawn shops." The authors "note with interest that no residences were deliberately burned, that damage to schools, libraries, public buildings was minimal and that certain types of business establishments, notably service stations and automobile dealers, were for the most part unharmed." It is also worth noting that the rioters were much more inclined to destroy the stock of the liquor stores they broke into than to steal it, and that according to the McCone Report, "there is no evidence that the rioters made any attempt to steal narcotics from pharmacies . . . which were looted and burned."

This is hardly a description of a Negro community that has run amok. The largest number of arrests were for looting—not for arson or shooting. Most of the people involved were not habitual thieves; they were members of a deprived group who seized a chance to possess things that all the dinning affluence of Los Angeles had never given them. There were innumerable touching examples of this behavior. One married couple in their sixties was seen carrying a couch to their home, and when its weight became too much for them, they sat down and rested on it until they could pick it up again. Langston Hughes tells of another woman who was dragging a sofa through the streets and who stopped at each intersection and waited for the traffic light to turn green. A third woman went out with her children to get a kitchen set, and after bringing it home, she discovered they needed one more chair in order to feed the whole family together; they went back to get the chair and all of them were arrested.

If the McCone Report misses the point of the Watts riots, it shows even less understanding of their causes. To place these in perspective, the authors begin by reviewing the various outbursts in the Negro ghettoes since the summer of 1964 and quickly come up with the following explanations: "Not enough jobs to go around, and within this scarcity not enough by a wide margin of a character which the untrained Negro could fill . . . . Not enough schooling to meet the special needs of the disadvantaged Negro child whose environment from infancy onward places him under a serious handicap." Finally, "a resentment, even hatred, of the police as a symbol of authority."

For the members of the special commission these are the fundamental causes of the current Negro plight and protest, which are glibly summed up in the ensuing paragraph by the statement that "Many Negroes moved to the city in the last generation and are totally unprepared to meet the conditions of city life." I shall be discussing these "causes" in detail as we go along, but it should be noted here that the burden of responsibility has already been placed on these hapless migrants to the cities. There is not one word about the conditions, economic as well as social, that have pushed Negroes out of the rural areas; nor is there one word about whether the cities have been willing and able to meet the demand for jobs, adequate housing, proper schools. After all, one could as well say that it is the *cities* which have been "totally unprepared" to meet the "conditions of *Negro* life," but the moralistic bias of the McCone Report, involving as it does an emphasis on the decisions of men rather than the pressures of social forces, continually operates in the other direction.

The same failure of awareness is evident in the report's description of the Los Angeles situation (the Negro areas of Los Angeles "are not urban gems, neither are they slums," the Negro population "has exploded," etc.). The authors do concede that the Los Angeles transportation system is the "least adequate of any major city," but even here they fail to draw the full consequences of their findings. Good, cheap transportation is essential to a segregated working-class population in a big city. In Los Angeles a domestic worker, for example, must spend about $1.50 and 1½ to 2 hours to get a job that pays $6 or $7 a day. This both discourages efforts to find work and exacerbates the feeling of isolation.

A neighborhood such as Watts may seem beautiful when compared to much of Harlem (which, in turn, is an improvement over the Negro section of Mobile, Alabama)—but it is still a ghetto. The housing is run-down, public services are inferior, the listless penned-in atmosphere of segregation is oppressive. Absentee landlords are the rule, and most of the businesses are owned by whites; neglect and exploitation reign by day, and at night as one Watts Negro tersely put it, "There's just the cops and us."

The McCone Report, significantly, also ignores the political atmosphere of Los Angeles. It refers, for example, to the repeal in 1964 of the Rumford Act—the California fair-housing law—in these words: "In addition, many Negroes here felt and were encouraged to feel that they had been affronted by the passage of Proposition 14." Affronted, indeed! The largest state in the Union, by a three-to-one majority, abolishes one of its own laws against discrimination and Negroes are described as regarding this as they might the failure of a friend to keep an engagement. What they did feel—and without any need of encouragement—was that while the rest of the North was passing civil-rights laws and improving opportunities for Negroes, their own state and city were rushing to reinforce the barriers against them.

The McCone Report goes on to mention two other "aggravating events in the twelve months prior to the riot." One was the failure of the poverty program to "live up to [its] press notices," combined with reports of "controversy and bickering" in Los Angeles over administering the program. The second "aggravating event" is summed up by the report in these words:

> Throughout the nation unpunished violence and disobedience to law were widely reported, and almost daily there were exhortations here and elsewhere, to take the most extreme and illegal remedies to right a wide variety of wrongs, real and supposed.

It would be hard to frame a more insidiously equivocal statement of the Negro grievance concerning law enforcement during a period that included the release of the suspects in the murder of the three civil-rights workers in Mississippi, the failure to obtain convictions against the suspected murderers of Medgar Evers and Mrs. Violet Liuzzo, the Gilligan incident in New York, the murder of Reverend James Reeb, and the police violence in Selma, Alabama—to mention only a few of the more notorious cases. And surely it would have been more to the point to mention that throughout the nation Negro demonstrations have almost invariably been non-violent, and that the major influence on the Negro community of the civil-rights movement has been the strategy of discipline and dignity. Obsessed by the few prophets of violent resistance, the McCone Commission ignores the fact that never before has an American group sent so many people to jail or been so severely punished for trying to uphold the law of the land.

It is not stretching things too far to find a connection between these matters and the treatment of the controversy concerning the role of the Los Angeles police. The report goes into this question at great length, finally giving no credence to the charge that the police may have contributed to the spread of the riots through the use of excessive force. Yet this conclusion is arrived at not from the point of view of the Watts Negroes, but from that of the city officials and the police. Thus, the report informs us, in judicial hearings that were held on 32 of the 35 deaths which occurred, 26 were ruled justifiable homicides, but the report—which includes such details as the precise time Mayor Yorty called Police Chief Parker and when exactly the National Guard was summoned—never tells us what a "justifiable homicide" is considered to be. It tells us that "of the 35 killed, one was a fireman, one was a deputy sheriff, and one was a Long Beach policeman," but it does not tell us how many Negroes were killed or injured by police or National Guardsmen. (Harry Fleischman of the American Jewish Committee reports that the fireman was killed by a falling wall; the deputy sheriff, by another sheriff's bullet; and the policeman by another policeman's bullet.) We learn that of the 1,032 people reported injured, 90 were police officers, 36 were firemen, 10 were National Guardsman, 23 were from government agencies. To find out that about 85 per cent of the injured were Negroes, we have to do our own arithmetic. The report contains no information as to how many of these were victims of police force, but one can surmise from the general pattern of the riots that few could have been victims of Negro violence.

The report gives credence to Chief Parker's assertion that the rioters were the "criminal element in Watts" yet informs us that of the 3,438 adults arrested, 1,164 had only minor criminal records and 1,232 had never been arrested before. Moreover, such statistics are always misleading. Most Negroes, at one time or another, have been picked up and placed in jail. I myself have been arrested twice in Harlem on charges that had no basis in fact: once for trying to stop a police officer from arresting the wrong man; the second time for asking an officer who was throwing several young men into a paddy wagon what they had done. Both times I was charged with interfering with an arrest and kept overnight in jail until the judge recognized me and dismissed the charges. Most Negroes are not fortunate enough to be recognized by judges.

Having accepted Chief Parker's view of the riots, the report goes on to absolve him of the charge of discrimination: "Chief Parker's statements to us and collateral evidence, such as his fairness to Negro officers, are inconsistent with his having such an attitude ['deep hatred of Negroes']. Despite the depth of feeling against Chief Parker expressed to us by so many witnesses, he is recognized even by many of his vocal critics as a capable Chief who directs an efficient police force and serves well this entire community."

I am not going to stress the usual argument that the police habitually mistreat Negroes. Every Negro knows this. There is scarcely any black man, woman, or child in the land who at some point or other has not been mistreated by a policeman. (A young man in Watts said, "The riots will continue because I, as a Negro, am immediately considered to be a criminal by the police and, if I have a pretty woman with me, she is a tramp even if she is my wife or mother.") Police Chief Parker, however, goes beyond the usual bounds. He does not recognize that he is prejudiced, and being both naïve and zealous about law and order, he is given to a dangerous fanaticism. His reference to the Negro rioters as "monkeys," and his "top . . . and bottom" description of the riots, speak for themselves, and they could only have further enraged and encouraged the rioters. His insistence on dealing with the outbreak in Watts as though it were the random work of a "criminal element" threatened to lead the community, as Martin Luther King remarked after the meeting he and I had with Chief Parker, "into potential holocaust." Though Dr. King and I have had considerable experience in talking with public officials who do not understand the Negro community, our discussions with Chief Parker and Mayor Samuel Yorty left us completely nonplussed. They both denied, for example, that there was any prejudice in Los Angeles. When we pointed to the very heavy vote in the city for Proposition 14, they replied, "That's no indication of prejudice. That's personal choice." When I asked Chief Parker about his choice of language, he implied that this was the only language Negroes understood.

The impression of "blind intransigence and ignorance of the social forces involved" which Dr. King carried away from our meeting with Chief Parker is borne out by other indications. The cast of his political beliefs, for example, was evidenced during his appearance last May on the Manion Forum, one of the leading platforms of the radical right, in which (according to newspaper reports) he offered his "considered opinion that America today is in reality more than half pagan" and that "we have moved our form of government to a socialist form of government." Such opinions have a good deal of currency today within the Los Angeles police department. About a month before the riots, a leaflet describing Dr. King as a liar and a Communist was posted on the bulletin board of a Los Angeles police station, and only after the concerted efforts of various Negro organizations was this scurrilous pamphlet removed.

Certainly these were "aggravating factors" that the McCone Report should properly have mentioned. But what is more important to understand is that even if every policeman in every black ghetto behaved like an angel and were trained in the most progressive of police academies, the conflict would still exist. This is so because the ghetto is a place where Negroes do not want to be and are fighting to get out of. When someone with a billy club and a gun tells you to behave yourself amid these terrible circumstances, he becomes a zoo keeper, demanding of you, as one of "these monkeys" (to use Chief Parker's phrase), that you accept abhorrent conditions. He is brutalizing you by insisting that you tolerate what you cannot, and ought not, tolerate.

In its blithe ignorance of such feelings, the McCone Report offers as one of its principal suggestions that speakers be sent to Negro schools to teach the students that the police are their friends and that their interests are best served by respect for law and order. Such public-relations gimmicks, of course, are futile—it is hardly a lack of contact with the police that creates the problem. Nor, as I have suggested, is it only a matter of prejudice. The fact is that when Negroes are deprived of work, they resort to selling numbers, women, or dope to earn a living; they must gamble and work in poolrooms. And when the policeman upholds the law, he is depriving them of their livelihood. A clever criminal in the Negro ghettoes is not unlike a clever "operator" in the white business world, and so long as Negroes are denied legitimate opportunities, no exhortations to obey the rules of the society and to regard the police as friends will have any effect.

This is not to say that relations between the police and the Negroes of Watts could not be improved. Mayor Yorty and Police Chief Parker might have headed off a full-scale riot had they refrained from denouncing the Negro leaders and agreed to meet with them early on. Over and over again—to repeat the point with which we began—the rioters claimed that violence was the only way they could get these officials to listen to them. The McCone Commission, however, rejects the proposal for an independent police review board and instead recommends that the post of Inspector General be established—under the authority of the Chief of Police—to handle grievances.

The conditions of Negro life in Watts are not, of course, ignored by the McCone Report. Their basic structure is outlined in a section entitled "Dull,

Devastating Spiral of Failure." Here we find that the Negro's "homelife destroys incentive"; that he lacks "experience with words and ideas"; that he is "unready and unprepared" in school; and that, "unprepared and unready," he "*slips* into the ranks of the unemployed" (my italics).

I would say, *is shoved*. It is time that we began to understand this "dull, devastating spiral of failure" and that we stopped attributing it to this or that characteristic of Negro life. In 1940, Edward Wight Bakke described the effects of unemployment on family structure in terms of the following model: The jobless man no longer provides, credit runs out, the woman is forced to take a job; if relief then becomes necessary, the woman is regarded even more as the center of the family; the man is dependent on her, the children are bewildered, and the stability of the family is threatened and often shattered. Bakke's research dealt strictly with white families. The fact that Negro social scientists like E. Franklin Frazier and Kenneth Clark have shown that this pattern is typical among the Negro poor does not mean, then, that it stems from some inherent Negro trait or is the ineluctable product of Negro social history. If Negroes suffer more than others from the problems of family instability today, it is not because they are Negro but because they are so disproportionately unemployed, underemployed, and ill-paid.

Anyone looking for historical patterns would do well to consider the labor market for Negroes since the Emancipation. He will find that Negro men have consistently been denied the opportunity to enter the labor force in anything like proportionate numbers, have been concentrated in the unskilled and marginal labor and service occupations, and have generally required wartime emergencies to make any advances in employment, job quality, and security. Such advances are then largely wiped out when the economy slumps again.

In 1948, for example, the rates of Negro and white unemployment were roughly equal. During the next decade, however, Negro unemployment was consistently double that of whites, and among Negro teenagers it remained at the disastrously high figure which prevailed for the entire population during the Depression. It is true that the nation's improved economic performance in recent years has reduced the percentage of jobless Negroes from 12.6 percent, which it reached in 1958 (12.5 percent in 1961) to roughly 8.1 percent today. Despite this progress, the rate of Negro unemployment continues to be twice as high as white (8.13 percent as against 4.2 percent). In other words, job discrimination remains constant. These statistics, moreover, conceal the persistence of Negro youth unemployment: in 1961, 24.7 per cent of those Negro teenagers not in school were out of work and it is estimated that in 1966 this incredible rate will only decline to 23.2 per cent. What this figure tells us is that the rise in Negro employment has largely resulted from the calling of men with previous experience back to work. This is an ominous trend, for it is estimated that in the coming year, 20 percent of the new entrants into the labor force will be Negro (almost twice as high as the Negro percentage of the population). Approximately

half of these young Negroes will not have the equivalent of a high-school education and they will be competing in an economy in which the demand for skill
and training is increasing sharply.

Thus there is bound to be a further deterioration of the Negro's economic—
and hence social—position, despite the important political victories being
achieved by the civil-rights movement. For many young Negroes, who are learning that economic servitude can be as effective an instrument of discrimination
as racist laws, the new "freedom" has already become a bitter thing indeed. No
wonder that the men of Watts were incensed by reports that the poverty program was being obstructed in Los Angeles by administrative wrangling. (As I
write this, the New York *Times* reports that political rivalries and ambitions have
now virtually paralyzed the program in that area.)

How does the McCone Report propose to halt this "dull, devastating spiral of
failure"? First, through education—"our fundamental resource." The commission's analysis begins with a comparison of class size in white and Negro areas
(the latter are referred to throughout as "disadvantaged schools"). It immediately notes that classes in the disadvantaged schools are slightly smaller; on the
other hand, the more experienced teachers are likely to be found in the *non*-
disadvantaged areas, and there is tremendous overcrowding in the disadvantaged
schools because of double sessions. The buildings in the "disadvantaged areas are
in better repair"; on the other hand, there are "cafeterias in the advantaged
schools" but not in the disadvantaged schools, which also have no libraries. This
random balance sheet of "resources" shows no sense of priorities; moreover,
despite the alarming deficiencies it uncovers in the "disadvantaged schools," the
McCone Report, in consistent fashion, places its emphasis on the Negro child's
"deficiency in environmental experiences" and on "his homelife [which] all too
often fails to give him incentive. . . ."

The two major recommendations of the commission in this area will hardly
serve to correct the imbalances revealed. The first is that elementary and junior
high schools in the "disadvantaged areas" which have achievement levels substantially below the city average should be designated "Emergency Schools." In each
of these schools an emergency literacy program is to be established with a
maximum of 22 students in each class and an enlarged and supportive corps of
teachers. The second recommendation is to establish a permanent pre-school
program to help prepare three and four-year-old children to read and write.

W. T. Bassett, executive secretary of the Los Angeles AFL-CIO, has criticized
the report for its failure to deal with education and training for adolescents and
adults who are no longer in school. Another glaring omission is of a specific plan
to decrease school segregation. While most of us now agree that the major goal
of American education must be that of quality integrated schools, we cannot, as
even the report suggests, achieve the quality without at the same time moving
toward integration. The stated goal of the McCone Commission, however, is to
"reverse the trend of de facto segregation" by improving the quality of the

Negro schools; in short, separate but equal schools that do not disturb the existing social patterns which isolate the Negro child in his "disadvantaged areas."

That the commission's explicit concern for Negro problems falls short of its implicit concern for the status quo is also evident in its proposals for housing. It calls for the liberalization of credit and FHA-insured loans in "disadvantaged areas," the implementation of rehabilitation measures and other urban-renewal programs and, as its particular innovation, the creation of a "wide area data bank." Meanwhile it refuses to discuss, much less to criticize, the effect of Proposition 14 or to recommend a new fair-housing code. To protect the Negro against discrimination, the McCone Report supports the creation of a Commission on Human Relations, but does not present any proposals that would enable it to do more than collect information and conduct public-relations campaigns.

The most crucial section of the report is the one on employment and, not unexpectedly, it is also the most ignorant, unimaginative, and conservative—despite its dramatic recommendation that 50,000 new jobs be created. On the matter of youth unemployment, the report suggests that the existing federal projects initiate a series of "attitudinal training" programs to help young Negroes develop the necessary motivation to hold on to these new jobs which are to come from somewhere that the commission keeps secret. This is just another example of the commission's continued reliance on public relations, and of its preoccupation with the "dull, devastating spiral" of Negro failure. The truth of the matter is that Negro youths cannot change their attitudes until they see that they can get jobs. When what they see is unemployment and their Economic Opportunity programs being manipulated in behalf of politicians, their attitudes will remain realistically cynical.

Once again, let me try to cut through the obscurantism which has increasingly come to cloud this issue of Negro attitudes. I am on a committee which administers the Apprenticeship Training Program of the Workers Defense League. For many years the League had heard that there were not enough Negro applicants to fill the various openings for apprenticeship training and had also repeatedly been told by vocational-school counselors that Negro students could not pay attention to key subjects such as English and mathematics. The League began its own recruitment and placement program two years ago and now has more than 500 apprentice applicants on file. When, last fall, Local 28 of the Sheetmetal Workers Union—to take one example—announced that a new admission test for apprentices was to be given soon, the League contacted those applicants who had indicated an interest in sheetmetal work. The young men came to the office, filled out a 10-page application form, filed a ten-dollar fee, and returned it to the Local 28 office. Then, five nights a week for three weeks, they came to Harlem, in many cases from Brooklyn and Queens, to be tutored. Most of the young men showed up for all fifteen sessions, and scored well on the test. At their interviews they were poised and confident. Eleven of these men finally were admitted to a class of 33. The WDL doesn't attribute this success to a miraculous program; it merely knows that when young people are told that at the end of a given period of study those who perform well will obtain decent work, then their attitudes will be markedly different from those who are sent off to a work camp with vague promises.

To cut the cost of job training programs, the McCone Commission avers that compensation "should not be necessary for those trainees who are receiving welfare support." Earlier in the report the authors point out that welfare services tend to destroy family life by giving more money to a woman who lives alone; yet they have the audacity to ask that the practice of not allowing men who are on family relief to earn an additional income be maintained for young men who are working and being trained. How is a young man to be adequately motivated if he cannot feel that his work is meaningful and necessary? The McCone Report would have us say to him, "There, there, young man, we're going to keep you off the streets—just putter around doing this make-work." But the young man knows that he can collect welfare checks and also hustle on street corners to increase his earnings. A man's share of a welfare allotment is pitifully small, but more than that, he should be paid for his work; and if one is interested in his morale, he should not be treated as a charity case.

Continuing with the problem of employment, the report recommends that "there should immediately be developed in the affected area a job training and placement center through the combined efforts of Negroes, employers, labor unions and government." In the absence of actual jobs, this would mean merely setting up a new division, albeit voluntary, of the unemployment insurance program. "Federal and state governments should seek to insure through development of new facilities and additional means of communication that advantage is taken of government and private training programs and employment opportunities in our disadvantaged communities." Perhaps the only thing the Job Corps program doesn't lack is publicity: last summer it received ten times as many applications as it could handle. Nor can new types of information centers and questionnaires provide 50,000 new jobs. They may provide positions for social workers and vocational counselors, but very few of them will be unemployed Negroes.

The report goes on: "Legislation should be enacted requiring employers with more than 250 employees and all labor unions to report annually to the state Fair Employment Practices Commission, the racial composition of the work force and membership." But an FEP Commission that merely collects information and propaganda is powerless. And even with the fullest cooperation of labor and management to promote equality of opportunity, the fact remains that there are not enough jobs in the Los Angeles area to go around, even for those who are fortunate enough to be included in the retraining programs. As long as unions cannot find work for many of their own members, there is not much they can do to help unemployed Negroes. And the McCone Report places much of its hope in private enterprise, whose response so far has been meager. The highest estimate of the number of jobs given to Los Angeles Negroes since the Watts crisis is less than 1,000.

The Negro slums today are ghettoes of despair. In Watts, as elsewhere, there are the unemployable poor: the children, the aging, the permanently handicapped. No measure of employment or of economic growth will put an end to their misery, and only government programs can provide them with a decent way of life. The care of these people could be made a major area of job growth. Los Angeles officials could immediately train and put to work women and unemployed youths as school attendants, recreation counselors, practical nurses, and community workers. The federal government and the state of California could aid the people of Watts by beginning a massive public-works program to build needed housing, schools, hospitals, neighborhood centers, and transportation facilities; this, too, would create new jobs. In short, they could begin to develop the $100-billion freedom budget advocated by A. Philip Randolph.

Such proposals may seem impractical and even incredible. But what is truly impractical and incredible is that America, with its enormous wealth, has allowed Watts to become what it is and that a commission empowered to study this explosive situation should come up with answers that boil down to voluntary actions by business and labor, new public-relations campaigns for municipal agencies, and information-gathering for housing, fair-employment, and welfare departments. The Watts manifesto is a response to realities that the McCone Report is barely beginning to grasp. Like the liberal consensus which it embodies and reflects, the commission's imagination and political intelligence appear paralyzed by the hard facts of Negro deprivation it has unearthed, and it lacks the political will to demand that the vast resources of contemporary America be used to build a genuinely great society that will finally put an end to these deprivations. And what is most impractical and incredible of all is that we may very well continue to teach impoverished, segregated, and ignored Negroes that the only way they can get the ear of America is to rise up in violence.

Louis Wirth

Urbanism as
a way of life

The central problem of the sociologist of the city is to discover the forms of
social action and organization that typically emerge in relatively permanent,
compact settlements of large numbers of heterogeneous individuals. We must also
infer that urbanism will assume its most characteristic and extreme form in the
measure in which the conditions with which it is congruent are present. Thus the
larger, the more densely populated, and the more heterogeneous a community,
the more accentuated the characteristics associated with urbanism will be. It
should be recognized, however, that in the social world institutions and practices
may be accepted and continued for reasons other than those that originally
brought them into existence, and that accordingly the urban mode of life may
be perpetuated under conditions quite foreign to those necessary for its origin.
    Some justification may be in order for the choice of the principal terms com-
prising our definition of the city. The attempt has been made to make it as in-
clusive and at the same time as denotative as possible without loading it with
unnecessary assumptions. To say that large numbers are necessary to constitute a
city means, of course, large numbers in relation to a restricted area or high density of settlement. There are, nevertheless, good reasons for treating large numbers and density as separate factors, since each may be connected with significantly different social consequences. Similarly the need for adding heterogeneity
to numbers of population as a necessary and distinct criterion of urbanism might
be questioned, since we should expect the range of differences to increase with
numbers. In defense, it may be said that the city shows a kind and degree of
heterogeneity of population which cannot be wholly accounted for by the law
of large numbers or adequately represented by means of a normal distribution
curve. Since the population of the city does not reproduce itself, it must recruit
its migrants from other cities, the countryside, and—in this country until
recently—from other countries. The city has thus historically been the melting-
pot of races, peoples, and cultures, and a most favorable breeding-ground of new
biological and cultural hybrids. It has brought together people from the ends of

Reprinted in abridged form from *The American Journal of Sociology,* 1938, 44:9-14;
20-22, with permission of The University of Chicago Press. Footnotes omitted.

the earth *because* they are different and thus useful to one another, rather than because they are homogeneous and like-minded.

There are a number of sociological propositions concerning the relationship between (*a*) numbers of population, (*b*) density of settlement, (*c*) heterogeneity of inhabitants and group life, which can be formulated on the basis of observation and research.

SIZE OF THE POPULATION AGGREGATE

Ever since Aristotle's *Politics*, it has been recognized that increasing the number of inhabitants in a settlement beyond a certain limit will affect the relationships between them and the character of the city. Large numbers involve, as has been pointed out, a greater range of individual variation. Furthermore, the greater the number of individuals participating in a process of interaction, the greater is the *potential* differentiation between them. The personal traits, the occupations, the cultural life, and the ideas of the members of an urban community may, therefore, be expected to range between more widely separated poles than those of rural inhabitants.

That such variations should give rise to the spatial segregation of individuals according to color, ethnic heritage, economic and social status, tastes and preferences, may readily be inferred. The bonds of kinship, of neighborliness, and the sentiments arising out of living together for generations under a common folk tradition are likely to be absent or, at best, relatively weak in an aggregate the members of which have such diverse origins and backgrounds. Under such circumstances competition and formal control mechanisms furnish the substitutes for the bonds of solidarity that are relied upon to hold a folk society together.

Increase in the number of inhabitants of a community beyond a few hundred is bound to limit the possiblity of each member of the community knowing all the others personally. Max Weber, in recognizing the social significance of this fact, pointed out that from a sociological point of view large numbers of inhabitants and density of settlement mean that the personal mutual acquaintanceship between the inhabitants which ordinarily inheres in a neighborhood is lacking. The increase in numbers thus involves a changed character of the social relationships.

● ● ●

The multiplication of persons in a state of interaction under conditions which make their contact as full personalities impossible produces that segmentalization of human relationships which has sometimes been seized upon by students of the mental life of the cities as an explanation for the "schizoid" character of urban personality. This is not to say that the urban inhabitants have fewer acquaintances than rural inhabitants, for the reverse may actually be true; it means rather that in relation to the number of people whom they see and with whom they rub elbows in the course of daily life, they know a smaller proportion, and of these they have less intensive knowledge.

Characteristically, urbanites meet one another in highly segmented roles. They are, to be sure, dependent upon more people for the satisfactions of their life-needs than are rural people and thus are associated with a greater number of organized groups, but they are less dependent upon particular persons, and their dependence upon others is confined to a highly fractionalized aspect of the other's round of activity. This is essentially what is meant by saying that the city is characterized by secondary rather than primary contacts. The contacts of the city may indeed be face to face, but they are nevertheless impersonal, superficial, transitory, and segmental. The reserve, the indifference, and the blasé outlook which urbanites manifest in their relationships may thus be regarded as devices for immunizing themselves against the personal claims and expectations of others.

The superficiality, the anonymity, and the transitory character of urban-social relations make intelligible, also, the sophistication and the rationality generally ascribed to city-dwellers. Our acquaintances tend to stand in a relationship of utility to us in the sense that the role which each one plays in our life is overwhelmingly regarded as a means for the achievement of our own ends. Whereas, therefore, the individual gains, on the one hand, a certain degree of emancipation or freedom from the personal and emotional controls of intimate groups, he loses, on the other hand, the spontaneous self-expression, the morale, and the sense of participation that usually comes with living in an integrated society. This constitutes essentially the state of *anomie* or the social void to which Durkheim alludes in attempting to account for the various forms of social disorganization in technological society.

The segmental character and utilitarian accent of interpersonal relations in the city find their institutional expression in the proliferation of specialized tasks which we see in their most developed form in the professions. The operations of the pecuniary nexus leads to predatory relationships, which tend to obstruct the efficient functioning of the social order unless checked by professional codes and occupational etiquette. The premium put upon utility and efficiency suggests the adaptability of the corporate device for the organization of enterprises in which individuals can engage only in groups. The advantage that the corporation has over the individual entrepreneur and the partnership in the urban-industrial world derives not only from the possibility it affords of centralizing the resources of thousands of individuals or from the legal privilege of limited liability and perpetual succession, but from the fact that the corporation has no soul.

The specialization of individuals, particularly in their occupations, can proceed only, as Adam Smith pointed out, upon the basis of an enlarged market, which in turn accentuates the division of labor. This enlarged market is only in part supplied by the city's hinterland; in large measure it is found among the large numbers that the city itself contains. The dominance of the city over the surrounding hinterland becomes explicable in terms of the division of labor which urban life occasions and promotes. The extreme degree of interdependence and the unstable equilibrium of urban life are closely associated with the division of labor and the specialization of occupations. This interdependence and instability is increased by the tendency of each city to specialize in those functions in which it has the greatest advantage.

In a community composed of a larger number of individuals than can know one another intimately and can be assembled in one spot, it becomes necessary to communicate through indirect mediums and to articulate individual interests by a process of delegation. Typically in the city, interests are made effective through representation. The individual counts for little, but the voice of the representative is heard with a deference roughly proportional to the numbers for whom he speaks.

While this characterization of urbanism, in so far as it derives from large numbers, does not by any means exhaust the sociological inferences that might be drawn from our knowledge of the relationship of the size of a group to the characteristic behavior of the members, for the sake of brevity the assertions made may serve to exemplify the sort of propositions that might be developed. . . .

• • •

URBANISM AS A FORM OF SOCIAL ORGANIZATION

The distinctive features of the urban mode of life have often been described sociologically as consisting of the substitution of secondary for primary contacts, the weakening of bonds of kinship, and the declining social significance of the family, the disappearance of the neighborhood, and the undermining of the traditional basis of social solidarity. All these phenomena can be substantially verified through objective indices. Thus, for instance, the low and declining urban-reproduction rates suggest that the city is not conducive to the traditional type of family life, including the rearing of children and the maintenance of the home as the locus of a whole round of vital activities. The transfer of industrial, educational, and recreational activities to specialized institutions outside the home has deprived the family of some of its most characteristic historical functions. In cities mothers are more likely to be employed, lodgers are more frequently part of the household, marriage tends to be postponed, and the proportion of single and unattached people is greater. Families are smaller and more frequently without children than in the country. The family as a unit of social life is emancipated from the larger kinship group characteristic of the country, and the individual members pursue their own diverging interests in their vocational, educational, religious, recreational, and political life.

Such functions as the maintenance of health, the methods of alleviating the hardships associated with personal and social insecurity, the provisions for education, recreation, and cultural advancement have given rise to highly specialized institutions on a community-wide, statewide, or even national basis. The same factors which have brought about greater personal insecurity also underlie the wider contrasts between individuals to be found in the urban world. While the city has broken down the rigid caste lines of pre-industrial society, it has sharpened and differentiated income and status groups. Generally, a larger proportion of the adult-urban population is gainfully employed than is the case with the adult-rural population. The white-collar class, comprising those employed in trade, in clerical, and in professional work, are proportionately more numerous in large cities and in metropolitan centers and in smaller towns than in the country.

On the whole, the city discourages an economic life in which the individual in time of crisis has a basis of subsistence to fall back upon, and it discourages self-employment. While incomes of city people are on the average higher than those of country people, the cost of living seems to be higher in the larger cities. Home ownership involves greater burdens and is rarer. Rents are higher and absorb a larger proportion of the income. Although the urban-dweller has the benefit of many communal services, he spends a large proportion of his income for recreation and advancement and a smaller proportion for food. What the communal services do not furnish the urbanite must purchase, and there is virtually no human need which has remained unexploited by commercialism. Catering to thrills and furnishing means of escape from drudgery, monotony, and routine thus become one of the major functions of urban recreation, which at its best furnishes means for creative self-expression and spontaneous group association, but which more typically in the urban world results in passive spectatorism on the one hand, or sensational record-smashing feats on the other.

Being reduced to a stage of virtual impotence as an individual, the urbanite is bound to exert himself by joining with others of similar interest into organized groups to obtain his ends. This results in the enormous multiplication of voluntary organizations directed toward as great a variety of objectives as there are human needs and interests. While on the one hand the traditional ties of human association are weakened, urban existence involves a much greater degree of interdependence between man and man and a more complicated, fragile, and volatile form of mutual interrelations over many phases of which the individual as such can exert scarcely any control. Frequently there is only the most tenuous relationship between the economic position or other basic factors that determine the individual's existence in the urban world and the voluntary groups with which he is affiliated. While in a primitive and in a rural society it is generally possible to predict on the basis of a few known factors who will belong to what and who will associate with whom in almost every relationship of life, in the city we can only project the general pattern of group formation and affiliation, and this pattern will display many incongruities and contradictions.

Hugh H. Smythe
James A. Moss

Human relations
among the culturally deprived

The war on poverty is one of the most widely discussed items of the day. The difficulties and conflicts of interest that eddy around President Lyndon B. Johnson's economic opportunity effort, popularly known as the "antipoverty program," make news continuously. Yet most of this publicity is concerned with the political and power aspects rather than with the human element which forms its substance and which should be the truly important focus of attention. One of the grave errors made repeatedly in good goal-oriented programs such as the present one is that the programs are developed and initiated with good intent but without real comprehension of that which is to be improved. And good intentions are not enough, especially when one is dealing with something as basic and important, as emotional and sensitive as human beings who for generation after generation have lived under the pall of hopelessness and despair, of feeling unclean and unwanted, so that they come to accept a self-image of "I am nothing."

Much of this destructive nothingness configuration derives from an entrenched habit of concerned professions of not giving those most affected an opportunity to participate as an integral part of whatever is proposed or done to ameliorate the condition of the underprivileged. Some old line social service professionals are dedicated, but they also have developed rigid attitudes and opinions and tend to resist change and new ideas. For traditional social work philosophy has some of the archaic evangelical religious missionary coloration in that the professional feels he must *do for* those he serves rather than *work with* and let them help themselves. This is one reason why in the antipoverty program so much emphasis is placed on giving the poor of the depressed areas the opportunity to help solve their own problems. For they are the ones who know what it is like not to have their garbage picked up and to have landlords cheat them with high rents, school teachers ignore their children, the labor market shun them as unemployable, and public officials refuse to listen to their troubles. If we are to bring about some lasting fundamental changes in these people and their environs, then we need to know as much as we can about the atmosphere

Reprinted with permission from *Journal of Human Relations*, 1965, 13(4):524-537. Footnotes omitted.

in which they exist. Thus the purpose of this two-part analysis is to look at human relations, broadly conceived, among the culturally deprived, first at the cultural atmosphere existing in the depressed areas where the poor live, and second, to examine some of the other facets of life there which tend to make them "culturally deprived."

THE SOCIOLOGICAL ATMOSPHERE

The atmosphere of a locality can be either the spark that motivates and encourages one to move ahead towards a better life from the onset of birth, or it can be the crusher that kills the spirit and dooms a person to nonachievement from the start of human existence. The child of the depressed area is a child of the slums. The barriers that confront this youngster, that weight it down with millstones which dampen its ardor and choke off its drive to do things, are numerous and insinuating. They are ever-present, pervasive, and debilitating, destructive both to body and morale, generally degenerative. They both quietly and loudly flagellate those who reside in this type of neighborhood complex as long as they reside in it. It is a residential community not consonant with race, for all racial groups live there. It is a human habitat that has nothing to do with religion, for those of all faiths are found a part of the locale. It is a community in which ethnicity plays no favorites, for it is a conglomeration of cultural segments. In sum, it is a locality in which all kinds of people are forced to have to eke out a miserable existence and suffer the consequences that dull their lives, limit their life chances, and start them off as outcasts of society and with a handicap so tremendous that most of them never are able to overcome it.

The sociologist Zorbaugh vividly set forth the component-quality of this type of locale in his book *The Gold Coast and the Slums*:

> The common denominator of the slum is its submerged aspect and its detachment from the city as a whole. The slum is a bleak area of segregation of the sediment of society; an area of working mothers and children, of high rates of birth, infant mortality, illegitimacy, and death; an area of pawnshops and second-hand stores, of gangs, of "flops" where every bed is a vote.
>
> The life of the slum is lived almost entirely without the conventional world. Practically its only contacts with the conventional world are through the social agency and the law. The social agency is looked upon as a sort of legitimate graft whereby small incomes may be considerably supplemented; and the law, symbolized by the "copper," the "bull," the "flivver," and the "wagon" is to the dweller in the slum a source of interference and oppression, a cause of interrupted incomes, a natural enemy.

Obviously any complex so infected with both material and human qualities of this nature is characterized by a particular mood, and it is this tonal touch that plays such a significant role in the motivational pattern and aspirational aspect of depressed area inhabitants. This "feel" of the slum is as important for us to know as almost any other single thing about it. This emotional temper, this tonal color has been strikingly construed for us in word-pictures and brought into stark reality by Jacob Riis. His sensitive projection of such a community at the end of the last century conveyed a feeling then that is as true for current conditions as when he wrote it in the 1890's. Here he says

all the influences make for evil; because they are hot beds of the epidemics that carry death to rich and poor alike; the nurseries of pauperism and crime that fill our jails and police courts; that throw off a scum of . . . human wrecks to the . . . asylums and workhouses year by year; that turned out . . . beggars to prey upon our charities; that maintain a standing army of . . . tramps with all that implies; because, above all, they touch the family life with deadly moral contagion. This is their worst crime, inseparable from the system. . . .

Thus, this environment in which people must move about trying to relate with one another is a gloomy place and has been called by many names—a "blighted area," a "deteriorated neighborhood," the "gray area," "lower class neighborhood," or simply a "low income locality." But whatever it is called, the term carries meaning in both depth and scope that makes sense both to the literate and illiterate and tells them that it is a place characterized by certain sociological factors negative in impact upon the human personality and upon its social development. What are some of these sociological factors?

Those who are professionals concerned with the elimination of slums see the area as an unstable community, due not only to the type of traits already noted, but also because it is *an area of transition* within the over-all spatial environs. Competition for favorable sites by business, industry, and residents gives rise to a continuous process of change which affects the people who live in these insecure and shaky localities. Owners of land in them, realizing it is soon going to be put to different use, tend to neglect their property, allowing it to run down as they squeeze out the the maximum rental revenue. Thus the physical deterioration makes the area relatively unappealing as a residential area, except for those unable to afford any better. For this reason the depressed area has come to be *the home of those who cannot afford to live elsewhere*. Thus poverty and physical deterioration go hand in hand. It is a hole empty of "culture" and entertainment devices, except of the most lurid type. Here almost no intellectual and cultural institutions are found, and the "civic center" is notable for its total absence from such spots.

The depressed area is a focal point that fosters unconventional behavior, or at least tolerates it. It is *a social reservoir for the uprooted*, for there is a continual inflow of impoverished young and old from the South, from the mountains; they pour in from the rurals and exhausted farms, as wetbacks (itinerant farm laborers) from across the Rio Grande River, from the slum barrios of San Juan and other locales of the island of Puerto Rico. Here one finds an unhealthy quota of social misfits and pariahs, winos, other alcoholics, established prostitutes and new ones on the make, overt homesexuals, and hardened criminals. Thus, as expected it has the familiar facade of alliance between crime and politics, between crime and business, networks maintained by racketeers and other denizens of the underworld. It is a community of high adult and juvenile delinquency rates, and substantial problems of underachievement. It is a living space marked by a flexible tolerance of nonmarital sexual relationships and an abnormal rate of children born out of wedlock, hence a high rate of unwed mothers. It is true that the area may contain a segment of those from each of its total socioreligious-ethnic composition who adhere to the middle-class American image—educated, upward aspiring, good-livers. But the vast majority of the residents move about in a pattern of discrimination and deprivation well known to those who are hemmed in by slum walls. Hence, in spite of the few islands of positive community life and a partial sense of community cohesiveness, it is a locality whose outstanding features lean towards deterioration, stagnation, helplessness, waste, and hoplessness. The police are the enemy, the businessmen the exploiters; the welfare agency an easy way of making it [*sic*].

THE PEOPLE

Who exists within such a social framework? The slum area has been *a port of entry for millions* of impoverished and dispossessed migrants: Old World immigrants, Negroes from the South, uprooted village and farm folk, Mexican laborers from across the border, West Indians from the crowded Caribbean islands, some Cubans, Puerto Ricans, Japanese, Chinese, Indians, Filipinos, and smatterings of other Orientals from Asia. But there are others, too, who do not "fit" the dream pattern of the "normal individual" as society pictures that figment of the imagination. For the area is likely also to be inhabited by students, artists, "bohemians," and some intellectuals, all attracted there by its low rents and other factors such as anonymity due to density of population and lack of organized resistance to their coming in. This is also the residential abode or the hangout for those who thrive in a social climate that encourages and fosters the unconventional. Here is to be found organized groups of delinquents and criminals. All these are people who do not conform to the expected norm of middle-class behavior, or of their standards of propriety and respectability. They are, in a sense, the "nonpeople" of modern society.

Although it is clear that depressed areas contain people or "nonpeople" of every race, religion, ethnic strain in the United States, race is a potent factor in *the ghetto process* that encompasses the poor. Since 1950 the largest cities in America have continually been adding more color to their urban overtones. A faster increasing income for whites has enabled them to move up and out into the outlying, more pleasant suburbs. They left behind their well-used shelters for those in lower income brackets—Negroes, Puerto Ricans, Latin Americans, Orientals, and poorly educated whites and hillbillies. Thus Chicago has its well-known South Side for Negroes and West Side for semi-literate and illiterate poor whites from the mountains and rural countryside of the South. East Los Angeles is a Mexican area, while in San Antonio, Texas, they are wedged into the eastern part of the city, and Phoenix, Arizona, packs them into the rundown South Side. As for New York's East Harlem, Puerto Ricans have and continue to replace Italians, while upper Manhattan's world-famed Harlem is the jammed space for Negroes, although Bedford-Stuyvesant in a sister borough of Brooklyn is another rapidly filling black ghetto. A remnant of lower class Jews remain in the deteriorated houses of the lower East Side of New York, but the community is now more of a medley of Puerto Ricans, Negroes, and a few other peoples who also do not share fully in the goodies of America. The Chinatowns of San Francisco and New York are still crowded, unique tourist spots for these people, while other Asian-descents live in and around these depleted areas of habitation no longer desired by more affluent whites. Although poor southern whites, East Europeans, Italians, and the Irish are also ghetto tenants, their numbers are small in relation to the large nonwhite masses crushed into depressed areas. For it is the nonwhites who in every aspect of the society encounter difficulty and find real barriers to their efforts to break out of the oldest neighborhoods.

This is a familiar pattern revealing that *race difference is a prime indicator of a lower place* on the social and economic scale, and knowledge and awareness of it by the residents creates a setting for tension and trouble. For stereotypes have been developed to stamp these people as atypical to the WASP (white-Anglo-Saxon-Protestant) complex that creates the prototypes for all America as people who are "intelligent, industrious, materialistic, progressive, and ambitious." Opposed to this, the depressed area persons, especially the nonwhite groups, are pictured as "superstitious, lazy, dirty, ignorant, musical, violent, unambitious, and oversexed." These stereotypes still exist and influence negatively the possibilities of depressed area inhabitants moving into nonghetto residential areas. In addition, this is a personality-devastating thing to have to be born into or reared in, or in which to experience one's adolescence. For all the negativity inherent in these stereotypes and reflected in the racial tension that is ever present in these ghetto communities seeps into the consciousness of the depressed area child at a very early age. Thus the child of the blighted area soon recognizes that his shabby living space is a place where certain kinds of people are forced to live; but what is worse, they are looked down upon by the larger community. It matters not that the child may come to realize that most of those like himself who live in the shoddy surroundings are "forced" to live there by circumstances—they are poor, without work skills, unsophisticated as to how to get ahead in American society, ill-educated, and trapped by housing restrictions of one kind or another. What sears him the most is that he is branded, and he recognizes that his ethnicity or religion, but mainly his race and color set him apart as less good, as something inferior to the rest of the human community.

The result of this psychosocial factor of race, religion, and ethnicity is tragic.

A scene emerges from the depressed area in which poverty and the "cult of color" appear to infuse the area. Its over-all low socioeconomic condition impairs and impedes physical, educational, and economic improvement and forces many of its people to exist on levels below those necessary for the maintenance of human decency, leaving them ill-nourished, poorly housed, badly educated, and without adequate medical care. This color cult has been injurious to the personality of the masses, saddling them with a "self-hate" complex and a sense of impotence and inferiority which tend to destroy upward aspirations and to develop a feeling of imprisonment and of being unwanted, from which it is almost impossible to escape. They become angry about the discrimination by labor unions and industry that systematically prevent them from becoming members of crafts, from learning skills, and from attaining white-collar jobs. They become furious about the inadequacy of existing educational facilities and the neglect of the schools their children are compelled to attend. They resent the continuous portrayal of their locale as inherently an inferior neighborhood. The total atmosphere eventually is climaxed by the characteristic of bitterness over the high rents one must pay for only dilapidated housing in their segregated area, a bitterness which any moment may erupt into violence.

THE HOUSING

One residence in a slum area has much that is representative of nearly all shelter in a depressed community. Sometimes the essence of enclosures in which these "nonpeople" live can be conveyed more vividly by the writer of fiction than one can find in the bland, prosaicly written analytical treatises of social scientists on the subject:

> The Chester, a building standing next to a Broadway cake shop with cakes in the window that look as though they've been baked in a plastic factory. . . . [The manager of the Chester says] "I wouldn't live in this neighborhood any more if you gave me a penthouse free. This is shot, killed dead. These buildings are rat holes. You need a machine gun in your pocket after six o'clock."
> I had grown accustomed to the broken mailboxes where the names piled up like junked cars. The hallways that smelled of urine and pork. But I could never get accustomed to the fat lumbering rats with enlarged stomachs who looked as though they had just swallowed a baby whole.
> I knew the building from the face of Mrs. Owens, who smoked all brands. She had fifty families in the building, and she carried them like a woman going inter [into her] tenth month. The building had been taken over by operators. The great six and eight room apartments were demolished. The kitchens were turned into community kitchens with a padlock on the refrigerator. A coat of green paint buried the old plaster work. The rooms were filled with families on assistance paying $16.00 to $25.00 a week for a room. The view out of the windows was the Hudson River. But no one ever saw the

river. I never heard a single client mention the river. The Hudson just didn't exist. The operators of the building were two men who looked as though they had spent their childhood drowning their playmates. They wrote rent receipts the Supreme Court couldn't decipher. I'm sure that more care was taken of the garbage collected in New York than the people in that building. The building was massive. For me it was always toppling. I could see it falling into the river. The building had no life, no living people in it. Not a single person with a plan for tomorrow morning. And the children in the building raced through the corridors like wild horses going over a cliff.

From such a picture one gets the "feel," can smell the odors that issue forth from the dried dirt and decaying filth that strews the halls and clutters the corners of the soiled rooms. But housing in depressed areas varies, even though the place is a slum. In some places one will find that the "streets are almost completely unimproved, many dwellings will have pit privies for toilets, even running water may not be available." In another sector one may find "examples of what are called 'corrals,' in which up to twenty or thirty families share one pit privy and a single cold-water tap." There are sometimes shacks without inside plumbing. Some areas of "newer" housing have been ramshackle slums from the day they were constructed, and their undersized septic tanks in clay soil may have rendered the inside plumbing almost unusable. In still another slum many more of the dwellings can be seen to be dilapidated, without private toilet or bath; some places have no electricity; some are "shotgun" hovels—one, two, or three rooms one behind another.

Further along one may find this type of rundown neighborhood to be a place jammed with a "great number of hotels and rooming houses." And there is another type of habitation found in the slums, too, "furnished rooms or apartments," terms which are more legal definitions than practical ones, for the furniture "generally consists of a bed, a table, a few chairs, a few other odds and ends, all usually in poor condition"; and in these living quarters what helps to run them down is "all the sharing of cooking facilities and almost all the sharing of bath and toilet facilities." For these dwellings overcrowding is customary. There are always more persons than rooms, and some "brownstones," intended to house a single family, have been subdivided so that "they now house fifteen to twenty families," and there is "generally one bathroom to a floor," with three or more families to each floor. And the same thing has occurred in much larger multiple dwellings, formerly quite elegant with large apartments of six or more rooms, but they, too, have been cut up into "furnished rooms" with the kitchen now communal, or hotplates in each room. Thus half a dozen families may now occupy the space originally designed for one. The effects of such housing on people who must inhabit them—interpreting broadly to include the neighborhood surroundings in which these residences are located—have been well spelled out by one specialist:

The following effects may spring from poor housing: a perception of one's self that leads to pessimism and passivity, stress to which the individual cannot adapt, poor health, and and a state of dissatisfaction; pleasure in company but not in solitude, cynicism about people and organizations, a high degree of sexual stimulation without legitimate outlet, and difficulty in household management and child rearing; and relationships that tend to spread out in the neighborhood rather than deeply into the family. Most of these effects in turn place obstacles in the path of improving one's financial circumstances. Obstacles such as those presented by poor health or inability to train children are obvious. Those presented by having ties centered in one's neighborhood rather than in one's wife and children are less direct, but significant. Such a family, for example, is less likely to move if a better job requires it.

THE POOR

Thus these people are trapped in these shelters, for without "a better job" they remain poor. Now poverty can be defined in many ways, although income level has been the most common basis to make projections. But however different sources interpret the concept, the meaning and the impact of the term are all too clear and all too constant, no matter how it is defined. Those in poverty number in the millions, no matter whose criteria are used. For the United States some say that at least 40 percent of the people live in poverty or deprivation, with President Lyndon B. Johnson saying, in his Economic Report to Congress on January 20, 1964, that 35 million people live without hope, below minimum standards of decency. Poverty always means people who lack enough food, enough clothing, who have no bright tomorrow to wake up to—it means the hopeless ones whether they are a part of "the other America," or Mexicans who are "the children of Sanchez." All of them have traits in common the world over.

In general *the horizon of the poor is limited*, and they are provincial in outlook, people only partially integrated into national institutions. The poor are marked by a low level of education and literacy; characterized by much unemployment and underemployment, they rarely belong to labor unions, while politicians habitually use them as pawns in the political process. Living as marginal people in the heart of big cities, on the fringes of a community as a rural slum, or as distinctive pockets of poverty attached to middle-class suburbs, or as the low-paid dependents attached to large farms, ranches, and haciendas, they rarely are participants in such protective social security devices as medical care, old age benefits, maternity care programs. The poor are people who make limited use of such things as local hospitals, banks, department and other stores, museums, airports, railroad stations, and art galleries. Those who live in poverty the world over are occupationally the unskilled, and child labor is not uncommon among them, even in nations with laws prohibiting such exploitation.

Further, the poor are *people without savings,* are chronically without cash, short of food reserves in the home, and accustomed to pawning personal goods in order to have a moment with money. Everywhere they are victims of usurious rates through being forced to borrow small sums to help eke out their lives. Their crowded slum living quarters contain secondhand furniture, while used clothing covers their bodies. Privacy is something almost unknown to their way of life, while alcoholism is common, and dope addiction a part of the environment. There is resort to violence to settle disputes, real or imaginary, and child training involves violence as a teaching method with wife beating a part of the mores. Free union or "consensual" marriage is widely patterned, and early sex experience a part of growing up. Characteristically desertion of wives and children is in the culture, so mother-centered families are many in the social structure. Authoritarianism is the household mode, with family solidarity emphasized but an ideal rarely achieved.

People who live in poverty are people of the present; *they live for today,* for there is a sense of resignation and fatalism about them that arises from their understanding of the harsh realities of their very difficult and very real life situation. There is likely to be a belief in male superiority on the part of the frustrated men, while a martyr complex envelops the women. A high tolerance exists for psychological pathology of all kinds, while for the established order there is a mistrust of government, a hatred of the police, and an over-all pessimism which gives the culture of poverty a potential to be used in various kinds of movements against the existing social order. Some communities that wallow in poverty may contain all of these traits or only some of them, but in one way or another across the face of the earth people who are poor suffer from these qualities in varying degrees.

SOCIAL CLASS OF THE POOR

People burdened with such demarcated signs of deprivation of course are at the bottom of the human heap in any social hierarchy. In America the traditional myth is that we like to pretend we do not have social classes. And to those who say otherwise, the usual reply is that while it is true some citizens are better off than others, this is because of their drive, initiative, and individual capacity; that everyone has an equal chance to rise because ours is an "open society." We say that we do not stop people from rising by such artificial categories as serfdom, peonage, royalty, slavery, or caste. But more and more we are forced to face up to the facts, that any dispassionate assessment of life as lived in modern America reveals that we do have social classes; and if you are poor, you suffer and may slide all the way down to "skid row."

Being poor flattens you on the floor of the stratified social cake. Over-all class is something that puts people into categories ranging from top to bottom, and no one denies that this ranking has implications for what people do, where they live, how they think, their level of aspiration, and so on. For the person in the depressed area, lower social class is a reality in terms of things that can be concretized. "The typical lower class person," says one professional with much experience in slum neighborhoods in the United States, "has had less than eighth grade education, is employed as an unskilled or service worker, and lives in a family whose income per person is less than the minimum wage." From this and all that has been said previously, it is evident that people who are entrapped on the ground floor of society find themselves the products of a system in which their lower class status is a prime factor in controlling what happens to them and to the future of their children, with an outlook that is bleak and uninspiring. The slums are full of these low status people—individuals with few occupational skills, little education, and low incomes—a combination sure to chain them in their present places; and unless they can better themselves in almost all of them, the chances of moving out of their environment and up the ladder of human betterment are practically nonexistent. By definition, therefore, their position approaches that known as "outcast." The unhappy fact is that these people number in the millions all over the world.

And what are the characteristics of those so fated? One student says those lumped together on the lowest level of the social continuum are defined by a series of "focal concerns": *trouble*—getting into and staying out of it; *toughness*—physical prowess, masculinity, endurance, strength; *smartness*—being more clever than the other guy, duping the teacher, avoiding being duped by others; *excitement*—the search for thrills and stimulation, goading the authorities, participating in a rumble; *fate*—Lady Luck as reigning goddess and the shaper of your destiny; *autonomy*—"no one is going to boss me," and an overt expression of disdain and dislike for external control. One specialist adds to these qualitites low paid, unskilled, and irregular employment, while still another stresses an unstable family pattern and things related to what he calls "personal" instability. There is also one student who uses such things as the display and defense of masculinity; the core role of the peer group; the subordinate role of children, and a lack of interest in them as individuals; freedom for boys while girls are kept home-bound; separate social lives for men and women; vivid, actual, and anecdotal conversation; detachment from the job but concern with job security; a negative view of white-collar workers and employer superiors; a lack of trust of the "outside world"; a personalization of government and antagonism towards legal authority and government. All of these things overlap and cut across race, creed, color, religion, and ethnicity, and are pertinent to insight and understanding of the people for whom they serve as a canopy.

THE EFFECT OF CONGESTION

These characteristics are jelled into a spatial situation that allows little or no room for social breathing, for the underprivileged person lives usually in a high density of population. This common condition of overcrowding comes from putting too many people into buildings that are in neighborhoods that already have too many overpacked buildings without proper cleaning, maintenance, and repair services. Although some of the more privileged people in society also inhabit high density areas, there is a difference in their surroundings and in the quality of the abodes they inhabit from that of the jam-packed conditions peculiar to the slum. In the latter there is a lack of privacy, noise is generic all about, nuisance and violence are present and are likely to be multiplied and enhanced by the neighborhood density.

The things we have discussed so far reveal a bleak, bleary blot of people who are oppressed and who must continue to move about in types of human relationships and environments which are not conducive to uplift of the human spirit or improvement of one's material station in life. The world continues to change, and for the better, so some say; yet it appears that those who seem doomed to spend their life-span in the gloomy confines of depressed areas are receiving little benefit from the positive results of this change. New laws are passed, new inspiring moods are developed, the national spirit is recharged with promises of greater equality, abundance, and a sharing of the good things of life. Still the slum person continues to feel he is not touched by this program or the spirit which prompts it. What are some of the other factors responsible for this attitude and the difficulty now faced in trying to overcome it? In a subsequent section we shall try to deal with some of these factors, especially those related to social pathology and human variables of people who live in depressed areas.

David Boesel

Richard Berk   Bettye Eidson

W. Eugene Groves   Peter H. Rossi

White institutions and black rage

Five summers of black rebellion have made it clear that the United States is facing a crisis of proportions not seen since the Great Depression. And one of the root causes of this crisis, it has also become clear, is the performance of white institutions, especially those institutions in the ghetto. Some of these institutions—police and retail stores, for example—have done much to antagonize Negroes; others, such as welfare departments and black political organizations, have tried to help and have failed.

Why have these white institutions helped engender black rage? One way to find out might be to study the attitudes of the men working for them—to discover what their personnel think about the racial crisis itself, about their own responsibilities, about the work they are doing. Therefore, at the request of the National Advisory Commission on Civil Disorders (the riot commisssion), we at Johns Hopkins University visited 15 Northern cities and questioned men and women working for six different institutional groups: major employers, retail merchants, teachers, welfare workers, political workers (all Negro), and policemen. All of the people we questioned, except the employers, work right in the ghetto, and are rank-and-file employees—the cop on the beat, the social caseworker, and so on.

EMPLOYERS' SOCIAL RESPONSIBILITY

The "employers" we questioned were the managers or personnel officers of the ten institutions in each city that employed the most people, as well as an additional 20 managers or personnel officers of the next 100 institutions. As such, they represented the most economically progressive institutions in America. And in their employment policies we could see how some of America's dominant corporate institutions impinge on the everyday lives of urban Negroes.

Businessmen are in business to make a profit. Seldom do they run their enterprises for social objectives. But since it is fashionable these days, most of the managers and personnel officers we interviewed (86 percent, in fact) accepted the proposition that they "have a social responsibility to make strong efforts to provide employment for Negroes and other minority groups." This assertion, however, is contradicted by unemployment in the Negro community today, as well as by the hiring policies of the firms themselves.

Businessmen, as a whole, do not exhibit openly racist attitudes. Their position might best be described as one of "optimistic denial"—the gentlemanly white racism evident in a tacit, but often unwitting, acceptance of institutional practices that subordinate or exclude Negroes. One aspect of this optimistic denial is a nonrecognition of the seriousness of the problems that face black people. Only 21 percent of our sample thought that unemployment was a very serious problem in the nation's cities, yet 26 percent considered air pollution very serious and 31 percent considered traffic very serious. The employers' perspective is based upon their limited experience with blacks, and that experience does not give them a realistic picture of the plight of Negroes in this country. Employers don't even think that racial discrimination has much to do with the Negroes' plight; a majority (57 percent) felt that Negroes are treated at least as well as other people of the same income, and an additional 6 percent felt that Negroes are treated *better* than any other part of the population.

This optimistic denial on the part of employers ("things really aren't that bad for Negroes") is often combined with a negative image of Negroes as employees. Half of those employers interviewed (51 percent) said that Negroes are likely to have higher rates of absenteeism than whites, so that hiring many of them would probably upset production schedules. Almost a third thought that, because Negro crime rates are generally higher than white crime rates, hiring many Negroes could lead to increased theft and vandalism in their companies. About a fifth (22 percent) thought that hiring Negroes might bring "agitators and troublemakers" into their companies, and another one-fifth feared that production costs might rise because Negroes supposedly do not take orders well.

The employer's views may reflect not only traditional white prejudices, but also some occasional experience he himself has had with Negroes. Such experiences, however, may stem as much from the employer's own practices and misconceptions as from imputed cultural habits of Negroes. As Elliott Liebow observed in his study of Negro street-corner men (*Tally's Corner*), blacks have learned to cope with life by treating menial, low-status, degrading jobs in the same way that the jobs treat them—with benign nonconcern.

Most of the employers believe that Negroes lack the preparation for anything but menial jobs. A full 83 percent said that few Negroes are qualified for professional jobs, and 69 percent thought that few are qualified for skilled positions. When it comes to unskilled jobs, of course, only 23 percent of the employers held this view. The employers seem to share a widespread assumption—one frequently used as a cover for racism—that for historical and environmental reasons Negroes have been disabled to such an extent as to make them uncompetitive in a highly competitive society. And while it is certainly true that black people have suffered from a lack of educational and other opportunities, this line of thinking—especially among whites—has a tendency to blame the past and the ghetto environment for what is perceived as Negro incompetence, thus diverting attention from *present* institutional practices. So, many employers have developed a rhetoric of concern about upgrading the so-called "hard-core unemployed" in lieu of changing their employment policies.

To a considerable extent our respondents' assessment of Negro job qualifications reflects company policy, for the criteria used in hiring skilled and professional workers tend to exclude Negroes. The criteria are (1) previous experience and (2) recommendations. It is evident that because Negroes are unlikely to have *had* previous experience in positions from which they have long been excluded, and because they are unlikely to have had much contact with people in the best position to recommend them, the criteria for "qualification" make it probable that employers will consider most Negroes unqualified.

NEGROES GET THE WORST JOBS

In short, the employers' aversion to taking risks (at least with people), reinforced by the pressure of labor unions and more general discriminatory patterns in society, means that Negroes usually get the worst jobs.

Thus, although Negroes make up 20 percent of the unskilled workers in these large corporations, they fill only a median of one percent of the professional positions and only 2 percent of the skilled positions. Moreover, the few Negroes in the higher positions are unevenly distributed among the corporations. Thirty-two percent of the companies don't report Negroes in professional positions, and 24 percent do not report any in skilled positions. If these companies are set aside, in the remaining companies the median percentage of Negroes in the two positions rises to 3 percent and 6 percent, respectively. Further, in these remaining companies an even larger percentage (8 percent in both cases) of *current* positions are being filled by Negroes—which indicates, among other things, that a breakthrough has been accomplished in some companies, while in others Negro employment in the upper level remains minimal or nonexistent.

Even among those companies that hire blacks for skilled jobs, a Negro applicant's chances of getting the job are only one-fourth as good as those of his white counterpart. For professional positions, the chances are more nearly equal: Negro applicants are about three-fourths as likely to get these jobs as are white applicants. It seems that Negroes have come closest to breaking in at the top (though across all firms only about 4 percent of the applicants for professional positions are Negro). The real stumbling-block to equal employment opportunities seems to be at the skilled level, and here it may be that union policies—and especially those of the craft unions—augment the employers' resistance to hiring Negroes for and promoting Negroes to skilled positions.

What do urban Negroes themselves think of employers' hiring practices? A survey of the same 15 cities by Angus Campbell and Howard Schuman, for the riot commission, indicates that one-third (34 percent) of the Negro men interviewed reported having been refused jobs because of racial discrimination, and 72 percent believed that some or many other black applicants are turned down for the same reason. Almost as many (68 percent) think that some or many black people miss out on promotions because of prejudice. And even when companies do hire Negroes (presumably in professional positions), this is interpreted as tokenism: 77 percent of the black respondents thought that Negroes are hired by big companies for show purposes.

The companies we studied, which have little contact with the ghetto, are very different from the other institutions in our survey, whose contact with the ghetto is direct and immediate. The corporations are also up-to-date, well-financed, and innovative, while the white institutions inside the ghetto are outdated, underfinanced, and overloaded. In historical terms, the institutions in the ghetto represent another era of thought and organization.

GHETTO MERCHANTS

The slum merchants illustrate the tendency of ghetto institutions to hark back to earlier forms. While large corporations cooperate with one another and with the government to exert substantial control over their market, the ghetto merchant still functions in the realm of traditional laissez-faire. He is likely to be a small operator, economically marginal and with almost no ability to control his market. His main advantage over the more efficient, modern retailer is his restricted competition, for the ghetto provides a captive market. The difficulty that many blacks have in getting transportation out of the ghetto, combined with a lack of experience in comparative shopping, seems to give the local merchant a competitive aid he sorely needs to survive against the lower prices and better goods sold in other areas of the city.

The merchants in our study also illustrate the free-enterprise character of ghetto merchandising. They run very small operations—grocery stores, restaurants, clothing and liquor stores, and so on, averaging a little over three employees per business. Almost half of them (45 percent) find it difficult to "keep up with their competition" (competition mainly *within* the ghetto). Since there are almost no requirements for becoming a merchant, this group is the most heterogeneous of all those studied. They have the widest age range (from 17 through 80), the highest percentage of immigrants (15 percent), and the lowest educational levels (only 16 percent finished college).

Again in contrast to the large corporations, the ghetto merchant must live with the harsh day-to-day realities of violence and poverty. His attitudes toward Negroes, different in degree from those of the employers, are at least partly a function of his objective evaluations of his customers.

Running a business in a ghetto means facing special kinds of "overhead."
Theft is an especially worrisome problem for the merchants; respondents mentioned it more frequently than any other problem. There is, of course, some basis
in fact for their concern. According to the riot commission, inventory losses—
ordinarily under 2 percent of sales—may be twice as great in high-crime areas
(most of which are in ghettos). And for these small businesses such losses may
cut substantially into a slender margin of profit.

Thus it is not surprising that, of all the occupational groups interviewed in
this study, the retail merchants were among the most likely to consider Negroes
violent and criminal. For example, 61 percent said that Negroes are more likely
to steal than whites, and 50 percent believed that Negroes are more likely to pass
bad checks. No wonder, then, that black customers may encounter unusual surveillance and suspicion when they shop.

Less understandable is the ghetto merchant's apparent ignorance of the plight
of ghetto blacks. Thus, 75 percent believe that blacks get medical treatment that
is equal to or better than what whites get. A majority think that Negroes are not
discriminated against with regard to treatment by the police, recreation facilities,
and so forth. Logically enough, 51 percent of the merchants feel that Negroes
are making too many demands. This percentage is the second-highest measured
(the police were the least sympathetic). So the merchants (like all other groups
in the survey except the black politicians) are inclined to emphasize perceived
defects in the black community as a major problem in their dealings with Negroes.

The shaky economic position of the merchants, their suspicion of their Negro
customers, and the high "overhead" of doing business in the ghetto (because of
theft, vandalism, bad credit risks) lead many merchants to sell inferior merchandise at higher prices—and to resort to other strategems for getting money out of
their customers. To elicit responses from the merchants on such delicate matters,
we drew up a series of very indirect questions. The responses we obtained,
though they no doubt understate the extent to which ghetto merchants provide
a poor dollar value per unit of goods, are nevertheless revealing. For example, we
asked the merchants to recommend various ways of "keeping up with business
competition." Some 44 percent said that you should offer extra services; over a
third (36 percent) said you should raise prices to cover unusually high overhead;
and the same number (36 percent) said that you should buy "bargain" goods at
lower prices, then sell them at regular prices. (To a small merchant, "bargain
goods" ordinarily means "seconds," or slightly spoiled merchandise because he
doesn't do enough volume to gain real discounts from a wholesaler.) A smaller
but still significant segment (12 percent) said that one should "bargain the selling price with each customer and take whatever breaks you can get."

The Campbell-Schuman study indicates that 56 percent of the Negroes interviewed felt that they had been overcharged in neighborhood stores (24 percent
said often); 42 percent felt that they had been sold spoiled or inferior goods (13

percent said often). Given the number of ghetto stores a customer may visit every week, these data are entirely compatible with ours. Since one-third of the merchants indicated that they were not averse to buying "bargain" goods for sale in their stores, it is understandable that 42 percent of the Negroes in these areas should say that at one time or another they have been sold inferior merchandise.

It is also understandable that during the recent civil disorders many Negroes, unable to affect merchants by routine methods, struck directly at the stores, looting and burning them.

TEACHERS IN THE GHETTO

Just as ghetto merchants are in a backwater of the economy, ghetto schools are in a backwater of the educational system, experimental efforts in some cities not withstanding.

Negroes, of course, are most likely to be served by out-moded and inadequate schools, a fact that the Coleman Report has documented in considerable detail. In metropolitan regions of the Northeast, for example, 40 percent of the Negro pupils at the secondary level attended schools in buildings over 40 years old, but only 15 percent of the whites did; the average number of pupils per room was 35 for Negroes but 28 for whites.

The teachers covered in our survey (half of whom were Negro) taught in ghetto schools at all levels. Surprisingly, 88 percent said that they were satisfied with their jobs. Their rate of leaving, however, was not consistent with this. Half of the teachers had been in their present schools for no more than four years. Breaking the figures down year by year, we find that the largest percentage (17 percent) had been there only one year. In addition, the teachers' rate of leaving increased dramatically after they had taught for five years.

While the teachers thought that education was a major problem for the cities and especially for the ghettos, they did not think that ghetto schools were a source of the difficulty. A solid majority, comparing their own schools with others in the city, thought that theirs were average, above average, or superior in seven out of eight categories. The one doubtful area, according to the teachers, was the physical plant, which seemed to them to be just barely competitive; in this respect, 44 percent considered their own schools below average or inferior.

The teachers have less confidence in their students than in themselves or their schools. On the one hand, they strongly reject the view that in ghetto schools education is sacrificed to the sheer need for order: 85 percent said it was not true that pupils in their schools were uneducable, and that teachers could do little more than maintain discipline. On the other hand, the teachers as a group could not agree that their students were as educable as they might be. There was little consensus on whether their pupils were "about average" in interest and ability: 28 percent thought that their pupils were; 41 percent thought it was partially true that they were; and 31 percent thought it was not true. But the teachers had less difficulty agreeing that their students were *not* "above average in ability and . . . generally co-operative with teachers." Agreeing on this were 59 percent of the teachers, with another 33 percent in the middle.

The real problem with education in the ghetto, as the teachers see it, is the ghetto itself. The teachers have their own version of the "Negro disability" thesis: the "cultural deprivation" theory holds that the reason for bad education in the ghetto is the student's environment rather than the schools. (See "How Teachers Learn to Help Children Fail," by Estelle Fuchs, September, 1968.) Asked to name the major problems facing their schools, the teachers most frequently mentioned community apathy; the second most-mentioned problem, a derivation of the first, was an alleged lack of preparation and motivation in the students. Fifty-nine percent of the teachers agreed to some extent that "many communities provide such a terrible environment for the pupils that education doesn't do much good in the end."

Such views are no doubt detrimental to education in the ghetto, for they imply a decided fatalism as far as teaching is concerned. If the students are deficient—improperly motivated, distracted, and so on—and if the cause of this deficiency lies in the ghetto rather than in the schools themselves, then there is little reason for a teacher to exert herself to set high standards for her students.

There is considerable question, however, whether the students in ghetto schools are as distracted as the teachers think. Events in the last few years indicate that the schools, especially the high schools and the junior high schools, are one of the strongest focuses of the current black rebellion. The student strike at Detroit's Northern High School in 1966, for example, was cohesive and well-organized. A boycott by some 2,300 students, directed against a repressive school administration, lasted over two weeks and resulted in the dismissal of the principal and the formation of a committee, including students, to investigate school conditions. The ferment in the ghetto schools across the country is also leading to the formation of permanent and independent black students' groups, such as the Modern Strivers in Washington, D.C.'s Eastern High, intent on promoting black solidarity and bringing about changes in the educational system. In light of such developments, there is reason to think that the teachers in the survey have overestimated the corrosive effects of the ghetto environment on students—and underestimated the schools' responsibility for the state of education in the ghetto.

SOCIAL WORKERS AND THE WELFARE ESTABLISHMENT

Public welfare is another area in which old ideas have been perpetuated beyond their time. The roots of the present welfare-department structure lie in the New Deal legislation of the 1930s. The public assistance provisions of the Social Security Act were designed to give aid to the helpless and the noncompetitive: the aged, the blind, the "permanently and totally" disabled, and dependent children. The assumption was that the recipient, because of personal disabilities or inadequacies, could not make his way in life without outside help.

The New Deal also provided work (e.g., the W.P.A.) for the able-bodied who were assumed to be unemployed only temporarily. But as the Depression gave way to the war years and to the return of prosperity, the massive work programs for the able-bodied poor were discontinued, leaving only those programs that were premised on the notion of personal disability. To a considerable extent today's Negro poor have had to rely on the latter. Chief among these programs, of course, is Aid for Dependent Children, which has become a mainstay of welfare. And because of racial discrimination, especially in education and employment, a large part of the Negro population also experiences poverty as a permanent state.

While most of the social workers in our survey showed considerable sympathy with the Negro cause, they too felt that the root of the problem lay in weaknesses in the Negro community; and they saw their primary task as making up the supposed deficiency. A hefty majority of the respondents (78 percent) thought that a large part of their responsibility was to "teach the poor how to live"—rather than to provide the means for them to live as they like. Assuming disability, welfare has fostered dependency.

The social workers, however, are unique among the groups surveyed in that they are quite critical of their own institution. The average welfare worker is not entirely at one with the establishment for which she works. She is likely to be a college graduate who regards her job as transitional. And her lack of expertise has its advantages as well as its disadvantages, for it means that she can take a more straightforward view of the situations she is confronted with. She is not committed to bureaucracy as a way of life.

The disparity between the welfare establishment and the average welfare worker is evident in the latter's complaints about her job. The complaints she voices the most deal *not* with her clients, but with the welfare department itself and the problems of working within its present structure—the difficulty of getting things done, the red tape, the lack of adequate funds, and so on. Of the five most-mentioned difficulties of welfare work, three dealt with such intra-agency problems; the other two dealt with the living conditions of the poor.

There is a good deal of evidence to support the social worker's complaints. She complains, for example, that welfare agencies are understaffed. The survey indicates that an average caseload is 177 people, each client being visited about once a month for about 50 minutes. Even the most conscientious of caseworkers must be overwhelmed by such client-to-worker ratios.

As in the case of the schools, welfare has engendered a countervailing force among the very people it is supposed to serve. Welfare clients have become increasingly hostile to the traditional structure and philosophy of welfare departments and have formed themselves into an outspoken movement. The welfare-rights movement at this stage has aims: to obtain a more nearly adequate living base for the clients, and to overload the system with demands, thus either forcing significant changes or clearing the way for new and more appropriate institutions.

BLACK POLITICAL PARTY WORKERS

Usually when segments of major social institutions become incapable of functioning adequately, the people whom the institutions are supposed to serve have recourse to politics. In the ghetto, however, the political machinery is no better off than the other institutions. Around the turn of the century Negroes began to carve out small niches for themselves in the politics of such cities as Chicago and New York. Had Negro political organizations developed along the same lines as those of white ethnic groups, they might today provide valuable leverage for the ghetto population. But this has not happened. For one thing, the decline of the big-city machine, and its replacement in many cities by "nonpolitical" reform governments supported by a growing middle class, began to close off a route traditionally open to minority groups. Second, black politicians have never been regarded as fullfledged political brokers by racist whites, and consequently the possibility of a Negro's becoming a powerful politician in a predominantly white city has been foreclosed (the recent election of Carl Stokes as Mayor of Cleveland and Richard D. Hatcher, Mayor of Gary, Indiana, would be exceptions). Whites have tended to put aside their differences when confronting Negro political efforts; to regard Negro demands, no matter how routine, as racial issues; and hence to severely limit the concessions made to black people.

Today the sphere of Negro politics is cramped and closely circumscribed. As Kenneth B. Clark has observed, most of the Negroes who have reached high public office have done so *not* within the context of Negro politics, but through competition in the larger society. In most cities Negro political organizations are outmoded and inadequate. Even if, as seems probable, more and more Negro mayors are elected, they will have to work within the antiquated structure of urban government, with sharply limited resources. Unless things change, the first Negro mayor of Newark, for example, will preside over a bankrupt city.

Our survey of Negro political workers in the 15 cities documents the inadequacy of Negro politics—and the inadequacy of the larger system of urban politics. The political workers, understandably, strongly sympathize with the aspirations of other black people. As ghetto politicians, they deal with the demands and frustrations of other blacks day after day. Of all the groups surveyed, they were the most closely in touch with life in the ghetto. Most of them work in the middle and lower levels of municipal politics; they talk with about 75 voters each week. These political workers are, of course, acutely aware of the precipitous rise in the demands made by the black community. Most (93 percent) agreed that in the last few years people in their districts have become more determined to get what they want. The strongest impetus of this new determination comes from the younger blacks: 92 percent of the political workers agreed that "young people have become more militant." Only a slight majority, however (56 percent), said the same of middle-aged people.

Against the pressure of rising Negro demands, urban political organizations formed in other times and on other assumptions, attentive to other interests, and constrained by severely limited resources, find themselves unable to respond satisfactorily. A majority of the political workers, in evaluating a variety of services available to people in their districts, thought that all except two—telephone service and the fire department—were either poor or fair. Worst of the lot, according to the political workers, were recreation, police protection, and building inspection.

In view of these respondents, the black community has no illusions about the ability of routine politics to meet its needs. While only 38 percent of the political workers thought that the people in their districts regarded their councilmen as friends fighting for them, 51 percent said that the people considered their councilmen "part of the city government which must be asked continually and repeatedly in order to get things done." (Since the political workers were probably talking about their fellow party members, their responses may have been more favorable than frank. A relatively high percentage of "don't know" responses supports this point.)

Almost all the Negro politicians said that they received various requests from the voters for help. Asked whether they could respond to these requests "almost always, usually, or just sometimes," the largest percentage (36 percent) chose "sometimes"—which, in context, is a way of saying "seldom." Another 31 percent said they "usually" could respond to such requests, and 19 percent said "almost always." Logically enough, 60 percent of the political workers agreed that in the last few years "people have become more fed up with the system, and are becoming unwilling to work with politicians." In effect, this is an admission that they as political workers, and the system of urban politics to which they devote themselves, are failing.

When economic and social institutions fail to provide the life-chances that a substantial part of a population wants, and when political institutions fail to provide a remedy, the aspirations of the people begin to spill over into forms of activity that the dominant society regards either as unacceptable or illegitimate—crime, vandalism, noncooperation, and various forms of political protest.

Robert M. Fogelson and Robert D. Hill, in the *Supplemental Studies* for the riot commission, have reported that 50 percent to 90 percent of the Negro males in ten cities studied had arrest records. Clearly, when the majority of men in a given population are defined as criminals—at least by the police—something more than "deviant" behaviour is involved. In effect, ghetto residents—and especially the youth—and the police are in a state of subdued warfare. On the one hand, the cities are experiencing a massive and as yet inchoate social rising of the Negro population. On the other hand, the police—devoted to the racial status quo and inclined to overlook the niceties of mere law in their quest for law and order—have found a variety of means, both conventional and otherwise, for countering the aims of Negroes. In doing so, they are not only adhering to the norms of their institution, but also furthering their personal goals as well. The average policeman, recruited from a lower- or middle-class white background, frequently of "ethnic" origins, comes from a group whose social position is marginal and who feel most threatened by Negro advances.

The high arrest rate in the Negro community thus mirrors both the push of Negroes and the determined resistance of the police. As the conflict intensifies, the police are more and more losing authority in the eyes of black people; the young Negroes are especially defiant. Any type of contact between police and black people can quickly lead to a situation in which the policeman gives an order and the Negro either defies it or fails to show sufficient respect in obeying it. This in turn can lead to the Negro's arrest on a disorderly conduct charge or on a variety of other charges. (Disorderly conduct accounted for about 17 percent of the arrests in the Fogelson-Hill study.)

POLICE HARASSMENT TECHNIQUES

The police often resort to harassment as a means of keeping the Negro community off-balance. The riot commission noted that:

> Because youths commit a large and increasing proportion of crime, police are under growing pressure from their supervisors—and from the community—to deal with them forcefully. "Harassment of youths" may therefore be viewed by some police departments—and members even of the Negro community—as a proper crime prevention technique.

The Commission added that "many departments have adopted patrol practices which, in the words of one commentator, have 'replaced harassment by individual patrolmen with harassment by entire departments.' "

Among the most common of the cops' harassment techniques are breaking up street-corner groups and stop-and-frisk tactics. Our study found that 63 percent of the ghetto police reported that they "frequently" were called upon to disperse loitering groups. About a third say they "frequently" stop and frisk people. Obviously then, the law enforcer sometimes interferes with individuals and groups who consider their activities quite legitimate and necessary. Black people in the ghetto—in the absence of adequate parks, playgrounds, jobs, and recreation facilities, and unwilling to sit in sweltering and overcrowded houses with rats and bugs—are likely to make the streets their front yards. But this territory is often made uninhabitable by the police.

Nearly a third of the white policemen in our study thought that most of the residents of their precinct (largely Negro) were not industrious. Even more striking about the attitudes of the white police working in these neighborhoods is that many of them deny the fact of Negro inequality: 20 percent say the Negro is treated better than any other part of the population, and 14 percent say he is treated equally. As for their own treatment of Negroes, the Campbell-Schuman survey reported that 43 percent of the black men, who are on the streets more than women, thought that police use insulting language in their neighborhood. Only 17 percent of the white males held this belief. Of the Negro men, 20 percent reported that the police insulted them personally and 28 percent said they knew someone to whom this had happened; only 9 percent and 12 percent, respectively, of the whites reported the same. Similarly, many more blacks than whites thought that the police frisked and searched people without good reason (42 percent compared to 12 percent); and that the police roughed up people unnecessarily (37 percent as compared to 10 percent). Such reports of police misconduct were most frequent among the younger Negroes, who, after all, are on the receiving end most often.

The policeman's isolation in the ghetto is evident in a number of findings. We asked the police how many people—of various types—they knew well enough in the ghetto to greet when they saw them. Eighty-nine percent of the police said they knew six or more shopowners, managers, and clerks well enough to speak with, but only 38 percent said they knew this many teenage or youth leaders. At the same time, 39 percent said that most young adults, and 51 percent said that most adolescents, regard the police as enemies. And only 16 percent of the white policemen (37 percent of the blacks) either "often" or "sometimes" attended meetings in the neighborhood.

The police have wound up face to face with the social consequences of the problems in the ghetto created by the failure of other white institutions—though, as has been observed, they themselves have contributed to those problems in no small degree. The distant and gentlemanly white racism of employers, the discrimination of white parents who object to having their children go to school with Negroes, the disgruntlement of white taxpayers who deride the present welfare system as a sinkhole of public funds but are unwilling to see it replaced by anything more effective—the consequences of these and other forms of white racism have confronted the police with a massive control problem of the kind most evident in the riots.

In our survey, we found that the police were inclined to see the riots as the long range result of faults in the Negro community—disrespect for law, crime, broken families, etc.—rather than as responses to the stance of the white community. Indeed, nearly one-third of the white police saw the riots as the result of what they considered the basic violence and disrespect of Negroes in general, while only one-fourth attributed the riots to the failure of white institutions. More than three-fourths also regarded the riots as the immediate result of agitators and criminals—a suggestion contradicted by all the evidence accumulated by the riot commission. The police, then, share with the other groups—excepting the black politicians—a tendency to emphasize perceived defects in the black community as an explanation for the difficulties that they encounter in the ghetto.

The state of siege evident in many police departments is but an exaggerated version of a trend in the larger white society. It is the understandable, but unfortunate, response of people who are angry and confused about the wide-spread disruption of traditional racial patterns and who feel threatened by these changes. There is, of course, some basis for this feeling, because the Negro movement poses challenges of power and interest to many groups. To the extent that the movement is successful, the merchants, for example, will either have to reform their practices or go out of business—and for many it may be too late for reform. White suburbanites will have to cough up funds for the city, which provides most of them with employment. Police departments will have to be thoroughly restructured.

The broad social rising of Negroes is beginning to have a substantial effect upon all white institutions in the ghetto, as the situation of the merchants, the schools, and the welfare establishment illustrates. Ten years ago, these institutions (and the police, who have been affected differently) could operate pretty much unchecked by any countervailing power in the ghetto. Today, both their excesses and their inadequacies have run up against an increasingly militant black population, many of whom support violence as a means of redress. The evidence suggests that unless these institutions are transformed, the black community will make it increasingly difficult for them to function at all.

Max Weber

Characteristics
of bureaucracy

Modern officialdom functions in the following specific manner:

I. There is the principle of fixed and official jurisdictional areas, which are generally ordered by rules, that is, by laws or administrative regulations.

1. The regular activities required for the purposes of the bureaucratically governed structure are distributed in a fixed way as official duties.

2. The authority to give the commands required for the discharge of these duties is distributed in a stable way and is strictly delimited by rules concerning the coercive means, physical, sacerdotal, or otherwise, which may be placed at the disposal of officials.

3. Methodical provision is made for the regular and continuous fulfillment of these duties and for the execution of the corresponding rights; only persons who have the generally regulated qualifications to serve are employed.

In public and lawful government these three elements constitute 'bureaucratic authority.' In private economic domination, they constitute bureaucratic 'management.' Bureaucracy, thus understood, is fully developed in political and ecclesiastical communities only in the modern state, and, in the private economy, only in the most advanced institutions of capitalism. Permanent and public office authority, with fixed jurisdiction, is not the historical rule but rather the exception. This is so even in large political structures such as those of the ancient Orient, the Germanic and Mongolian empires of conquest, or of many feudal structures of the state. In all these cases, the ruler executes the most important measures through personal trustees, table-companions, or court-servants. Their commissions and authority are not precisely delimited and are temporarily called into being for each case.

II. The principles of office hierarchy and of levels of graded authority mean a firmly ordered system of super- and subordination in which there is a supervision of the lower offices by the higher ones. Such a system offers the governed the possibility of appealing the decision of a lower office to its higher authority, in a definitely regulated manner. With the full development of the bureaucratic type, the office authority is found in all bureaucratic structures: in state and ecclesiastical structures as well as in large party organizations and private enterprises. It does not matter for the character of bureaucracy whether its authority is called 'private' or 'public.'

When the principle of jurisdictional 'competency' is fully carried through, hierarchical subordination—at least in public office—does not mean that the 'higher' authority is simply authorized to take over the business of the 'lower.' Indeed, the opposite is the rule. Once established and having fulfilled its task, an office tends to continue in existence and be held by another incumbent.

III. The management of the modern office is based upon written documents ('the files'), which are preserved in their original or draught form. There is, therefore, a staff of subaltern officials and scribes of all sorts. The body of officials actively engaged in a 'public' office, along with the respective apparatus of material implements and the files, make up a 'bureau.' In private enterprise, 'the bureau' is often called 'the office.'

In principle, the modern organization of the civil service separates the bureau from the private domicile of the official, and, in general, bureaucracy segregates official activity as something distinct from the sphere of private life. Public monies and equipment are divorced from the private property of the official. This condition is everywhere the product of a long development. Nowadays, it is found in public as well as in private enterprises; in the latter, the principle extends even to the leading entrepreneur. In principle, the executive office is separated from the household, business from private correspondence, and business assets from private fortunes. The more consistently the modern type of business management has been carried through the more are these separations the case. The beginnings of this process are to be found as early as the Middle Ages.

It is the peculiarity of the modern entrepreneur that he conducts himself as the 'first official' of his enterprise, in the same way in which the ruler of a specifically modern bureaucratic state spoke of himself as 'the first servant' of the state. The idea that the bureau activities of the state are intrinsically different in character from the management of private economic offices is a continental European notion and, by way of contrast, is totally foreign to the American way.

IV. Office management, at least all specialized office management—and such management is distinctly modern—usually presupposes thorough and expert training. This increasingly holds for the modern executive and employee of private enterprises, in the same manner as it holds for the state official.

V. When the office is fully developed, official activity demands the full working capacity of the official, irrespective of the fact that his obligatory time in the bureau may be firmly delimited. In the normal case, this is only the product of a long development, in the public as well as in the private office. Formerly, in all cases, the normal state of affairs was reversed: official business was discharged as a secondary activity.

VI. The management of the office follows general rules, which are more or less stable, more or less exhaustive, and which can be learned. Knowledge of these rules represents a special technical learning which the officials possess. It involves jurisprudence, or administrative or business management.

The reduction of modern office management to rules is deeply embedded in its very nature. The theory of modern public administration, for instance, assumes that the authority to order certain matters by decree—which has been legally granted to public authorities—does not entitle the bureau to regulate the matter by commands given for each case, but only to regulate the matter abstractly. This stands in extreme contrast to the regulation of all relationships through individual privileges and bestowals of favor, which is absolutely dominant in patrimonialism, at least in so far as such relationships are not fixed by sacred tradition.

THE POSITION OF THE OFFICIAL

All this results in the following for the internal and external position of the official:

I. Office holding is a 'vocation.' This is shown, first, in the requirement of a firmly prescribed course of training, which demands the entire capacity for work for a long period of time, and in the generally prescribed and special examinations which are prerequisites of employment. Furthermore, the position of the official is in the nature of a duty. This determines the internal structure of his relations, in the following manner: Legally and actually, office holding is not considered a source to be exploited for rents or emoluments, as was normally the case during the Middle Ages and frequently up to the threshold of recent times. Nor is office holding considered a usual exchange of services for equivalents, as is the case with free labor contract. Entrance into an office, including one in the private economy, is considered an acceptance of a specific obligation of faithful management in return for a secure existence. It is decisive for the specific nature of modern loyalty to an office that, in the pure type, it does not establish a relationship to a *person,* like the vassal's or disciple's faith in feudal or in patrimonial relations of authority. Modern loyalty is devoted to impersonal and functional purposes. Behind the functional purposes, of course, 'ideas of culture-values' usually stand. These are *ersatz* for the earthly or supra-mundane personal master: ideas such as 'state,' 'church,' 'community,' 'party,' or 'enterprise' are thought of as being realized in a community; they provide an ideological halo for the master.

The political official—at least in the fully developed modern state—is not considered the personal servant of a ruler. Today, the bishop, the priest, and the preacher are in fact no longer, as in early Christian times, holders of purely personal charisma. The supra-mundane and sacred values which they offer are given to everybody who seems to be worthy of them and who asks for them. In former times, such leaders acted upon the personal command of their master; in principle, they were responsible only to him. Nowadays, in spite of the partial survival of the old theory, such religious leaders are officials in the service of a functional purpose, which in the present-day 'church' has become routinized and, in turn, ideologically hallowed.

II. The personal position of the official is patterned in the following way:

1. Whether he is in a private office or a public bureau, the modern official always strives and usually enjoys a distinct *social esteem* as compared with the governed. His social position is guaranteed by the prescriptive rules of rank order and, for the political official, by special definitions of the criminal code against 'insults of officials' and 'contempt' of state and church authorities. . . .

Social control
of riots

Official and academic conceptions of riots have strongly influenced the assumptions underlying governmental response to civil disorders in the past. We have argued that these conceptions seriously misconstrue the meaning of riots on several counts. It follows that riot-control efforts based on these conceptions may be inadequate and often self-defeating.

No recent treatment advocates a purely repressive approach to riot control. On the contrary, official conceptions of riots have usually been translated into recommendations combining a program for the reduction of social tensions with a call for the development of strategy and technology to contain disruption. On its face, this dual approach seems both reasonable and feasible. It suggests sympathetic response to legitimate grievances, and at the same time it offers the prospect of sophisticated, measured, and controlled force to protect civic order. After considerable analysis, however, we have come to question whether this two-pronged approach is ultimately workable.

PROSPECTS OF SUPPORT

First, implicit in the two-pronged theory is the assumption that, in practice, reform measures have about the same prospect of gaining executive and legislative support as control and firepower measures. Historical experience, however, suggests no such parity. On the contrary, commissions from the Chicago Commission of 1919 to the Kerner Commission have adopted the dual approach and have lived to observe control recommendations being implemented without concomitant implementation of social reform measures. Although it has generally been recognized that riots are motivated in part by legitimate grievances, the ensuing political response clearly reveals that order has been given priority over justice. After the Harlem riot in 1935, it was reported that "extra police stand guard on the corners and mounted patrolmen ride through the streets . . . . To

Reprinted from *The Politics of Protest: Violent Aspects of Protest and Confrontation,* Staff Report No. 3, prepared by Jerome Skolnick, to the National Commission on the Causes and Prevention of Violence, Washington, D.C., U.S. Government Printing Office, 1969:260-262. Footnotes omitted.

the citizens of Harlem they symbolize the answer of the city authorities to their protest. . . . It offers no assurance that the legitimate demands of the community for work and decent living conditions will be heeded." Yet the Harlem Commission warned that riots would recur so long as basic grievances were not answered. Over thirty years later, the Kerner Commission reported a similar finding that "in several cities, the principal official response has been to train and equip the police with more sophisticated weapons." Following the Kerner Commission, there has been considerable development to riot-control weapons and programs in urban areas, without similar efforts, recommended by the Commission, to meet underlying and legitimate grievances. From the evidence, it appears that it has been found more expedient to implement recommendations for control than recommendations for altering the social structure. There is little evidence that a call for social reform, on the one hand, and for the development of sophisticated riot-control techniques and weaponry, on the other, will not suffer the same fate today.

We may suggest as a general rule that a society which must contemplate massive expenditures for social control is one which, virtually by definition, has not grappled with the necessity of massive social reform. There are various possible levels of social reform, ranging from merely token and symbolic amelioration of fundamental problems to significant changes in the allocation of resources—including political power. We feel that contemporary efforts at reform in this country remain largely at the first level. Precisely because society leaves untouched the basic problems, the cycle of hostility spirals: there is protest, violence, and increased commitment to social control: as we spiral in this direction, the "need" for massive social control outstrips the capacity of democratic institutions to maintain both social order and democratic values. Little by little, we move toward an armed society which, while not clearly totalitarian, could no longer be called consensual.

We need to reverse the spiral. A genuine commitment to fundamental reform will have positive effects, both reducing the need for massive social control and altering the quality and character of social control. We do not, of course, suggest that every demand of every protester or protest group be met. We do suggest, however, that a distinction be drawn between *demands* and *underlying grievances* and that grievances be considered on their merits. Too often attention is paid to disruption, but not to the reasons for it.

Law enforcement should be taken seriously. By this we mean to suggest that policing should take place within the framework of due process of law, using the minimum force required to effect the establishment of order. When actual crimes are committed, suspects should be arrested, charged, and tried in a court of law, not beaten in the streets. We should support reform of control agencies, not simply the addition of weaponry. The reduction and reformation of control should also occasion positive benefits by reducing polarization and hostility; that, in turn, should decrease disaffection, thus decreasing the need for force, and so forth. Only if the roots of disorder are attacked can the spiral be reversed and the problem of social order rendered manageable within a democratic framework.

The ramifications of reducing force and reforming the social structure, including the established policing services, are evident if we examine the connection between anti-war, student, and black protest. For example, a reduction of military spending and involvement overseas would reduce the level of anti-war and student protest, freeing resources that could then be used to combat the problems of the black communities. A greater understanding of black problems by control agents—a sympathetic understanding—would, in turn, also reduce the need for massive force.

STRATEGIES OF CONTROL

The escalation of violence is related to strategies of social control. Our evidence suggests that a diversion of resources into domestic force and away from redress of social grievances is not only costly but self-defeating, since the heightening of force is likely to be a factor in creating still more violence. The ultimate result of force will probably *not*, in the long run, be to "channel the energy of collective outbursts into more modest kinds of behavior"; the eventual effects may be directly contrary.

Because the police are received with hostility in the black communities of America, the introduction of more and better-armed police will, we believe, only aggravate the situation. The contemporary ideology and behavior of police across America make it difficult to think otherwise. Furthermore, the introduction of sophisticated weaponry will likely be seen by protesting groups as evidence of governmental duplicity. The development of "nonlethal" weapons, for example, will not be perceived by the young man in the ghetto as a humane response to his condition; to him they will still be weapons—aimed at him—and will be viewed with hostility. Finally, as we have developed at length, the police, the military, and other agents of social control may themselves be implicated in triggering riots and in building up long-term grievances.

THE POLITICAL SIGNIFICANCE OF RIOTS

The conventional approach underestimates the political significance of riots. Even given the possibility of efficient short-term control of riots, and ignoring its immediate destructive effects, the political nature of riots suggests that forceful riot-control techniques may channel expressive protest into more organized forms of political violence, thus requiring greater military and paramilitary force with its inescapable monetary and social costs. Thus it is not surprising that one expert finds that riots may be "giving way to more specific, more premeditated and more regularized uses of force." What is surprising, however, is his conclusion that "only surveillance and covert penetration supplies an effective technique of management."

We have learned from the Vietnam War that power and covert surveillance may well have the unanticipated effect of increasing resistance. Indeed, the literature of guerrilla warfare stresses that revolutionaries are made through violence. So, too, the young man who encounters the hostile actions of a policeman is likely to increase his hostility toward the society and to be attracted to groups that express such hostility. Moreover, in measuring the consequences of escalating domestic force, we must add the political and social dangers of depending on espionage as an instrument of social control, including its potential for eroding constitutional guarantees of political freedom.

For these reasons, we question the conventional two-pronged approach to contemporary American protest. An approach that gives equal emphasis to force and reform fails to measure the anticipated consequences of employing force; and it fails to appreciate the political significance of protest. If American society concentrates on the development of more sophisticated control techniques, it will move itself into a destructive and self-defeating position. A democratic society cannot depend upon force as its recurrent answer to long-standing and legitimate grievances. This nation cannot have it both ways: either it will carry through a firm commitment to massive and widespread political and social reform, or it will develop into a society of garrison cities where order is enforced without due process of law and without the consent of the governed.

SELECTED BIBLIOGRAPHY

Agger, Robert E., Goldrich, Daniel, and Swanson, Bert. *The Rulers and the Ruled.* New York: Wiley, 1964.

Banfield, Edward, and Wilson, James Q. *City Politics.* Cambridge, Mass.: Harvard University Press, 1963.

Bloomberg, Warner. "Community Organization." In Becker, Howard S. (ed.), *Social Problems.* New York: Wiley, 1966, pp. 359-425.

Bruyn, Severyn T. *Communities in Action.* New Haven: College and University Press, 1963.

Clark, Kenneth. *Dark Ghetto.* New York: Harper & Row, 1965.

Coleman, James S. *Community Conflict.* Glencoe, Ill.: Free Press, 1957.

Conot, Robert. *Rivers of Blood, Years of Darkness.* New York: Bantam, 1967.

Drake, St. Clair, and Cayton, Horace. *Black Metropolis,* two vols. New York: Harcourt Brace Jovanovich, 1962.

Duhl, Leonard (ed.). *The Urban Condition.* New York: Basic Books, 1963.

Form, William H., and Miller, Delbert. *Industry, Labor, and Community.* New York: Harper & Row, 1960.

Glazer, Nathan, and Moynihan, Daniel. *Beyond the Melting Pot.* Cambridge, Mass.: M.I.T. Press, 1963.

Gordon, Mitchell. *Sick Cities.* Baltimore: Penguin, 1966.

HARYOU-ACT, *Youth in the Ghetto.* New York: HARYOU-ACT, 1964.

Jacobs, Jane. *The Death and Life of Great American Cities.* New York: Random House, 1961.

Jacobs, Paul. *Prelude to Riot: A View of Urban American from the Bottom*. New York: Random House, 1967.

Katz, F. E. "Social Participation and Social Structure," *Social Forces*, 45 (December 1966), 199-210.

Koenig, Rene. *The Cummunity*. New York: Humanities, 1968.

Kuper, Leo. *Living in Towns*. London: Cresset, 1953.

Lowry, Nelson, Ramsey, C.E., and Verner, C. *Community Structure and Change*. New York: Macmillan, 1960.

Lyford, Joseph. *The Air-Tight Cage*. New York: Harper & Row, 1966.

Martin, Roscoe, et al. *Decisions in Syracuse*. New York: Doubleday, 1961.

Marx, Gary. *Protest and Prejudice: A Study of Belief in the Black Community*. New York: Harper & Row, 1967.

Morris, Robert (ed.). *Centrally Planned Change*. New York: National Association of Social Workers, 1964.

Park, Robert E., and Burgess, Ernest W. *The City*. Chicago: University of Chicago Press, 1925.

Parsons, Talcott, and Clark, Kenneth (eds.). *The Negro American*. Boston: Daedalus, 1966.

Riis, Jacob. *How the Other Half Lives*. New York: Hill & Wang, 1957.

Schnore, Leo T. (ed.). *Social Science and the City: A Survey of Urban Research*. New York: Praeger, 1967.

Seeley, John. "The Slum: Its Nature, Use and Users," *Journal of the American Institute of Planners*, 25 (February 1959), 7-14.

Silberman, Charles. *Crisis in Black and White*. New York: Random House, 1964.

Skolnick, Jerome. *The Politics of Protest*. New York: Ballantine, 1969.

Trans-action, VI (February 1969), whole issue, *"The American Under-Class."*

Valentine, Charles. *Culture and Poverty: Critique and Counter-Proposals*. Chicago: University of Chicago Press, 1968.

Vidich, A.J., and Bensman, J. *Small Town in Mass Society*. New York: Doubleday (Anchor), 1958.

Warren, Roland. *The Community in America*. Chicago: Rand-McNally, 1963.

Wheeler, Harvey. "A Moral Equivalent for Riots," *Saturday Review* (May 11, 1968), 19-22, 51, 52.

Wilkins, Leslie. *Social Deviance: Social Policy, Action, and Research*. Englewood Cliffs, N.J.: Prentice-Hall, 1965.

Williams, Robin. *Strangers Next Door*. Englewood Cliffs, N.J.: Prentice-Hall, 1964.

Wirth, Louis. *The Ghetto*. Chicago: University of Chicago Press, 1928.

Wright, Nathan. *Black Power and Urban Unrest: Creative Possibilities*. New York: Hawthorn, 1968.

Wright, Nathan. *Ready to Riot*. New York: Holt, Rinehart & Winston, 1968.

Zorbaugh, Harvey. *The Gold Coast and the Slum*. Chicago: University of Chicago Press, 1929.

2

Education

The education system, both public and private, has been until recently reasonably successful with the cognitive instruction that has prepared educable youths for successful college entrance and equally successful performance in those vocations and professions requiring trained intellectual capabilities. In the past, a parallel system of trade and vocational schools has also performed well in equipping the hand-minded, providing them with useful skills and work habits that have aided graduates in securing jobs and performing their tasks successfully. On-the-job training and apprenticeship programs in business and industry have supplemented public school offerings. Those who did not succeed in the cognitive mode or vocational training track left school and joined an army of semiliterate, unskilled, and semiskilled workers, which the economy, until recently, needed in large numbers.

Public schools in the inner city perform creditably with the first model, assuming that students are still motivated and prepared by home and peer culture to be educable. The second level of training is still successful, but major technological changes are making what was once very relevant less so, and vocational education is now undergoing significant change.

As for the third group, the number of opportunities for the unskilled and the semiskilled has diminished drastically. Urban schools are now compelled to educate those with whom they have never before been successful. This need arose when employment opportunities for the unskilled became seriously restricted. An increasingly demanding urban population, making for a series of small and large disasters, is now shaking inner-city education to its foundations.

LIFESTYLE OF EDUCATORS

Urban schools in the North, and to some degree in other parts of the country, have traditionally been a means of upward mobility for the lower socioeconomic classes and ethnic groups. To a considerable extent, school teachers of recent vintage have been the daughters and sons of European immigrants. This is still the case today, but pressures on school personnel to move on and out are being generated by the new militancy of previously submerged groups—among them Negroes, Puerto Ricans, and Mexican-Americans. Courteous waiting in line until retirement of present incumbents is no longer the order of the day, reflected in the serious conflict of group interests between the "ins" and those who wish to take over.

Public-school teachers have traditionally been among the most conforming of middle-class groups. School norms of behavior—physical, emotional, social, intellectual—are more in harmony with middle-class values than any other American social group, with the exception of the clergy. Present ghetto school conflicts involving students, parents, and teachers stem from challenges to the authority of middle-class culture. Although physical and verbal violence have been anathema to middle-class teachers, present conflicts between teachers and parents and students are creating battlegrounds of many big-city schools.

EDUCATION AS A POLITICAL FUNCTION

The outstanding development in public education in the inner city during the past decade has been its politicization. Education has always had political aspects, but these have been muted and implicit, not subject to mass involvement of parents, community, teachers, and students. Public education, traditionally an instrument of social control, is now subjected to the militant demands and actions of those who before had been subjects of its control. Consequently, the conditions of teaching and learning have undergone drastic changes, with more yet to come. Racial and ethnic politics always associated with the governance of the schools are now explicit, and violent confrontations are common.

The past decade has witnessed two apparently contradictory approaches which, stripped of their untested educational assumptions, are the means by which the black population has begun an ironic test of the educational conundrum, "Can the schools change the social order?" The first plan, desegregation (northern), succeeded in reversing in New York City, the largest city in the country, the per-pupil expenditure from the traditional beneficiary of educational largess, the middle-class child, to greater financial commitment to the ghetto schools. It also added to the flight from the inner city of middle-class white families and a significant percentage of Negro middle-class families as well. The second objective, local or community control reflecting an ideology of deliberate racial self-segregation, produced revolutionary challenges to the authority and competence of classroom teachers and principals, as well as to the overall authority of the boards of education and the superintendents' administrative cadres. Although the most publicized conflicts have been in New York City, other urban communities have been significantly affected.

CONCEPTS IN EDUCATION

The educational system comprises all kinds of issues and problems, from those of the teacher in the classroom, through organizational problems of the local school district, to vast philosohpical debates over what the society ought to expect from its schools in the way of preparation of the next generation of students. Estelle Fuchs' descriptive article uses the concepts of a good school, the individual child or teacher, the class as a social group, the good class, and the slow class.

The variety of approaches and meanings of segregation, desegregation, integration, or racial balance are clearly revealed in the two articles on these issues, "Fake Panaceas for Ghetto Education" and "Ghetto Education." Powerful examples of conflicting arguments, these pieces argue for and against desegregation or racial balance as the factor that will provide the best education for black America. Is interracial contact essential for good education or not? Is the pupil-teacher ratio the significant variable? What about proper equipment, buildings, visual aids, and libraries as crucial ingredients for education of the disadvantaged?

So, we present two theoretical illustrations. Taking the concept already used by Suttles in Chapter 1 to describe local community behavior, Birnbaum transforms the notion of group identification to the national level. Values are those central goals that are pursued by religious groups or ethnic groups. The theoretical proposition that a plural society in terms of political and organizational structures must have a plural value system is used in this article to throw light on the educational system. Each ethnic group expects that education of children in the classrooms of its neighborhood schools will reenforce its own particular definition of the patriotism of a good American. Finally, an abbreviated version of how one contemporary sociological theorist, Talcott Parsons, views the classroom in American society is presented. This excerpt looks at the same world as does Estelle Fuchs, the world of teachers and children interacting in the elementary school classroom.

Estelle Fuchs

Teaching the teacher

Ideally, the public schools exist to provide equal educational opportunity for all, and to provide opportunity for each to develop according to his capacity. The following excerpts, which follow the experience of a first-grade teacher and her class through the first semester, illustrate the way in which the bureaucratic structure of the school frustrates the attainment of ideal goals. This case indicates the way in which, through both informal and formal mechanisms, the teacher comes to accept the mores of the slum school, which tend to project the cause of school failure upon the children or their families and away from the school.

October 26. Mrs. Jones, the sixth-grade teacher, and I went on to discuss the problems of reading. I said, "I wonder about my children. They don't seem too slow; they seem average. Some of them even seem to be above average. I can't understand how they can grow up to be fifth- and sixth-grade children in school and still be reading on the second-grade level. It seems absolutely amazing."

Mrs. Jones explained about the environmental problems that these children have. "Some of them never see a newspaper. Some of them have never been on the subway," she said. "The parents are so busy having parties and things that they have no time for their children. They can't even take them to a museum or anything. It's very important that the teacher stress books."

Mrs. Jones tells her class, "If anyone asks you what you want for Christmas, you can say you want a book." She told me that she had a 6/1 class last year and it was absolutely amazing how many children never even saw a newspaper. They can't read Spanish either. So she said that the educational problem lies with the parents. They are the ones that have to be educated.

It's just a shame that the children suffer. I guess this problem will take an awful lot to straighten it out. I guess it won't take one day or even a year; it will take time.

December 14. Here I am a first-grade teacher. I get a great thrill out of these children being able to read, but I often wonder, "Am I teaching them how to

Reprinted from Estelle Fuchs, *Teachers Talk*, Doubleday Anchor Books, 1969, Garden City, N.Y., pp. 172-184. Copyright © 1967, 1969 by Estelle Fuchs. Reprinted by permission of Doubleday & Company, Inc.

read or are they just stringing along sight words that they know?" I never had a
course in college for teaching phonetics to children. In this school we have had
conferences about it, but I really wish that one of the reading teachers would
come in and specifically show me how to go about teaching phonics. I have
never gotten a course like this and it is a difficult thing, especially when there is
a language barrier and words are quite strange to these children who can't speak
English. How can they read English? So we have a great responsibility on our
shoulders, and teachers should take these things seriously.

January 4. Something very, very important and different has happened to me in
my school. It all happened in our last week before the vacation, on Tuesday. Mr.
Frost, our principal, came over to me and asked me if I would be willing to take
over a second-grade class starting after the vacation. Well, I looked at him and I
said, "Why?"

He told me briefly that the registers in the school have dropped and according
to the Board of Education the school must lose a teacher. Well, apparently he
was getting rid of a second-grade teacher and he wanted to combine two of the
first-grade classes. The registers on the first grade were the lowest in the school, I
believe. Anyway, he told me that he was going to all the afternoon first-grade
teachers asking if any of them would be willing to change in the middle of the
term. He said that he thought perhaps someone really would want it and, instead
of his just delegating a person, it would be better if he asked each one individually.

I was torn between many factors. As you know, I enjoyed my class very, very
much and I enjoy teaching the first grade. But because I was teaching afternoon
session (our school runs on two different sessions) I was left out of many of the
goings on within the school, as my hours were different, and it also sort of con-
flicted with my home responsibilities. Well, with these two points in mind, I
really felt that I would rather stay with my class than to switch over in the
middle of the term. But he explained further that some of the classes would not
remain the same because there would be many changes made. So, being the type
of person that I am, I felt that, even though I did want to stay with my class and
the children and the first grade, if something had to be done in the school, there
was no way of stopping it and I might as well do it. I explained to Mr. Frost that
even though I wouldn't want to change in the middle—after all, it would be a
whole new experience, two classes of children would be suffering by the change—
but if it had to be done I would be willing to take on the new responsibility.

With that, Mr. Frost said, "Thank you," and said he would go around to the
other teachers to see if anyone really wanted to change. Well, already I felt that
it was going to be me, but I wasn't sure.

A little later on in the day I was taking my class to recess and we were lining
up. We had just gotten into the hall. I had spoken to Miss Lane, another teacher,
about what had happened. He had also spoken to her. She told me that she
didn't quite understand what Mr. Frost was talking about, so I explained it to

her in more detail. At that point Mr. Frost came over and spoke to me and told me that he was sorry but that I had been the one elected. Well, I said that I hoped that I would be able to do a good job, and that was that.

From that point on there was an awful lot of talk in the school. Everybody was talking about it, at least, everyone who knew something about the matter. So all the afternoon first-grade teachers and all the morning first-grade teachers knew and many of the new teachers (those that I came into the school with), and apparently there was a lot of business going on that I can't begin to describe because I don't know how the whole thing started in the first place. However, from the office I did find out that it wasn't Mr. Frost's fault or anything that the second-grade teacher was going to be dismissed. It was a directive from higher up that stated he would lose a teacher. How he chose this particular teacher to let go I really can't say. I understand that they really didn't get along too well and neither of them was too happy in the school working together.

Everything went so quickly and everybody was talking to me. Mrs. Parsons spoke to me. She is my assistant principal. She was supervisor of the first grade and she will be in charge of the second grade also. I was told that I would have to take over the new class on January 2, the first day that we return from the vacation. I really felt terrible about my children, but it was something that had to be done and I did it.

Thursday, Mr. Frost talked to the other afternoon teachers and myself. He referred to me as the hero and he said, "Now it is your turn to be heroes also." He asked the afternoon first-grade teachers if they would be willing to have their registers become higher by having my twenty-seven children split up among the four remaining afternoon classes, or did they think he should have them split up among all the first-grade classes, some of which met in the morning.

He was straightforward, saying that he didn't think it would be a good idea for the children to be split up among all the first-grade teachers. I agreed with him. He felt that it would be trying on the parents and on the children to have a whole new schedule worked out. After all, if you're used to going to school from twelve to four, coming to school from seven-thirty to twelve is quite a differ-ence. It would be very, very hard on the parents. Especially in this neighbor-hood, where sometimes you have a few children in the same grade, a few in different grades. These parents do bring them to school and take them home. So I agreed with Mr. Frost. The other teachers didn't seem too happy about the idea, but they said they would go along with it.

Mr. Frost and Mrs. Parsons worked out a plan whereby the 1/1 class register would go up to thirty-five, which is generally what a 1/1 class has (thirty-four or thirty-five, I can't remember exactly), and the 1/3 class register would go up to thirty-two or thirty-three. And so forth down the line. Class 1/5 (my class) would be erased, and then came 1/7. Their register would go up to about thirty; and then came 1/9, which would go up to about twenty-six or so. The teachers didn't think it was so bad then, but we all did have added responsibilities.

Mr. Frost then added that if at this time we had any children in our classes that we felt did not belong, this was our chance to have them changed, since there would be many interclass transfers in order to make more homogeneous classes and he would be willing to grant these changes now. So we all had to sit down and think—"Who belongs? Who doesn't belong?"—and I, of course, had to decide where twenty-seven children would belong. I went through my class and divided them into groups to the best of my ability. I put them where I felt they would belong. In the 1/1 class, I put Joseph R., who scored the highest on the reading readiness test, and as a result of his score on the test and his work in class I felt Joseph did belong in the 1/1 class. Then again, I looked further and Lydia A., who I believe is a very smart girl and who wasn't really working as well as she could in my class, I felt she belonged in the 1/1 class. Lydia scored second highest on the reading readiness test. In the 1/1 class I also put Anita R. Anita is a bit older than the rest of the children, but she has caught on most beautifully to most phases of school work even though she just came to the United States last March. Also, she scored the same as Lydia on the reading readiness test.

Then I looked further and I decided that I would put Robert M. in the 1/1 class. I felt strongly that Robert was by far the best child in my class. Robert did every bit of the work ever assigned. He caught on very, very quickly to all phases of work besides doing his work well, quickly, efficiently, and neatly. Even though on the reading readiness he only scored in the fiftieth percentile, I felt he really stood out and *I also felt that once you're in a "1" class, unless you really don't belong, you have a better chance. For some reason the "1" class on the grade is really the only class that you could term a "good" class.* [Author's emphasis] So those four children I recommended for the 1/1 class.

Then I went down the line, and for the 1/3 class I picked nine children, really good children who on the whole listened and did their work. Most of them scored in the fiftieth and fortieth percentile on the reading readiness and they were coping with school problems very, very well. In the 1/7 class I put the slower children, and in the 1/9 class, of course, which is Mrs. Gould's, I put all the children that really weren't doing well in schoolwork at all. I think I should tell you some of the children that I placed in that class. First, of course, Alberto. Alberto is still not able to write his name, so he was in that class. Then I put Beatrice, Stella, Pedro, and several others who really were not working as well as the other children in the class.

I know that the other teachers do have a big job before them because whichever class these children are place in will not have been doing exactly the same work. The children either have much to catch up on or they might review some of the work and the teachers will have to be patient either way. On the whole, I really don't think anyone will have serious discipline problems except perhaps in the 1/1 class where Lydia and Anita have been placed.

The time came when I had to tell the children that I would not be their teacher any more. Well, as young as they are I think that many of them caught on immediately and before I could say anything, faces were very, very long and the children were mumbling, "But I wanted you for a teacher."

That was all I needed! I felt even worse than I felt when I found out that I wouldn't be with them any more. So I continued talking and I told them that it's just something that happens and that I would still be in the school and maybe next year they would get me when they go to the second grade. I told them that I would miss them all, that they would have a lot of fun in their new classes and they would learn a lot. And, of course, I said, "You know all the other teachers. Some of you will get Mrs. Lewis. Some will get Miss Lane, some will get Miss Taylor, and some will get Mrs. Gould."

To my astonishment, Anita kept saying over and over, "But I want you for a teacher. But I want you for a teacher."

I looked around the room. Most of the children were sitting there with very, very long faces. Joseph C. was sitting there with the longest face you could imagine and Robert G. said he didn't want another teacher and all of a sudden Joseph started crying and just didn't stop. He cried all the way out into the hall when we got dressed to go home. I spoke to him softly and said, "Joseph, wouldn't you like Miss Lane for a teacher?" She was standing right near me and finally he stopped crying.

I said goodbye to them and that I would see them all. And that was the end of my class. . . .

. . . Good schools. Poor schools. What is a good school? Is a good school one that is in a good neighborhood, that has middle-class children? Is that a good school? Is a poor school one in a depressed area where you have Negro and Puerto Rican children? These are common terms that people refer to all the time. They hear your school is on Wolf Street—"Oh, you must be in a bad school."

I don't really think that that is what a good or a bad school is. I think a good school is a school that is well run, has a good administration, has people that work together well, has good discipline, and where the children are able to learn and also, of course, where there are numerous facilities for the children and the teachers. In my estimation a poor or a bad school would be one in which the administration and the teachers do not work together, are not working in the best interests of the children, and where learning is not going on. Also, a poor school is one where you don't have proper facilities. I am not acquainted with many of the public schools and I really can't say that the ones that I know are better or worse. I believe my school is a pretty good school. It isn't in the best neighborhood. There are many, many problems in my school, but on the whole I think that the teachers and the administration work together and I do believe that they are doing the best they can with the problems that are around.

You have to remember that in a school such as ours the children are not as ready and willing to learn as in schools in middle-class neighborhoods. [Author's emphasis]

DISCUSSION

Although the human being is born with the capacity to function within a social group, his position within it and the forms of behavior and beliefs appropriate to his particular culture have to be learned. Socialization is the name given to the process by means of which the individual is integrated into his society. It is through this process that the individual adapts to fellow members of his group and is assigned or achieves the various status positions he will assume during his lifetime. These can vary with sex, age, kinship, etc.

Man must do an enormous amount of learning in order to achieve competency and acceptability in his culture. The process of learning the behavior and beliefs appropriate to the culture and to the position of the individual within it has been termed enculturation. It is through this process that the individual's behavior falls well within the limits of tolerance established by the culture, for the individual internalizes the values and beliefs, becomes possessed of the necessary skills and techniques to function within the society, and becomes capable of adjusting and adapting to his physical and social environment.

Enculturation proceeds throughout one's lifetime, for although by adulthood one has usually learned the culture so well that he need give it little thought, an individual has continually to learn the behavior and attitudes appropriate to the new situations in which he finds himself. Thus, although already socialized and learned in the ways of the culture as a student in college, the potential teacher must learn principles, methods, and an ideal role in regard to teaching. As a teacher within a school, he or she must learn the appropriate behavior, attitudes, and skills required in the new situation. Much of this learning is conscious. Some of it is not. What is significant is that, while on the job, the teacher is also socialized, i.e., she is integrated into the ongoing society of the school, and, in addition, the teacher is learning the values, beliefs, and attitudes which in reality govern the functioning of the institution.

The saga of class 1/5 illustrates the manner in which one teacher internalized the cultural characteristics of the slum school in which she is working, coming to accept its organization and the prevailing rationale for pupil failure. There are many lessons here for administrators of inner-city schools. If they wish to change the pattern of failure in schools in order to equip inner-city youngsters with the education to enable them to equitably participate in the opportunities provided by American society, they must become increasingly aware of the values and attitudes prevailing in the school milieu, as well as the educational implications of the organizational structure, for these conditions play a crucial role in the education of children.

The teacher of class 1/5 has warm, friendly relations with her youngsters. She respects and admires their abilities and is troubled by what she foresees in the future for them as she surveys the large amount of educational failure by the sixth grade evident in her school.

Very early in her teaching career, however, this new teacher is indoctrinated by a more experienced teacher in the belief, widely held, that the children come from inferior backgrounds and that it is the deficits in their homes—expressed here as being lack of newspapers and parental care—which prevent educational achievement. That the teachers and the school as an institution also operate as agents to ensure the failure of the children is never even implied or understood as a possible cause.

The beginning teacher, in her description of what happens to class 1/5, provides some insight into the genesis of failure that appears to be an almost inevitable consequence for most of the youngsters in the class.

First, their actual instruction should be examined. Early in her career, this new, very sincere teacher is painfully aware of her own deficits as a teacher. Unclear concerning her teaching of so fundamental a subject as reading, she raises serious questions about how effectively she is providing instruction. As yet, she has not internalized the notion that the failure of children stems from gaps in their backgrounds. She is too sensitive concerning her own inadequacies and expresses a desire for professional growth in the teaching of reading. Although no consensus exists concerning reading methodology, the teacher is telling us that there are serious weaknesses in evaluation and feedback, so that she is unable to know what the children have really been taught and have learned.

By the end of the term, however, all this has changed. By that time, the prognosis for failure is positive. The school practically ensures the failure of the children, and the teacher has been socialized to rationalize this in terms of pupil inadequacy.

An examination of the case will give insight into how this takes place. First, as a result of the drop in school register, the principal loses a teacher, which means the loss of a class, leading to the distribution of one class of children among other classes. The principal and the teachers have little control over this phenomenon. They are themselves manipulated by forces outside their direct control. Education budgets, tables of organization, or directions from headquarters, create conditions without regard for the views and advice of those people in closest relation to the children themselves.

A drop in pupil registers would seem to imply the opportunity to provide for a higher adult-pupil ratio and, consequently, the opportunity for more individualized instruction and pedagogical supports for the youngsters and teachers in this school. Instead it led to the loss of a teacher, higher registers, and, perhaps most important, increased time spent by the administrator and his staff on the mechanics of administration rather than on educational supervision—less time spent on professional growth of teachers and on the education of the children. Why one teacher rather than another was released is unclear, though the substitute status and lower rank of the dismissed teacher was probably involved. As a result of this situation, many classes are disrupted, several first-grade class registers increase, time for instruction is lost, and concern is felt by teachers and pupils alike.

Another even more significant clue to possible eventual failure for the children is described in poignant detail by our teacher when she tells how the youngsters in her class will be distributed among the other first-grade classes. All educators have learned about different maturation rates for children, differential rates of learning readiness, and the developmental differences between boys and girls relevant to learning. To determine the educational outcome for youngsters at this early stage of their development, without due provision for understanding of these normal growth variations, would seem to be a travesty of the educational process. Yet here, in the first half of the first grade, a relatively inexperienced young teacher, herself keenly aware of her own deficiencies as an educator, is placed in the position of literally deciding the educational future of her charges. A few are selected for success—"I felt that once you're in a '1' class, unless you really don't belong, you have a better chance. For some reason the '1' class on the grade is really the only class that you would term a 'good' class." Several children are placed in a class labeled "slow." The other youngsters are relegated to a state of limbo, and the middle range does not carry with it the hope of providing a "better chance."

Thus, before these youngsters have completed four months of schooling, their educational futures have been "tracked," for all through the grades the labels of their class placement will follow them, accompanied by teacher attitudes concerning their abilities. Some youngsters are selected very early for success, others written off as slow. The opportunity to move across is limited, for differential teaching occurs and helps to widen the gap between children. In addition, the children too become aware of the labels placed upon them. Their pattern for achievement in later years is influenced by the feelings of success or failure in these early school experiences.

As she reflects upon what a "good" school or a "bad" school is, our teacher continues to include the learning by children as a significant criterion, together with good relations between staff and administration. The children in the school in which she works do not achieve academically. When describing whether or not her own school is "good" or "bad" she stresses the good relations between the administration and the teachers. That the children do not learn does not now seem so important, for ". . . the children are not as ready and willing to learn as in schools in middle-class neighborhoods."

How well the teacher has internalized the attitude that child deficits explain the failure of children to succeed in school. How normal she now considers the administrative upheavals and their effects upon teachers and children. How perfectly ordinary she considers the tracking of youngsters so early in their school years. The teacher of class 1/5 has been socialized by the school to accept its structure and values. She is not likely to effect much change in the prognosis of failure for most of the children in this school, because she has come to accept the very structural and attitudinal factors which make failure nearly certain. In addition, with all the good intentions in the world, she has come to operate as an agent in the process of determining the life chances of the children in her class by distributing them as she does among the ranked classes on the grade.

This teacher came to her position with very positive impulses. She thought highly of her youngsters and was disturbed that, with what appeared to be good potential, there was so much failure in the school in the upper grades. She looked inward for ways in which she might improve her professional effectiveness in order to forestall retardation, and was not repelled by the neighborhood in which she worked. There is every indication that she had the potential of becoming a very desirable teacher of disadvantaged youngsters. However, her impulses were not enough. Unarmed with the strength that understanding the social processes involved might have given her, as well as having little power within the school hierarchy, this young teacher was socialized by the attitudes of those around her, by the administration and by the availability of a suitable rationale to explain her and the school's failure to fulfill ideal roles. As a result she came to accept traditional slum school attitudes toward the children, and traditional attitudes toward school organization as the way things have to be. She gives every indication of being a pleasant, flexible, co-operative young woman to have on one's staff. But at the same time, she has learned to behave and think in a way that perpetuates a process by which disadvantaged children continue to be disadvantaged.

Robert Schwartz
Thomas Pettigrew
Marshall Smith

Fake panaceas for ghetto education

America has educationally failed fourteen generations of Negro Americans, and has paid a high price for this failure. Currently, the nation is failing to educate the fifteenth generation, and the price in human tragedy promises to be even greater. *The New Republic* readers recently (July 22) received the benefit of Joseph Alsop's thinking on this subject. Stripped of its rhetoric, Alsop's argument reduces to six central propositions:

1. Negro children are not being adequately educated in America's schools.

2. Effective action must be initiated at once to correct this situation.

3. Ending *de facto* segregation is a "virtuous incantation" which cannot be a solution for many reasons. First, desegregation is not going to happen, "at any rate for a long time to come." Second, major federal studies which suggest the efficacy of interracial education in a variety of settings are either "extremely deficient" as in the case of the US Office of Education's monumental "Coleman Report," or "shocking," as in the case of the US Commission on Civil Rights' report on *Racial Isolation in the Public Schools.* Third, when Negroes are "unprepared" for desegregation, school quality goes "to Hell in a hack." Consequently, "unprepared desegregation" drives white parents to the suburbs, creates more school segregation, and causes our central cities to become increasingly Negro.

4. "Brilliant Negro achievements is *[sic]* the answer." Only when Negro American achievements, as in athletics and the army, are conspicuous can white Americans accept desegregation.

5. And brilliant Negro achievements will come only with quality ghetto education. Racially separate schools can do the job if only educators would take the newspaperman's advice and follow "a series of steps of the most ABC simplicity." These steps are demonstrated by the "complete victory" of New York City's "More Effective Schools" (MES) program.

6. As to costs, only "a monster" would deny funds to such a reasonably reliable "cancer cure" as MES.

Few would contest Alsop's first two propositions: a majority of Negro children *are* being cheated out of their American birthright to a full public education; and massive corrective action *is* desperately required. But from this point on he loses the thread.

The desegregation of the nation's public schools is indeed a slow process as long as the necessary structural changes, such as metropolitan consolidation, are not achieved. Although Alsop pays lip service to interracial education as "the ideal solution," his article resists these structural changes by obscuring them. For example, he asserts educational consolidation in metropolitan Washington would require a constitutional amendment. This is absurd, for effective consolidation by no means necessitates a single metropolitan school district as initial efforts in Boston, Hartford, and Rochester demonstrate. Admittedly, metropolitan consolidation is politically difficult to achieve, but the federal government could encourage it in education as it has effectively done in other realms through multi-district funding incentives. In any event, Alsop worries that any pursuit of desegregation will deter his version of "the practical solution." Instead, we worry that Alsop is supplying the self-fulfilling rationale for racially segregated schools "for years to come."

No studies are definitive, nor do the Coleman and Civil Rights Commission reports claim to be final. But no fair-minded observer can pass off the second largest study of American education as "extremely deficient" without a full explanation. Nor could such an observer attack the Commission monograph with libelous charges without detailed elaboration. Apparently, Alsop is peeved that the MES program was not included in the report on *Racial Isolation in the Public Schools*. Had he the courtesy to call down the street to the Commission staff, he would have learned the reasons: the first long-term evaluation of MES appeared too late for inclusion in the Commission report; and, as we shall note below, neither the mode of operation nor the test data of MES are basically different from compensatory programs which are described in the study.

Most serious of all is Alsop's implication that the report of the United States Commission on Civil Rights is racist, that it maintains if you "put Negro with Negro, you get stupidity." If Alsop eventually reads the report, he will encounter the following rejoinder from Commissioner Frankie M. Freeman:

> "The question is not whether in theory or in the abstract Negro schools can be as good as white schools. In a society free from prejudice in which Negroes were full and equal participants, the answer would clearly be 'Yes.' But we are forced, rather, to ask the harder question, whether in our present society, where Negroes are a minority which has been discriminated against, Negro children can prepare themselves to participate effectively in society if they grow up and go to school in isolation from the majority group. We must also ask whether we can cure the disease of prejudice and prepare all children for life in a multiracial world if white children grow up and go to school in isolation from Negroes."

Alsop would also discover the Commission finding that white children in mixed, predominantly white schools perform as well as those in all-white schools. He will learn, too, that only about one in 25 white suburbanites gives racial problems in central city schools as his reason for moving. Our largest cities are becoming increasingly Negro not because whites move to the suburbs at rates similar to those of other industrial nations, but because Negroes are not free to move with them.

Fortunately, neither Washington nor New York are prototypes of American cities. Urban areas with smaller ghettos can often desegregate without suburban cooperation—as Providence, Berkeley, White Plains, and Evanston illustrate. Cities with large ghettos, of course, pose the major difficulties. But metropolitan and public-private cooperation could do the job. Negroes comprise approximately the same percentage of metropolitan areas as they do in the entire nation—roughly 11 percent. And the six cities Alsop compares with Washington all have large Roman Catholic school systems that currently absorb large percentages of their school-aged whites. "The ideal solution" of desegregation *can* be accomplished but not by abandoning the goal and cursing reports which demonstrate its necessity.

Alsop's "brilliant Negro achievement" theory is an insult to the millions of Negro Americans who *have* achieved. Many achieving Negroes have painfully learned, however, that racial discrimination is still a part of their American experience. And this recipe for improved race relations blithely consigns yet another generation to ghetto schools while the brilliant achievers "inspire the next generation." As daily headlines make clear, America's racial problems will not wait that long. Desegregation is not something Negroes "earn" but is their right. Furthermore, Alsop's own examples of American institutions with remarkably reduced racial discrimination—"the hard-bitten army and harder-bitten professional sports teams"—forcefully demonstrate the efficacy of desegregation.

Alsop's belief in the possibility of quality segregated education seems to rest almost entirely on his impression of the achievements of New York City's More Effective Schools, an experimental program which was initiated in ten elementary schools in 1964-65 and expanded to eleven more in 1965-66. The idea originated with the city's teachers union, the United Federation of Teachers, and the UFT has made the further expansion of MES one of the key items in its current negotiations with the Board of Education. In Alsop's opinion the MES program, by starting in early childhood, providing small classes, employing backup teachers, and offering "all the obvious extras," has achieved a breakthrough: it is "literally the first to produce clear test results showing that ghetto children can be given a fully adequate education in ghetto schools."

The independent evaluations performed by New York's Center for Urban Education corroborate Alsop's favorable description of the climate and morale in the More Effective Schools. While the Center's most recent evaluation is careful to point out that there is considerable variation in quality among the 21 schools, most of the Center's observers agreed they would willingly send their children to the particular schools they visited. Given the apathy and despair that typically characterize ghetto schools, the optimism, sense of commitment and parental support that seem to prevail at most of the program's schools are in themselves significant achievements.

But what kind of academic success have these schools had? In Alsop's view, the test scores indicate "all [MES] children have shown a very great average improvement, and those children who have begun in pre-kindergarten and continued on from there are actually performing, on average, *at grade level or above*." (Italics his.) What exactly is Alsop asserting? What does it mean to say that *all* children have shown a very great *average* improvement? How is this improvement to be defined and what data does he have to support this high-sounding claim? His second assertion at least has the virtue of clarity: it should be quite easy to ascertain whether the children who enrolled in MES pre-kindergartens in 1964 are now performing at grade level. But since no citywide tests are administered until the second grade, it cannot possibly be supported or refuted.

The youngest MES children for whom we have three years of test scores are those who have just completed the fourth grade. When these children were first tested in October 1964, their median reading score was only .3 of a year below the city norm. At the end of the first year the gap had widened, but the hope was expressed in the Board of Education's preliminary evaluation that after another year or two of MES the gap would be closed. The sad fact is, however, that the April 1967 fourth grade scores reveal that in only two of the More Effective Schools is the average child reading at grade level. On further inquiry, one discovers that these two "above-average" schools are not ghetto schools at all, but are 70 percent white schools located in a predominantly middle-class section of the Bronx!

Stated flatly, the reading scores show that from the fourth grade on, no majority non-white school in the MES program is reading at grade level. Moreover, when we compare the slope of reading retardation in More Effective Schools with that in control schools (so designated by the Board of Education on the basis of comparable ethnic composition), we find little difference. At each grade level both sets of schools fall further and further behind the city and national norms. The second grade classes at the control schools are on average four months behind city norms, whereas the fifth grade classes are a year and four months behind. The MES second grade classes are one month behind the norm, while their fifth grade classes are a year and a month behind. Alsop is free to hail these scores as representing "a complete victory over that terrible educational lag that is the curse of America's Negro minority." He may well wish to publish them in "Mao-style Big Character posters," but we hope we may be pardoned for not joining in the celebration. It gives us no pleasure to have to state that the MES reading scores simply provide additional evidence to support one of the basic findings of the Civil Rights Commission Report: compensatory programs in predominantly non-white schools have so far had little sustained success in raising the achievement levels of their students.

FALSE EXPECTATIONS

The saddest consequence of Alsop's headlong foray into the educational arena is that by creating false expectations he may have done irreparable damage to a program that is worth encouraging. Anyone who has worked in schools knows that there are no instant miracles. For a program as ambitious as the More Effective Schools, a three-year trial period simply isn't sufficient. At the very least, the program should be continued until the first pre-kindergarten classes have completed their eight years. Unless MES is continued, we will never know whether it could have made a difference for those children caught early enough.

As the evidence now stands, however, the verdict is at best a mixed one. Here are the concluding sentences from the summary of the Center For Urban Education's most recent MES evaluation, conducted by Dr. David Fox of City University:

"In short, this evaluation suggests that the basic program introduced under the label 'MES' has had a favorable impact on the adults in these schools, in terms of their observed behavior, their views of the programs, and the general climate of the school. But it has not had a comparable impact on the observed behavior, perception, or achievement of the children who attended."

Interestingly, Alsop talked with Dr. Fox and his colleagues before going out to spend two hours at two schools, so he cannot plead ignorance of their conclusions. We quote from a report of the Alsop visit written by Joseph Krevisky, chairman of the Center's Field Research and Evaluation Committee, and published in *The Center Forum*, July 5th:

"All consultants stressed the very tentative nature of our findings, and the great difficulty of generalizing about the success of this program or about the broader implications that MES is a possible solution to the crucial problems of education of Negro and Puerto Rican children.

. . . .In general, these cautions made very little dent on Mr. Alsop, who disagreed with almost all the comments made and was irritated by some of them. He said at that point it was futile to discuss such points any more as *nobody would change his mind.*"

There is also the little matter of money. Alsop disposes of desegregation as impractical, but does not explain how practical it will be to get the nation to "invest until it hurts cruelly." MES costs $1,263 per child, $700 more than in regular primary schools in the New York system. It also requires 30 percent more schoolrooms and roughly twice the staff members of regular elementary schools in the city. And since MES has so far obtained only modest test score increments at best, these costs are gross underestimates for achieving Alsop's goal of average performance at grade level. The newspaperman is advocating a national educational program which, if possible at all, would cost well in excess of ten billion dollars annually. We salute Alsop's resolute refusal to choose between guns and butter, but the question remains: will even the richest country on earth simultaneously support the Vietnam war and a national MES program?

The MES requirement of 30 percent more schoolrooms raises yet another difficulty. So far in New York, only schools with underutilized facilities have taken part. But nationally the program would require many new schools; and Alsop would have them built deep within the ghetto. This would institutionalize racial segregation and seal Negro children in the ghetto for generations. Instead, new school construction must take the form of large complexes, such as campus parks, which draw upon wide attendance areas, guarantee quality education, and maximize desegregation.

WHY INTERRACIAL SCHOOLING?

But to dwell on costs and construction would be to allow ourselves to be deflected from the fundamental sources of our disagreement with Alsop. Let us suppose that his facts are right, that we do have evidence that by spending $1,263 per child we could raise the reading scores of ghetto children to the level of those of suburban children. This would indeed signify equality of educational opportunity, and it would be a distinct improvement over what we now have. But would this fulfill the primary aims of a public school system in a multiracial society? Reduced to its simplest terms, our belief is that interracial contact is an essential component of quality education, that schools which are isolated by virtue of race, social class, or religion deprive their students of adequate preparation for a diverse society and world.

We don't want to fall into the trap of seeming to assert that integrated education is by definition good education; obviously, the mere presence of whites and Negroes in the same classroom is no guarantee of anything. But when we compare the findings of the Coleman and Civil Rights Commission reports with those of such compensatory programs as the More Effective Schools, we must conclude that the evidence suggests that minority group students perform better in integrated than in isolated settings.

Are the reasons for this so hard to discern? To quote again from the Krevisky report of Alsop's visit to the MES schools:

"The teachers stressed that neither MES nor other programs have yet succeeded in overcoming the sense of hopelessness in the community, and the powerful barriers to incentives posed by discrimination in housing and jobs. . . ."

Unless we are willing to change the fundamental realities of ghetto life in America, aren't we deceiving ourselves to think that any amount of money can buy quality segregated education?

Let there be no misunderstanding. We believe MES and other dedicated remedial programs are necessary efforts at this desperate juncture in American race relations. But they constitute neither a national model nor a permanent solution. At best, they buy time until racial desegregation becomes a widespread fact of American public schools. Full desegregation must be the goal, and all efforts, including MES, must point toward it. Indeed, MES was originally conceived in this spirit, as the May 1964 program description made clear on its first page. And Alsop encountered on his hurried visit the same position from MES teachers:

> ". . .the teachers, mostly experienced and mostly Negro, sharply disagreed with Alsop's line. They refused adamantly to accept the solution of quality segregated education and questioned him insistently on what he was doing to educate white people to accept Negroes trying to break out of the 'ghetto'. They sharply challenged a statement he made that education was the only key to integration—by elevating the abilities of the Negro people, and leading to their acceptance by the white community." (*The Center Forum*, July 5.)

We agree with Mr. Alsop that "it is always wicked to hold out false hopes and offer fake panaceas to those in desperate need of hope and help." But even the best funded and most dedicated "compensatory" *ghetto* program is just such a "false hope" and "fake panacea" if it is advanced as a "complete victory."

Joseph Alsop

Ghetto education

Although some time has passed since the publication of "Fake Panaceas for Ghetto Education" (Sept. 23), this very strange document demands a reply, however belated. For the sake of those *New Republic* readers who may have missed the angry outburst by Messrs. Thomas Schwartz, Thomas Pettigrew and Marshall Smith, "Fake Panaceas" was an attack on an earlier article of mine. In this earlier article, I did no more than suggest that pursuit of the vital goal of school desegregation must not be permitted to interfere with a parallel effort— the urgently, even desperately needed effort to educate the millions of Negro children now in ghetto schools or soon to go to ghetto schools, who have little hope of experiencing integrated education either now or in the foreseeable future. I shall pass over everything that was personal to me, all of it grossly inaccurate, in this Schwartz-Pettigrew-Smith attack; for all this is of no special consequence. What is profoundly consequential is quite another point. To put it bluntly, Professor Pettigrew, the real author of the Civil Rights Commission's report on "Racial Isolation in the Public Schools," is either unwilling to look the harsh facts of ghetto education in the face, or has never troubled to gather these basic facts concerning the problem he discusses so glibly. If the real author of such an important government report does not know or refuses to consider the basic facts, we are in a pretty bad way.

The thrust of the Pettigrew argument is that emphasis on ghetto school improvement—emphasis, in fact, on truly educating the millions of children now in ghetto schools or destined to go to ghetto schools, where they are not now being truly educated—will provide "the self-fulfilling rationale for socially segregated schools for years to come." Hence the first basic facts to consider are those bearing on the question: how many Negro children actually have the faintest chance of escaping from segregated ghetto schools "for years to come"? Even the most eminent academics' desire to avoid "self-fulfilling rationales" must after all be subordinated to the needs of the children themselves—and their prime need is *decent education.*

Let us begin this part of the inquiry in 18 American cities—most of them among our largest cities. All of these 18 cities have total school populations that

Reprinted from *The New Republic*, Nov. 18, 1967:18-23, by permission of the author.

include at least 40 percent of Negro children. . . . In all cities, the percentage of Negro children in the primary and elementary schools is substantially higher than the percentage in the high schools. Thus, Cleveland, with a school population 49 percent Negro, has a Negro majority in the primary and elementary schools; and much the same upper-lower relationships may also be assumed for all the other cities in the 40-50 percent bracket. These few bits and pieces of data should be enough to indicate the total falsity of the Schwartz-Pettigrew-Smith assertion that "neither Washington nor New York are prototypes of American cities." New York is, indeed, not a prototype because its Negro percentage of the school population is no more than 28.4, hardly higher than Boston, which has 26 percent. (But in New York, the ghetto schools also include unusually large numbers of Puerto Ricans, who are . . . another major element of the ghetto school problem.) Washington *is* a prototype, alas, in the literal sense of the word; for Washington is merely the most advanced case of an urban demographic trend which will surely produce many other super-ghetto center-cities unless drastic steps are taken to solve the ghetto school problem. Where St. Louis and Baltimore are today, for instance, Washington was only a few years ago; and the same observation applies, in varying degree, to just about every other city in the table with 40 percent and more of Negro children in its schools.

[There] are 18 cities with the most acute current problem. In these 18 cities, there are now close to a million Negro children in the elementary schools alone. Officially, a school is defined as segregated if it is 50 percent Negro or above. Even if the entire school populations of all these cities could be automatically homogenized, so that each school would contain the exact citywide percentage of Negro pupils in the whole school system, every one of these cities would still have segregated or borderline-segregated primary and elementary schools; and in many of them, all the schools, including high schools, would still be segregated under the official definition. As a practical matter, of course, this kind of total homogenization of the entire school population is absolutely out of the question in any city of considerable size. It can be done—and often should be done—in small cities, and even in big cities where the Negro percentage of the school population is not too unwieldy. It has been done, for instance, in White Plains, N.Y., where the predominantly Negro center-city school was closed, and the center-city children are now being bused out to the four white, middle-class schools in White Plains' outer ring. But in White Plains, this involved no insurmountable physical problem, whereas in cities like Chicago and Detroit, mere physical problems put anything like the White Plains solution utterly beyond reach. In such cities, the great majority of ghetto children are inevitably going to be educated *in ghetto schools* for a very long time to come; and this is why the prospects of *improved education in the ghettos* now constitute a subject of such urgent interest and importance.

By "physical problems" I mean, for instance, the hopeless difficulty of busing scores and even hundreds of thousands of children back and forth, often for very long distances, over the length and breadth of such a city as Chicago. As the sinister example of Boston has all too plainly shown, meanwhile, no sane man who gives a tinker's damn for Negro education can dare to forget about political problems. In Boston, after all, there are only 26 percent of Negro children in the entire school population, and not much more than 30 percent in the primary and elementary school population. I do not admire Louise Day Hicks any more than Professor Pettigrew does. Thank God she was defeated, though by a disturbingly narrow margin. But the voters she appealed to are a fact of life, however sordid and regrettable this fact may be. In Boston, moreover the real problem was rather small in dimension, and should have been manageable by persons of reasonable goodwill. Thus it is obvious that situations even more threatening than Boston's can all too easily arise elsewhere. Unless, once again, swift and drastic steps to solve the ghetto school problem begin to be taken in the ghettos themselves.

In summary, school desegregation is literally impossible, even by forcible homogenization, in 18 cities which now have a Negro elementary school population of nearly a million, with scores of thousands more in high school. In 17 more cities—those with 20 percent of Negro schoolchildren or above—serious school desegregation is probably politically impossible; for a new Louise Day Hicks can all too easily emerge from limbo, in every one of these cities, if the right steps to solve the ghetto school problem in the ghettos are not taken in the first instance. And in only 12 cities on the Commissioner of Education's list— those with school populations under 20 percent Negro—is anything like truly and fully integrated schooling an imaginable feasible aim. Even where it is imaginably feasible, any realist must further note that the road to school integration can be all too rocky, although the task should theoretically be as easy as in White Plains.

Such, then, is the first set of basic demographic, practical and political facts tha Messrs. Schwartz, Pettigrew and Smith have either refused to face, or have failed to take the trouble to discover. If fear of "self-fulfilling rationales" is going to prevent radical ghetto school improvement in a large majority of the cities on the list, something like a million and a half Negro children will then be permanently condemned to grossly inadequate schooling—and thereby in turn condemned to permanent inability to compete in modern society. This seems a heartless and antisocial decision to take.

There are also some additional facts to consider, which are of very great interest. Let us begin with busing, which was recommended as the sovereign remedy for urban school segregation in the Civil Rights Commission report, to which Professor Pettigrew contributed so importantly. In my previous article I called that report "scandalous" because it offered busing as its prime remedy, yet was datelined Washington, D.C., where the public schools are almost entirely Negro. The report would not have been scandalous, to be sure, if it had included a recommendation for a constitutional amendment, permitting forcible imposition by the federal government of some sort of general homogenization of the school populations of the District of Columbia and its white middle-class suburbs—plus the same sort of thing, of course, in other cities nearly as deeply afflicted by the white suburban emigration. If this degree of honesty and fact-facing had been practiced, the Civil Rights Commission report would not have been scandalous; it would merely have been silly. The report would have been silly, in the first place, because it would then have asked the center-city and suburban parents to tolerate their children wasting anywhere up to three hours a day on buses, in order to achieve homogenization. And the report would have been silly in the second place, and above all, because there is not the remotest chance of carrying the necessary constitutional amendment, in the highly improbable event that it is ever offered. I strongly favor busing wherever it can be of any use; yet it is abundantly clear that busing is useless as a *general remedy*. It can produce modestly useful fringe results within center-cities, although even in the center-cities, the results are bound to be more and more marginal in proportion to increases in the percentages of Negro children in the school populations.

On busing from the center-cities to the suburbs, Messrs. Schwartz, Pettigrew and Smith reassuringly declared the "efforts . . . in Rochester demonstrate" that "effective consolidation" of center-city and suburban schools "by no means necessitates a single metropolitan school district." Note those words, "effective consolidation." As usual, Schwartz, Pettigrew and Smith either neglected to inform themselves about the proud case of Rochester, or else they were once again guilty of citing nonsense-evidence. In Rochester, to be sure, some hundreds of children are being bused within the center-city, and others are being bused to the suburbs. But those being bused to the suburbs number only 220, out of a total Negro grade school population in Rochester that is close to 10,000. The children being bused have been carefully chosen for good past performance and high future potential. Even so, the majority of Rochester's suburbs are now resisting a plan to bus out a few beggarly hundreds of additional children. If this kind of "initial effort" demonstrates anything at all, it demonstrates the precise point made in my earlier article. And in Hartford, Boston and all other cases known to me of center-city-surburban busing, it is again the same story of a few hundreds, usually specially selected, out of the many thousands of children who constitute the true problem. In short, center-city-suburban busing is no more than a very minor virtuous gesture. I must add that I am not against virtuous gestures of this sort, however minor; indeed, I favor them, because even the smallest addition to our future totals of effectively educated Negroes will also be an addition to the number of Negroes equipped to compete successfully and to achieve conspicuously. But the crucial difference between remedies and gestures is another key fact that Schwartz, Pettigrew and Smith have failed to face or have not bothered to figure out.

Finally, at the very heart of all the key facts the Schwartz-Pettigrew-Smith team have either failed to face or do not know about, there is the major role of *unprepared* school desegregation in transforming more and more of the great center-cities into proto-ghettos surrounded by rings of prosperous white middle-class suburbs. In my previous article, I cited the case of the nation's capital, which has 250,000 remaining white inhabitants, with only 13,500 children in the public schools, as against nearly 500,000 Negro inhabitants, with over 134,000 children in the schools. Obviously a white population of 250,000 with only 13,500 children in the public school system (including teachers' colleges) is a demographic monstrosity in normal circumstances. Obviously, this is the situation in Washington simply because virtually all white families with children in need of schooling have automatically moved to the suburbs, except for those few in neighborhoods where the schools are still predominantly white, plus another, even smaller group who can afford to send their children to private or parochial schools. In the same article, I also cited the really tragic case of PS 7 and PS 8 in Brooklyn—one segregated, one white—the pairing of which was sponsored by the PTA of the white school. The result, as I wrote, was that school quality declined very gravely, because no adequate measures had been taken to maintain both schools' educational effectiveness in the face of a heavy post-pairing admixture of extremely deprived children. In consequence, the very same white parents who had sponsored pairing either moved to the suburbs or put their children into private schools, leaving two segregated public schools where there had been only one before. This case is particularly significant because the white flight from the paired schools took place *before* any very striking change in the neighborhood the white children came from.

A large allowance for the influence of change in the neighborhood must be made, in contrast, in the cases of the schools in "transitional areas," also in New York City. In order to try to maintain a reasonable racial balance in these schools, New York has been spending some millions of dollars each year on extras intended to improve school quality. The extras have been valuable, but the improvements have been insufficient to hold the schools' white population, which has declined by one-half in three short years. The school principals themselves attribute this emigration only 50 percent to the change in their neighborhoods, and admit that the other 50 percent is attributable to continuing white dissatisfaction with the schools. Yet sufficient improvement can indeed be made to hold and even to increase the white population in a predominantly Negro school, as is proved by the case of PS 307, also in Brooklyn. Here the school principal, Dr. Irving Carlin, had to speak on the Brooklyn church-circuit to get his first 30 or so white pupils, when PS 307 was reopened as one of New York's More Effective Schools. In addition, he was able to offer the special inducement of pre-kindergarten, which is only provided in New York by schools in the MES program. But that was more than three years ago. Today, PS 307 has over 200 white children going to school—being bused in, too—in a near-complete ghetto neighborhood. Seventy of last year's kindergarten whites have stayed on into the first grade; these first-grade white children's parents show every sign of intending to keep them in PS 307 until their primary schooling is finished—always supposing school quality is maintained; and the school now *has a waiting list of another 100 white children* who cannot be accepted because there are no places for them. This is no trifling business, either, for with 200 white pupils at present, PS 307 is already above 20 percent white, solely by *reverse integration*, solely resulting from the attractive power of outstanding school quality.

Evidently, however, facts like these are either too unsettling for Messrs. Schwartz, Pettigrew and Smith to digest, or they are too troublesome for them to ascertain. In their article they passed over, in resounding silence, the uncomfortably difficult problems of Washington's strange demographic pattern and the story of PS 7 and PS 8. Probably they had not bothered to learn about the results of the New York program for schools in "transitional areas," and they had certainly failed to inquire into the achievement of PS 307. Without offering any sort of detailed proof, they contented themselves with grandly remarking that "only about one in 25 white suburbanites gives" racial problems in the schools as his reason for moving to the suburbs. If you can believe that this is indicative or meaningful, in the face of Washington's demographic pattern, for instance, you are capable of believing six impossible things before breakfast, in the manner of the White Queen in *Alice*. The plain fact of the matter is that unless radical measures to maintain school quality are taken in advance, white middle-class families will almost always begin to exercise the option to move away, either to the suburbs or to another center-city neighborhood, whenever the percentage of deprived children in a given school rises above a certain level— generally about one-quarter of the total. It is not so much a matter of race, either, as it is a matter of the effect on school quality of the addition of large numbers of children who are educationally retarded; for the white middle-class emigration has also occurred in numerous cases where the educationally retarded children were Mexican-Americans, Puerto Rican-Americans and Appalachian poor whites. In contrast, moreover, there is more than a glimmer of hope that extreme (and costly) attention to school quality can quite successfully maintain a reasonable racial balance. Here, see the case of PS 307.

Add it all up. For anyone who is willing to find out the facts and to face up to them, several conclusions are unavoidable. First, no amount of court-ordering, no further dubious report-writing by the Pettigrews of the academic community, nor any other influence that one can think of, will save millions of Negro children from receiving mainly segregated schooling, either now or for a long time to come. Second, providing those millions of Negro children with a decent education, and thereby fitting them to compete in our increasingly technological society, is therefore one of the most desperately urgent problems confronting this country, which *must be solved, no matter what the cost.* Third, however, for all the reasons cited, the problem *cannot be solved* by exclusive, too often vain pursuit of school desegregation; in fact, the only available *overall* solution is radical improvement of the ghetto schools, in parallel, of course, with efforts to obtain desegregation wherever this is practically feasible. To these all too amply buttressed conclusions, one may also add another, extremely tentative conclusion. It just may be that radical ghetto school improvement, on a very big scale, will not only help to secure the school integration that Professor Pettigrew and I both fervently believe in as the ideal result; in addition, this kind of school improvement in the center-cities may even tend to reverse the terrible demographic trend that is threatening to turn so many of our larger cities into super-ghettos surrounded by endless rings of rancidly complacent, fatly affluent white suburbs.

That leaves the question whether sufficiently radical improvement of ghetto schools is really possible, given the cruel character of the ghetto environment. The answer is, thus far, that we cannot be quite sure about this, because all experiments with really radical ghetto school improvement are too recent to have produced final results; yet we already have very good grounds for hope. As giving grounds for real hope (but no means as a "panacea" or even as a final model) I cited the longest established effort of really radical school improvement, the More Effective Schools program in New York City, which was only started in the 1964-65 school year. There is no space here for detailed refutation of the Schwartz-Pettigrew-Smith attack on the MES program. It is enough to make a single, very simple point. Briefly, one of the cardinal requirements—perhaps *the* cardinal requirement—of the MES program is to catch the children young, in order to overcome basic ghetto handicaps like speech difficulties when the children are still malleable and receptive. This is why all MES schools have an extra pre-kindergarten year. For this very reason, too, the earlier grades, whose children really were caught young, are the only fair tests of the MES schools that are as yet available, whereas the higher grades are not fair tests because the children were not caught young enough. For reasons which are extremely mysterious, the Center for Urban Education based its most recent report on the MES schools (though not its two earlier reports) exclusively on the higher grades. The explanation privately given at the Center was that in Grade II, variations in test results between MES and other schools were too trifling to be interesting. But this, as will be seen, is flatly untrue. Before using the Center's last report as their test, one must add that Schwartz, Pettigrew and Smith could have discovered the untruth by totaling up last year's test results.

The New York Board of Education has just made available its more recent sets of test results for all the schools in the city. In order to get a fair comparison, I have eliminated three schools in partly middle-class neighborhoods (originally included in the MES program to see whether they could hold their white pupils) which have shown extra-high performance. I have used as my bases of comparison only the 18 MES schools that were formerly "special service schools"—which in New York means ghetto schools—and the more than 200 non-MES ghetto schools still in the "special service" group—not excluding "special service" schools with university or college affiliations, unusually helpful neighborhood situations, or other advantages. As the new figures were barely in hand when this went to press, I have only the reading scores; but these are exceedingly impressive if correctly interpreted.

Let us begin with Grade II. At the opening of the 1966-67 school year, when the norm was 2, the children in the special service schools showed a reading average of 1.7. And when retested in April 1966, by which time the norm was 2.7, the special service school-children showed a reading average of 2.4. In other words, their reading skills were equal to those of more fortunate children with only two years and four months of schooling, instead of children with two years and seven months, as should have been the case. Serious retardation had therefore set in already. In contrast, in the schools in the MES program, the children also started the school year below norm, but they were only one month behind, with an average score on the reading tests of 1.9. On the April retest, moreover, they were performing above the norm—in fact, above the average of more fortunate children—with an average score of 2.9. Of the 18 schools, futhermore, only three were more than a point below the norm (all of them in particularly horrible neighborhoods); and a few were also really well above the norm. There are many reasons for variations from school to school, which are also dramatically present among New York's special service schools. Centralized direction of the More Effective Schools program—which the Board of Education has just struck down—is badly needed in order to get at those reasons and to secure better performance in the small minority of less successful schools. Overall, in any case, the MES children were performing above grade level, on average, when they were nearing the end of the second grade. In Grade III, again, where the children had been caught less young, but still young enough to show the effects of earlier learning and better work habits, the two groups of schools still showed nearly the same contrast. At the beginning of the school year, when the norm was 3, the reading tests of the special service school-children averaged 2.5, while those of the children in the MES program averaged 2.7. And in the April 1967 retests, when the norm had reached 3.7, the special service school-children averaged 3.3, while the children in the MES program averaged 3.7—on the nose of grade level, in fact. Finally, in Grade V, there was still a marked contrast, although the Grade V children had certainly not been caught young enough to offer a fair test of MES. At the beginning of the school year, the norm was by now 5, and both special service and MES schoolchildren scored only 4. But on the April retests, when the norm had reached 5.7, the special service school-children scored, on average, only 5, while the MES program children had an average score of 5.3.

This talk of test scores and grade levels may seem bewildering to the average reader, but the figures are bursting with significance, nonetheless. They mean that in the representative earlier grades, the average child in the MES program *does not show the terrible, progressive retardation which is the curse of ghetto schooling,* whereas in those same grades, the curse already begins to show very clearly in the average performance of the children in New York's other ghetto schools. Furthermore, I have talked or obtained opinions from a long series of principals of successful More Effective Schools; and they are unanimous that their second-graders will go forward, on average, at grade level or above—in other words, be educated like more fortunate children—as they move upward in their schools to the higher grades. If this proves true MES will then be a solution of the ghetto school problem—but one must wait and see.

At this juncture there is only one point, indeed, concerning which one does not need to wait and see. If millions of Negro children are highly unlikely to escape from segregated, ghetto education for years to come, something has got to be done to give those children an education, *in the ghettos if need be,* that will fit them to compete in modern American society. The present system, of allowing the heaviest kind of educational handicap to be regularly piled on top of the barriers of ugly prejudice, is simply an inbuilt design for perpetuating discrimination and injustice in our society. The system must therefore be reformed, no matter what the cost. Hence educational theorists would do better to stop belaboring the arguments so dear to Messrs. Schwartz, Pettigrew and Smith; and above all, they ought to begin to study and explore every imaginable method of securing radical improvement of *the schools where the children are.* To do less than this, is callously to condemn to defeat and despair millions of Negro children who have no practical hope of integrated education.

In conclusion, I must repeat with emphasis that fully integrated schools in a fully integrated sociey must always be the American aim. The question is not what the aim ought to be. The question is, really, how to attain that aim— whether, for example, ghetto school improvement to equip Negro children for equal future competition with their white middle-class contemporaries is not an unavoidable prerequisite to eventual attainment of the total aim. There are many ways to approach this central question. Only one thing is already certain. Any approach that is *not* based on all the facts, that ignores current urban demography, that lets "the best become the enemy of the good," that is self-serving and fundamentally dishonest in its formulation of the problem, will surely meet with disastrous failure. And when you can find great encouragement in Rochester; when you can forget about or overlook the million elementary school-children of Washington and 17 other major cities; when you can prate about busing as a general remedy and are driven to snide misstatement concerning the one promising in-ghetto solution that is well under way thus far, then your approach belongs in the class described above.

Max Birnbaum

Whose values
should be taught?

In a society in which there is general agreement on what constitutes the good, the true, and the beautiful, the task of teaching values is a simple one. The consensus is clear and, even if minority views exist, they do not challenge the majority judgment effectively. But in a pluralist society, in which no general agreement has been reached, the problem becomes infinitely more difficult.

Teaching values in American classrooms today, therefore, is an awesome assignment. For, as a nation, we are caught between the myths of a rural past that has all but disappeared, and the new urban present that has not yet achieved its final form. While our backs were turned, profound changes took place not only in our values, but in the very sources from which they come. While our sights were focused on older, simpler patterns of thought and conduct, far more complex problems and issues were beginning to challenge our society. No longer, for instance, can we teach the principle of equality for all without recognizing its unique meaning for the American Negro; nor can we discuss traditional concepts of religious liberty without taking into account the recent Supreme Court decisions on Bible reading and prayer in the classroom, and the role played by the new assertiveness of Catholics and Jews in many areas of our national life.

(Some teachers who live and work in areas of the country where religious, racial, and ethnic differences are not acute will insist that such problems are alien to the American Way. But many others have experienced the problems of emerging difference at first hand and are aware of the vast changes that have taken place.)

Yet the dramatic changes that have marked the development of contemporary attitudes did not come without warning. If we take even a brief backward look at our nation's history, we can see that they evolved over a period of several decades.

The American colonies were settled originally by Protestant, English-speaking people of Anglo-Saxon origin. Almost from the beginning this group was joined by those who were non-Protestant, non-Anglo-Saxon, and even non-English speaking. But the names of the signers of the Declaration of Independence and

Reprinted from *Saturday Review*, June 20, 1964: 60-62, 67.
Copyright © 1964 by Saturday Review, Inc.

the membership of the Constitutional Convention, almost 150 years after the earliest settlements, still reflected the continued dominance of the first group. This persistence of control is most remarkable in view of fairly sound historical evidence that almost 40 per cent of the inhabitants of the United States in 1790 were of non-English-speaking origin.

American culture, its values, institutions, and mores are primarily, although not exclusively, the creation of that remarkable group of men whose origins, immediate and remote, were the British Isles. To be sure, the group absorbed innumerable sons and daughters from other religions and cultures, but its Protestant Anglo-Saxon imprint continued to be highly visible.

The Civil War and the rise of industrial America contributed directly to changes in the religious and ethnic composition of the nation. Most new immigrants in the years immediately after the Civil War were German and Irish. These were followed by people from Southern and Eastern Europe, of Slavic and Italian origin and Jews from the Austro-Hungarian empire, Poland, and Russia. Part of the native American's horror-stricken reaction to the city of the late nineteenth century came from the fact that it was crowded by people with strange tongues and stranger behavior. By the turn of the century, when immigrants of English origin were fast becoming a minority, voices were saying that unless something were done to stem the tide, the character of our civilization would change drastically.

Just as the Civil War was in many ways the "Second American Revolution" in its impact on our society, so 1914 marked the end not only of our isolation from world involvement, but also of our unitary society. The values and mores derived from our historically dominant religious and ethnic groups were being challenged. As a result, in the years following 1914, we witnessed the imposition of immigration quotas based upon a philosophy of Nordic Supremacy, the Great Depression and the fundamental changes it brought in the relations of the state to our citizenry, and the successive challenges to the old order by Catholic, Jew, and now the Negro. In the light of these swift and truly revolutionary changes it is not remarkable that our schools have had difficulty in promulgating a common set of values. What is amazing is that they have done as well as they have.

Of the half century since 1914, perhaps the most significant years were the 1920's. For they marked a climactic period during which those conflicts that had raged sporadically just beneath the surface of public awareness were revealed publicly. The fears of those who felt that this country was theirs by right of birth and ancestral domain were intensified by the 1919 steel strike and rumors of Bolshevik infiltration. The American Legion had been organized in Paris in response to similar fears, when all of Europe appeared to be going communist. The United States, with its polyglot population, seemed a natural target for such subversion. But the most significant impact on America came from the immigration debates that raged for almost a decade in Congress and throughout the nation, in which terms such as the "alien flood," the "barbarian horders," and the "foreign tide" were freely used.

The debates when stripped to their essentials reveal that: 1) the dominant voices in our society used basically racist arguments to stigmatize those who had immigrated from Southern and Eastern Europe; 2) descent from English-speaking ancestors from the British Isles was deemed sufficient guarantee of superior capacity to assume the responsibilities and privileges of American citizenship; 3) American labor, despite its origins, was willing to be swayed by economic need to shut the doors of the nation even against its own kin; 4) the new American patriotic coalition, which emerged at this time, spearheaded the drive for restriction of immigration as an expression of nationalism and a fear of socialism and communism.

Although minority peoples formed protective organizations in response to a variety of special needs, the defensive character of these groups was intensified by the use of ethnic group classifications in the National Origins Act that determined all future quotas for immigration into the United States. From that point on, the right to enter America and become a citizen was defined not in individual but in group terms. The Irish had already learned the uses of ethnic group politics; other immigrant groups were now to follow in their footsteps, and group pressures soon became common in all areas of national life, including the schools.

The end of unrestricted immigration created a condition quite different from that which had been intended by the architects of the restrictive immigration policy. In two generations, all citizens of Eastern European descent had become native, rather than foreign-born Americans. But for many the group consciousness stimulated by the National Origins Act helped to strengthen rather than lessen their adherence to the values of the groups from which they sprang. Aided by awareness of service on behalf of country in two World Wars, the minority religious and ethnic groups began increasingly to assert their rights. Subsequently, the American Negro returned from the Allies' victory over German Nazism, determined to destroy racism here as well.

The decade of the Thirties witnessed two events of overwhelming importance to all Americans that had special poignancy for Catholics and Jews—and that also demonstrate the complexity of group loyalties in American society. The first was the Spanish Civil War. The nation, with the exception of the Catholics, was largely sympathetic to the Republican cause. The fact that Germany and Italy were aiding Franco, and Soviet Russia was aiding the Loyalists, created disastrous divisions among religious, ethnic, and political groupings. The issue was in large measure, for the Catholics and Jews, a matter of opposing the ally who was most threatening to them at the time. For the Jews it was obviously Hitler; for the Catholics it was Stalin; Protestants, and the unchurched generally, except for those who feared and hated the Soviet more than anything else, were either neutral or pro-Republican.

Then came the war against the Axis powers. A significant number of Americans, reflecting predominantly Catholic and Protestant groups, some of whom were of German ancestry, felt that we were fighting the wrong enemy. When Stalin and the Soviet Union became our major antagonists in the period after the Second World War, those groups that had opposed our fighting as an ally of Russia came into their own. Their passionate opposition to American foreign policy had been long pent-up and the beginning of the Cold War provided them with final justification for their feelings.

Senator McCarthy was in many respects a charismatic champion of this submerged cause. A Midwestern Irish Catholic, elected from a state with a very large German ethnic population, he provided precisely the kind of ruthless hostility toward Communism that would satisfy the loose coalition of those who had always felt that Russia was the true threat to America. A Gallup Poll during the period of McCarthy's greatest influence showed Jews overwhelmingly opposed to him, the Catholics strongly in his favor, and Protestants divided. The strongly Protestant hinterlands of the Middle West and Southwest supported him, and the urban, Northwestern, and Far Western Protestants strongly opposed him. The endurance of attitudes based on religious and ethnic considerations has rarely been more clearly demonstrated than during this conflict. And, as we shall see, recent problems in the teaching about communism and patriotism are still intertwined with this legacy of the past.

At this point it should be revealing to analyze three basic issues that have presented serious problems for teachers, in terms of the group forces operating in our contemporary society. Obviously, the most significant value-laden issues for public schools have been the place of religion and religious values in the curriculum, the teaching of patriotism, and the closely related issue of teaching about communism. The impact of race on our schools is also of prime importance, but this will be treated separately because of the unusual character of the group forces reflected in the racial crisis.

Before applying a group relations theory to explain these complicated issues, however, certain qualifications should be stated. No one theory can explain complex group behavior. Few observers after the election of 1960 would deny the persistence of religious, ethnic, and racial loyalties. The significant shift of Democratic Protestants to Nixon and a similar shift of Republican Catholics to Kennedy is evidence enough. What is not explained by any simple cause and effect analysis is why so many Protestants, for example, voted for Kennedy, and why so many Catholics voted for Nixon. Economic factors, ethnic backgrounds, regional biases, personal preferences largely free of group loyalties or pressures, would have to be investigated. Jews and Negroes, on the other hand, voted in overwhelming numbers for Kennedy. The Democratic Party, especially in the Northern cities, still retains the loyalty of these and other minority religious and racial groups. The appointment of two Jews to Kennedy's Cabinet, and the subsequent appointment to that powerful and symbolic body of an Italo-American and a Polish-American, with a tacit commitment to include a Negro eventually as well, makes very plain indeed that the old Protestant, Anglo-Saxon order has changed.

With this *caveat* stated, let us consider the two major problem areas that have both openly and subtly affected the teaching of values and value-laden subjects during the past two decades—religion and patriotism. Both problems differ markedly from region to region and stubbornly refuse to respond to simple analysis. But after saying this, we are also reasonably certain that on both issues Catholics and Jews have been overwhelmingly on opposite sides, and that Protestants, once again, have split down the middle, in a pattern very similar to that which prevailed during the 1930s and through the McCarthy period.

The growing agreement between the politically and theologically liberal Protestants and the Jews with similar views has been an important factor in Protestant sensitivity to Jewish hostility toward religious influences in the public schools. Prayer, Bible reading, and excessively Christological observance of Christmas and Easter are cases in point. And most of the leaders of the larger Protestant denominations, together with a few Catholics, have gone along with the recent Supreme Court decisions on prayer and Bible reading. (To be sure, the awareness of Protestant leaders that the more important issue is public support of parochial education undoubtedly influenced many to make what is a comparatively small sacrifice in order to build additional legal bulwarks against the potential diversion of public funds.) Common commitment to public education, similar attitudes on censorship, birth control, and a host of other religiously value-laden issues make for easy communication and accommodation between these Protestants and most Jewish groups.

Most Catholic spokesmen, on the other hand, originally opposed the Supreme Court decisions in terms that were surprisingly similar in tone to the declarations of the Protestant South and Middle West. Increased secularization of the public schools is seen as a direct threat to conservative Protestants, and as an attack on religion in public life by Catholics.

Beyond this point, however, the two groups differ. And unless the essentially unstable character of this coalition is comprehended, it is virtually impossible to understand the unpredictable strengths and weaknesses of its pressures on the schools. The largest segment of Protestants opposed to the elimination of prayer and other religious observances in the classroom also opposes with the greatest vigor any grant of public funds to Catholic parochial schools or any move that would increase Catholic influence. Fundamentally, the purely religious loyalties of the two parties to the coalition are directly opposed to each other. For instance, consider the Catholic opposition to public school baccalaureate services throughout the Middle West and the opposition of Protestants to an ambassador to the Vatican.

When the topics of divorce, family relationships, and the nature of authority arise, members of each of the two coalitions again find themselves in agreement. The question of school discipline is a revealing touchstone, for here, too, with some exceptions, the Jews and liberal Protestants tend to be more child-centered and less concerned with traditional forms of authority and discipline. The fundamentalist Protestants and most Catholics tend in the opposite direction. Attitudes toward the subject of mental health divide similarly. What we have in essence is a serious culture conflict, with powerful groups arrayed against each other along fairly distinct religious lines.

The issue of patriotism and the related problem of communism are directly associated with this culture conflict. Reliance on familiar religious forms, hostility to anti-religious forces, zealous support for traditional forms of authority, a highly developed sense of individual property rights, plus a strong nationalist bias would immediately predispose the conservative coalition to react to the serious threat of the cold war with traditional solutions. Their support for a program of indoctrination in the schools, the feeling that there should be no compromise with evil, and a strong sense of what is right and what is wrong, the insistence that there is good only on our side and nothing but evil "out there" are but a public restatement in pedagogical terms of the manner in which members of the coalition were reared—or believe they were reared.

The opposite approach is also easy to comprehend if we interpret the religious, ethnic, and regional influences on those who support it. The coalition of liberal Protestants and Jews reflects basically a yearning for peace, an effort to achieve possible accommodation with the cold war enemy, and a recognition that authoritarian solutions are difficult if not impossible to achieve. (To be sure, the liberal coalition has at times seemed to be so unaware of the harsher realities of peace and power politics as to cause their opponents to question both their patriotism and their competence to administer affairs of state.) This group also displays a considerably smaller degree of nationalism, and their support of the U.N. is, therefore, firm. In direct contrast, the conservative religious coalition reflects strong suspicion and outright hostility to the U.N. and its affiliated agencies, especially UNESCO. And finally, the liberal coalition's memory of Hitler predisposes its members to be especially vigilant in opposing any excessive anti-communism that tends to bracket communism with liberalism.

What impact the recent shift in emphasis and viewpoint within the Roman Catholic Church will have on issues that concern the public schools is a matter for speculation. Very likely, leading Catholic spokesmen will join with the liberal coalition on selected issues at first, but ultimately the full import of the Catholic Church's ecumenical effort to reorient itself for participation in a religiously and racially pluralist society will make itself felt—and with profound effects on the American public school scene. This realignment will not only have profound influence on the atmosphere in which values are taught—possibly making the job easier —but it may also lead to further experiments in closer cooperation between public and parochial schools such as shared-time programs.

The racial problem has been reserved for separate treatment for several reasons. Race in our culture has been an infinitely more difficult barrier to surmount than religious or ethnic background, and the Negro has been compelled to condense into a few short years what for other groups has been decades of organization and effort. The violence of the Negro thrust can only be understood when we remember what happens when a coiled spring, compressed to its utmost, is suddenly released. The election of 1960 was won with the strong surge of Negro votes in the major Northern city strongholds of the Democratic Party. What has happened since has been the presentation of a bill for payment for services rendered. This process is as old as the political realities of American elections.

The Negroes, who are primarily Protestant, although there is a sizable Catholic minority, have hardly engaged in "religious politics"; their overriding concern has been the question of race. So basic is the issue of color that increasingly the Negroes have become a separate entity, considered as a third force in addition to the two religious coalitions. This condition will undoubtedly continue for some time to come. Ironically, in the last few years the cause of equality for the Negro has become the first occasion for a remarkable degree of cooperation and collaboration among the three major religious faiths. Short of war, this has not happened before. (There are other signs that cooperation on behalf of the cause of the Negro may be the first of a series of collaborations on crucial issues, such as U.N. support and world peace.)

The Negro, with the help of his white allies, has turned to the schools with a host of demands that have upset public education as seldom before. This is true not only in the South, where the issue has been a matter of constitutional right, but also in the North, where the school has become the major instrumentality for the symbolic—if not actual—end of racial segregation. Balked at ending residential segregation immediately, and unable to secure the kinds of jobs that satisfy their rising expectations, the Negroes have turned on the schools with a series of demands. Almost overnight the problems of the education of deprived children and the school drop-out have become predominantly the problems of Negro children. They have also become the two most discussed educational problems since the post-Sputnik overhaul of science and mathematics teaching. The reverberation of this onslaught will affect the teaching of history and social problems, textbook revision, the nature of teaching, the organization of schools, and practically every other facet of education. But what is perhaps most meaningful for the teaching of social values is that the militancy of the civil rights movement has heightened our awareness of the fact that so many of our values reflect a white culture with unconscious as well as conscious biases. These will be repeatedly challenged from now on. Excessive sensitivity that has led to attacks on *Huckleberry Finn* and other classics will undoubtedly abate in the future, but the period immediately ahead promises to be a very stormy one for schools and teachers.

The gradual dissolution of a homogeneous, Anglo-Saxon, Protestant society, the appearance of the conservative and liberal religious coalitions, and the emergence of the racial crisis will necessarily lead either to a truly pluralist society or to chaos. The problem for the public schools, of course, is especially acute. Caught for the past two decades in a religio-ethnic crossfire, they are suddenly also beset by racial conflicts. Their only salvation is to begin immediately to bring to bear all our present knowledge and experience to develop ground rules for teaching and learning in a diverse society that will conserve our basic values and still accommodate the emerging social order. Fortunately, such a pluralist solution is in harmony with the spirit of our democratic ideal and the reality of our constitutional tradition. But the task will be a difficult one—far more difficult and complex than most of us have yet admitted.

Talcott Parsons

The school class
as a social system

This essay will attempt to outline, if only sketchily, an analysis of the elementary and secondary school class as a social system, and the relation of its structure to its primary functions in the society as an agency of socialization and
allocation. While it is important that the school class is normally part of the
larger organization of a school, the class rather than the whole school will be the
unit of analysis here, for it is recognized both by the school system and by the
individual pupil as the place where the "business" of formal education actually
takes place. In elementary schools, pupils of one grade are typically placed in a
single "class" under one main teacher.

. . . [From] the functional point of view the school class can be treated as an
agency of socialization. That is to say, it is an agency through which individual
personalities are trained to be motivationally and technically adequate to the
performance of adult roles. It is not the sole such agency; the family, informal
"peer groups," churches, and sundry voluntary organizations all play a part, as
does actual on-the-job training. But, in the period extending from entry into first
grade until entry into the labor force or marriage, the school class may be regarded as the focal socializing agency.

The socialization function may be summed up as the development in individuals of the commitments and capacities which are essential prerequisites of
their future role-performance. Commitments may be broken down in turn into
two components: commitment to the implementation of the broad *values* of
society, and commitment to the performance of a specific type of role within
the *structure* of society.

● ● ●

Capacities can also be broken down into two components, the first being
competence or the skill to perform the tasks involved in the individual's roles,

Reprinted in abridged form from Talcott Parsons, "The School Class as a Social System,"
Harvard Educational Review, 1959, 29(4):297-318.

and the second being "role-responsibility" or the capacity to live up to other people's expectations of the interpersonal behavior appropriate to these roles. Thus a mechanic as well as a doctor needs to have not only the basic "skills of his trade," but also the ability to behave responsibly toward those people with whom he is brought into contact in his work.

● ● ●

We are interested, then, in what it is about the school class in our society that determines the distinction between the contingents of the age-cohort which do and do not go to college.

● ● ●

Considerations like these lead me to conclude that the main process of differentiation (which from another point of view is selection) that occurs during elementary school takes place on a single main axis of *achievement*. Broadly, moreover, the differentiation leads up through high school to a bifurcation into college-goers and non-college-goers.

To assess the significance of this pattern, let us look at its place in the socialization of the individual. Entering the system of formal education is the child's first major step out of primary involvement in his family of orientation. Within the family certain foundations of his motivational system have been laid down. But the only characteristic fundamental to later roles which has clearly been "determined" and psychologically stamped in by that time is sex role. The postoedipal child enters the system of formal education clearly categorized as boy or girl, but beyond that his *role* is not yet differentiated. The process of selection, by which persons will select and be selected for categories of roles, is yet to take place.

On grounds which cannot be gone into here, it may be said that the most important single predispositional factor with which the child enters the school is his level of *independence*. By this is meant his level of self-sufficiency relative to guidance by adults, his capacity to take responsibility and to make his own decisions in coping with new and varying situations. This, like his sex role, he has as a function of his experience in the family.

The family is a collectivity within which the basic status-structure is ascribed in terms of biological position, that is, by generation, sex, and age. There are inevitably differences of performance relative to these, and they are rewarded and punished in ways that contribute to differential character formation. But these differences are not given the sanction of institutionalized social status. The school is the first socializing agency in the child's experience which institutionalizes a differentiation of status on nonbiological bases. Moreover, this is not an ascribed but an achieved status; it is the status "earned" by differential performance of the tasks set by the teacher, who is acting as an agent of the community's school system. Let us look at the structure of this situation.

● ● ●

THE STRUCTURE OF THE ELEMENTARY SCHOOL CLASS

In accord with the generally wide variability of American institutions, and of course the basically local control of school systems, there is considerable variability of school situations, but broadly they have a single relatively well-marked framework. Particularly in the primary part of the elementary grades, *i.e.*, the first three grades, the basic pattern includes one main teacher for the class, who teaches all subjects and who is in charge of the class generally. Sometimes this early, and frequently in later grades, other teachers are brought in for a few special subjects, particularly gym, music, and art, but this does not alter the central position of the main teacher. This teacher is usually a woman. The class is with this one teacher for the school year, but usually no longer.

The class, then, is composed of about 25 age-peers of both sexes drawn from a relatively small geographical area—the neighborhood. Except for sex in certain respects, there is initially no formal basis for differentiation of status within the school class. The main structural differentiation develops gradually, on the single main axis indicated above as achievement. That the differentiation should occur on a single main axis is ensured by four primary features of the situation. The first is the initial equalization of the "contestants' " status by age and by "family background," the neighborhood being typically much more homogeneous than is the whole society. The second circumstance is the imposition of a common set of tasks which is, compared to most other task-areas, strikingly undifferentiated. The school situation is far more like a race in this respect than most role-performance situations. Third, there is the sharp polarization between the pupils in their initial equality and the *single* teacher who is an adult and "represents" the adult world. And fourth, there is a relatively systematic process of evaluation of the pupils' performances. From the point of view of a pupil, this evaluation, particularly (though not exclusively) in the form of report card marks, constitutes reward and/or punishment for past performance; from the viewpoint of the school system acting as an allocating agency, it is a basis of *selection* for future status in society.

Two important sets of qualifications need to be kept in mind in interpreting this structural pattern, but I think these do not destroy the significance of its main outline. The first qualification is for variations in the formal organization and procedures of the school class itself. Here the most important kind of variation is that between relatively "traditional" schools and relatively "progressive" schools. The more traditional schools put more emphasis on discrete units of subject-matter, whereas the progressive type allows more "indirect" teaching through "projects" and broader topical interests where more than one bird can be killed with a stone. In progressive schools there is more emphasis on groups of pupils working together, compared to the traditional direct relation of the individual pupil to the teacher. This is related to the progressive emphasis on cooperation among the pupils rather than direct competition, to greater permissiveness as opposed to strictness of discipline, and to a de-emphasis of formal marking. In some schools one of these components will be more prominent, and in others, another. That it is, however, an important range of variation is clear. It has to do, I think, very largely with the independence-dependence training which is so important to early socialization in the family. My broad interpretation is that those people who emphasize independence training will tend to be those who favor relatively progressive education. The relation of support for progressive education to relatively high socio-economic status and to "intellectual" interests and the like is well known. There is no contradiction between these emphases both on independence and on co-operation and group solidarity among pupils. In the first instance this is because the main focus of the independence problem at these ages is vis-à-vis adults. However, it can also be said that the peer group, which here is built into the school class, is an indirect field of expression of dependency needs, displaced from adults.

The second set of qualifications concerns the "informal" aspects of the school class, which are always somewhat at variance with the formal expectations. For instance, the formal pattern of nondifferentiation between the sexes may be modified informally, for the very salience of the one-sex peer group at this age period means that there is bound to be considerable implicit recognition of it—for example, in the form of teachers' encouraging group competition between boys and girls. Still, the fact of coeducation and the attempt to treat both sexes alike in all the crucial formal respects remain the most important. Another problem raised by informal organization is the question of how far teachers can and do treat pupils particularistically in violation of the universalistic expectations of the school. When compared with other types of formal organizations, however, I think the extent of this discrepancy in elementary schools is seen to be not unusual. The school class is structured so that opportunity for particularistic treatment is severely limited. Because there are so many more children in a school class than in a family and they are concentrated in a much narrower age range, the teacher has much less chance than does a parent to grant particularistic favors.

Bearing in mind these two sets of qualifications, it is still fair, I think, to conclude that the major characteristics of the elementary school class in this country are such as have been outlined. It should be especially emphasized that more or less progressive schools, even with their relative lack of emphasis on formal marking, do not constitute a separate pattern, but rather a variant tendency within the same pattern. A progressive teacher, like any other, will form opinions about the different merits of her pupils relative to the values and goals of the class and will communicate these evaluations to them, informally if not formally. It is my impression that the extremer cases of playing down relative evaluation are confined to those upper-status schools where going to a "good" college is so fully taken for granted that for practical purposes it is an ascribed status. In other words, in interpreting these facts the selective function of the school class should be kept continually in the forefront of attention. Quite clearly its importance has not been decreasing; rather the contrary.

THE NATURE OF SCHOOL ACHIEVEMENT

What, now, of the content of the "achievement" expected of elementary school children? Perhaps the best broad characterization which can be given is that it involves the types of performance which are, on the one hand, appropriate to the school situation and, on the other hand, are felt by adults to be important in themselves. This vague and somewhat circular characterization may, as was mentioned earlier, be broken down into two main components. One of these is the more purely "cognitive" learning of information, skills, and frames of reference associated with empirical knowledge and technological mastery. The *written* language and the early phases of mathematical thinking are clearly vital; they involve cognitive skills at altogether new levels of generality and abstraction compared to those commanded by the pre-school child. With these basic skills goes assimilation of much factual information about the world.

The second main component is what may broadly be called a "moral" one. In earlier generations of schooling this was known as "deportment." Somewhat more generally it might be called responsible citizenship in the school community. Such things as respect for the teacher, consideration and co-operativeness in relation to fellow-pupils, and good "work-habits" are the fundamentals, leading on to capacity for "leadership" and "initiative."

The striking fact about this achievement content is that in the elementary grades these two primary components are not clearly differentiated from each other. Rather, the pupil is evaluated in diffusely general terms; a *good* pupil is defined in terms of a fusion of the cognitive and the moral components, in which varying weight is given to one or the other. Broadly speaking, then, we may say that the "high achievers" of the elementary school are both the "bright" pupils, who catch on easily to their more strictly intellectual tasks, and the more "responsible" pupils, who "behave well" and on whom the teacher can "count" in her difficult problems of managing the class. One indication that this is the case is the fact that in elementary school the purely intellectual tasks are relatively easy for the pupil of high intellectual ability. In many such cases, it can be presumed that the primary challenge to the pupil is not to his intellectual, but to his "moral," capacities. On the whole, the progressive movement seems to have leaned in the direction of giving enhanced emphasis to this component, suggesting that of the two, it has tended to become the more problematical.

The essential point, then, seems to be that the elementary school, regarded in the light of its socialization function, is an agency which differentiates the school class broadly along a single continuum of achievement, the content of which is relative excellence in living up to the expectations imposed by the teacher as an agent of the adult society. The criteria of this achievement are, generally speaking, undifferentiated into the cognitive or technical component and the moral or "social" component. But with respect to its bearing on societal values, it is broadly a differentiation of *levels* of capacity to act in accord with these values. Though the relation is far from neatly uniform, this differentiation underlies the processes of selection for levels of status and role in the adult society.

• • •

SOCIALIZATION AND SELECTION
IN THE ELEMENTARY SCHOOL

To conclude this discussion of the elementary school class, something should be said about the fundamental conditions underlying the process which is, as we have seen, simultaneously (1) an emancipation of the child from primary emotional attachment to his family, (2) an internalization of a level of societal values and norms that is a step higher than those he can learn in his family alone, (3) a differentiation of the school class in terms both of actual achievement and of differential *valuation* of achievement, and (4) from society's point of view, a selection and allocation of its human resources relative to the adult role system.

Probably the most fundamental condition underlying this process is the sharing of common values by the two adult agencies involved—the family and the school. In this case the core is the shared valuation of *achievement*. It includes, above all, recognition that it is fair to give differential rewards for different levels of achievement, so long as there has been fair access to opportunity, and fair that these rewards lead on to higher-order opportunities for the successful. There is thus a basic sense in which the elementary school class is an embodiment of the fundamental American value of equality of opportunity, in that it places value *both* on initial equality and on differential achievement.

As a second condition, however, the rigor of this valuational pattern must be tempered by allowance for the difficulties and needs of the young child. Here the quasi-motherliness of the woman teacher plays an important part. Through her the school system, assisted by other agencies, attempts to minimize the insecurity resulting from the pressures to learn, by providing a certain amount of emotional support defined in terms of what is due to a child of a given age level. In this respect, however, the role of the school is relatively small. The underlying foundation of support is given in the home, and as we have seen, an important supplement to it can be provided by the informal peer associations of the child. It may be suggested that the development of extreme patterns of alienation from the school is often related to inadequate support in these respects.

Third, there must be a process of selective rewarding of valued performance. Here the teacher is clearly the primary agent, though the more progressive modes of education attempt to enlist classmates more systematically than in the traditional pattern. This is the process that is the direct source of intra-class differentiation along the achievement axis.

The final condition is that this initial differentiation tends to bring about a status system in the class, in which not only the immediate results of school work, but a whole series of influences, converge to consolidate different expectations which may be thought of as the children's "levels of aspiration." Generally some differentiation of friendship groups along this line occurs, though it is important that it is by no means complete, and that children are sensitive to the attitudes not only of their own friends, but of others.

Within this general discussion of processes and conditions, it is important to distinguish, as I have attempted to do all along, the socialization of the individual from the selective allocation of contingents to future roles. For the individual, the old familial identification is broken up (the family of orientation becomes, in Freudian terms, a "lost object") and a new identification is gradually built up, providing the first-order structure of the child's identity apart from his originally ascribed identity as son or daughter of the "Joneses." He both transcends his familial identification in favor of a more independent one and comes to occupy a differentiated status within the new system. His personal status is inevitably a direct function of the position he achieves, primarily in the formal school class and secondarily in the informal peer group structure. In spite of the sense in which achievement-ranking takes place along a continuum, I have put forward reasons to suggest that, with respect to this status, there is an important differentiation into two broad, relatively distinct levels, and that his position on one or the other enters into the individual's definition of his own identity. To an important degree this process of differentiation is independent of the socio-economic status of his family in the community, which to the child is a prior ascribed status.

When we look at the same system as a selective mechanism from the societal point of view, some further considerations become important. First, it may be noted that the valuation of achievement and its sharing by family and school not only provides the appropriate values for internalization by individuals, but also performs a crucial integrative function for the system. Differentiation of the class among the achievement axis is inevitably a source of strain, because it confers higher rewards and privileges on one contingent than on another within the same system. This common valuation helps make possible the acceptance of the crucial differentiation, especially by the losers in the competition. Here it is an essential point that this *common* value on achievement is shared by units with different statuses in the system. It cuts across the differentiation of families by socio-economic status. It is necessary that there be realistic opportunity and that the teacher can be relied on to implement it by being "fair" and rewarding achievement by whoever shows capacity for it. The fact is crucial that the distribution of abilities, though correlated with family status, clearly does not coincide with it. There can then be a genuine selective process within a set of "rules of the game."

This commitment to common values is not, however, the sole integrative mechanism counteracting the strain imposed by differentiation. Not only does the individual pupil enjoy familial support, but teachers also like and indeed "respect" pupils on bases independent of achievement-status, and peer-group friendship lines, though correlated with position on the achievement scale, again by no means coincide with it, but cross-cut it. Thus there are cross-cutting lines of solidarity which mitigate the strains generated by rewarding achievement differentially.

It is only *within* this framework of institutionalized solidarity that the crucial selective process goes on through selective rewarding and the consolidation of its results into a status-differentiation within the school class. We have called special attention to the impact of the selective process on the children of relatively high ability but low family status. Precisely in this group, but pervading school classes generally, is another parallel to what was found in the studies of voting behavior. In the voting studies it was found that the "shifters"—those voters who were transferring their allegiance from one major party to the other—tended, on the one hand, to be the "cross-pressured" people, who had multiple status characteristics and group allegiances which predisposed them simultaneously to vote in opposite directions. The analogy in the school class is clearly to the children for whom ability and family status do not coincide. On the other hand, it was precisely in this group of cross-pressured voters that political "indifference" was most conspicuous. Non-voting was particularly prevalent in this group, as was a generally cool emotional tone toward a campaign. The suggestion is that some of the pupil "indifference" to school performance may have a similar origin. This is clearly a complex phenomenon and cannot be further analyzed here. But rather than suggesting, as is usual on common sense grounds, that indifference to school work represents an "alienation" from cultural and intellectual values, I would suggest exactly the opposite: that an important component of such indifference, including in extreme cases overt revolt against school discipline, is connected with the fact that the stakes, as in politics, are very high indeed. Those pupils who are exposed to contradictory pressures are likely to be ambivalent; at the same time, the personal stakes for them are higher than for the others, because what happens in school may make much more of a difference for their futures than for the others, in whom ability and family status point to the same expectations for the future. In particular for the upwardly mobile pupils, too much emphasis on school success would pointedly suggest "burning their bridges" of association with their families and status peers. This phenomenon seems to operate even in elementary school, although it grows somewhat more conspicuous later. In general I think that an important part of the anti-intellectualism in American youth culture stems from the *importance* of the selective process through the educational system rather than the opposite.

One further major point should be made in this analysis. As we have noted, the general trend of American society has been toward a rapid upgrading in the educational status of the population. This means that, relative to past expectations, with each generation there is increased pressure to educational achievement, often associated with parents' occupational ambitions for their children. To a sociologist this is a more or less classical situation of anomic strain, and the youth-culture ideology which plays down intellectual interests and school performance seems to fit in this context. The orientation of the youth culture is, in the nature of the case, ambivalent, but for the reasons suggested, the anti-intellectual side of the ambivalence tends to be overtly stressed. One of the reasons for the dominance of the anti-school side of the ideology is that it provides a means of protest against adults, who are at the opposite pole in the socialization situation. In certain respects one would expect that the trend toward greater emphasis on independence, which we have associated with progressive education, would accentuate the strain in this area and hence the tendency to decry adult expectations. The whole problem should be subjected to a thorough analysis in the light of what we know about ideologies more generally.

The same general considerations are relevant to the much-discussed problem of juvenile delinquency. Both the general upgrading process and the pressure to enhanced independence should be expected to increase strain on the lower, most marginal groups. The analysis of this paper has been concerned with the line between college and non-college contingents; there is, however, another line between those who achieve solid non-college educational status and those for whom adaptation to educational expectations at *any* level is difficult. As the acceptable minimum of educational qualification rises, persons near and below the margin will tend to be pushed into an attitude of repudiation of these expectations. Truancy and delinquency are ways of expressing this repudiation. Thus the very *improvement* of educational standards in the society at large may well be a major factor in the failure of the educational process for a growing number at the lower end of the status and ability distribution. It should therefore not be too easily assumed that delinquency is a symptom of a *general* failure of the educational process.

● ● ●

SELECTED BIBLIOGRAPHY

Alsop, Joseph. "No More Nonsense About Ghetto Education," *New Republic* (July 22, 1967), 18-23.
Becker, Howard. "The Career of the Chicago Public School Teacher," *American Journal of Sociology*, 57 (March 1952), 470 ff.
Becker, Howard. "Social Class Variations in the Teacher-Pupil Relationship," *Journal of Educational Sociology*, 25 (April 1952), 451-465.
Benne, Kenneth, and Birnbaum, Max. "Change Does Not Have to Be Haphazard," *The School Review*, 8, 3, 282-293.
Bernstein, Abraham. *The Education of Urban Populations*. New York: Random House, 1967.
Cervantes, Lucius F. *The Drop-Out: Causes and Cures*. Ann Arbor: University of Michigan Press, 1965.
Colemen, James S., et al. *Equality of Educational Opportunity*. Washington, D.C.: U.S. Office of Education, 1966.
Coles, Robert. *Children of Crisis: A Study of Courage and Fear*. Boston: Little, Brown, 1967.

Dentler, R. A., et al. *The Urban R's.* New York: Praeger, 1967.

Dentler, R. A., and Warshauer, Mary Ellen. *Big City Drop-Outs and Illiterates.* New York: Praeger, 1965.

Duncan, B. "Education and Social Background," *American Journal of Sociology,* 72 (January 1967), 363-372.

Dynes, W. "Education and Tolerance: An Analysis of Intervening Factors, " *Social Forces,* 46 (September 1967), 22-34.

Gittlell, Marilyn. *Participants and Participation.* New York: Praeger, 1967.

Gittlell, Marilyn. *Six Urban School Districts.* New York: Praeger, 1968.

Goldstein, Bernard, et al. *Low Income Youth in the Urban Area: Critical Review.* New York: Holt, Rinehart & Winston, 1967.

Halsey, H. H., Floud, Jean, and Anderson, C. A. (eds.). *Education, Economy, and Society.* New York: Free Press, 1960.

Hansen, Donald, and Gerstl, Joel. *On Education: Sociological Perspectives.* New York: Wiley, 1967.

Hillson, M. "Reorganization of the School," *Phylon,* 28 (Fall 1967), 230-245.

Hillson, M. "Social Functions of Education," *International Social Science Journal,* 19 (1967), 313-429.

Hurd, G. E., and Johnson, T. J. "Education and Development," *Sociological Review,* 15 (March 1967), 59-71.

Iannacone, Lawrence. *Politics In Education.* New York: Center for Applied Research in Education, 1967.

Kerber, August, and Bommarito, Barbara (eds.). *The Schools and the Urban Crisis.* New York: Holt, Rinehart & Winston, 1965.

Kohl, Herbert. *36 Children.* New York: New American Library, 1968.

Kozol, Jonathan. *Death at an Early Age.* Boston: Houghton Mifflin, 1967.

Leonard, George. *Education and Ecstasy.* New York: Delacorte, 1968.

Miller, Harry L., and Smiley, Marjorie. *Education in the Metropolis.* New York: Free Press, 1967.

Moles, Oliver C. "Training Children in Low Income Families for School," *Welfare in Review,* 3 (June 1965), 1-11.

Moore, Alexander. *Realities of the Urban Classroom: Observations in Elementary Schools.* New York: Doubleday (Anchor), 1967.

Morrison, R. "Education for Environmental Concerns," *Daedalus,* 12 (Fall 1967), 10-33.

Parsons, Talcott. "The School Class as a Social System: Some of Its Functions in American Society," *Harvard Educational Review,* 29 (Fall 1959), 297-318.

Passow, A. H. *Education in Depressed Areas.* New York: Columbia Teachers' College Press, 1963.

Reiss, Albert J. (ed.). *Schools in a Changing Society.* New York: Free Press, 1965.

Reissman, Frank. *The Culturally Deprived Child.* New York: Harper & Row, 1962.

Riesman, David. *Contrast and Variety in American Education.* New York: Doubleday, 1958.

Roberts, Joan (ed.). *School Children in the Urban Slums.* New York: Free Press, 1967.

Rogers, David. "NYC Schools: A Sick Bureaucracy," *Saturday Review,* (July 20, 1968), 47-50, 59-62.

Rosenthal, Alan. *Pedagogues and Power: Teacher Groups in School Politics.* Syracuse: Syracuse University Press, 1969.

Schrag, Peter. *Village School Downtown.* Boston: Beacon, 1967.

Schreiber, Daniel (ed.). *The School Drop-Out.* Washington, D.C.: National Education Association, 1964.

Schueler, H. "Education in the Modern Urban Setting," *Law and Contemporary Problems,* 30 (Winter 1965), 162-175.

Smith, Louis M., and Geoffrey, William. *The Complexities of an Urban Classroom: An Analysis Toward a General Theory of Teaching.* New York: Holt, Rinehart & Winston, 1968.

Snyder, E. E. "Sociology of Education," *Sociology and Social Research,* 52 (January 1968), 237-242.

Stinchcombe, A. L. *Rebellion in a High School.* Chicago: Quadrangle, 1964.

Strom, Robert (ed.). *The Inner City Classroom: Teacher Behaviors.* Columbus, Ohio: Merrill, 1966.

Toby, Jackson. "Orientation to Education as a Factor in School Maladjustment of Lower-Class Children," *Social Forces,* 35 (March 1957), 259-266.

Wise, Arthur E. *Rich Schools, Poor Schools: The Promise of Equal Educational Opportunity.* Chicago: University of Chicago Press, 1968.

3
The Police

The specific tasks of the teacher to educate pupils into literacy, skill with numbers, and desire to conform to an ideal concept of an American obscure the social-control aspects of his role. Not so for the police system: Their central objective is to *exercise* social control over deviant behavior, whether crime, misdemeanor, or simply annoyance to a citizen or a group of citizens. Preparation of the policeman for this function begins with selection and continues through training.

SELECTION OF POLICE

Candidates for the police force are in most cities subjected to an extremely strenuous series of character investigations. There appears to be evidence that those with pronounced liberal opinions or friends will find it difficult to make the grade. In some police systems this interdiction would extend to extremists of rightist persuasion as well. The contemporary need for more Negro police, however, has led to a significant amelioration of extremely harsh tests of personal probity, extending back into adolescent and preadolescent pecadilloes. With slum life so rife with chances for arrests and convictions, the acceptance of a more tolerant approach to early mistakes in prospective police employment may serve to reform the entire process of selection.

Most police, whether inner-city or rural, are recruited from lower socioeconomic groups (primarily upper-lower echelons) where the desire for job security provides a significant step up the social ladder. One reason given for the reluctance of middle-class individuals to enter police work is abhorrence of the use of force. Conversely, the lack of such reluctance among the lower classes generally eliminates this factor as a deterrent. As Neiderhoffer puts it, "Working-class background, high school education or less, average intelligence, cautious personality—these are the typical features of the modern police recruit."

Police manuals rarely discuss decisions that police must make every day. "Whether or not to break up a sidewalk gathering, whether or not to intervene in a domestic dispute, whether or not to silence a street corner speaker, whether or not to stop and frisk." The solidarity of the police and the fact that each police force acts almost as a closed system promotes unquestioned support for these individual actions.

POLICE TRAINING AND BEHAVIOR

Training is deliberately intended to wall off the recruit from his former associations and habitat. In a fashion somewhat comparable with that of the cadets in the most prestigious Service Academies or the less socially elect, but still prestigious, Marine boot camp, the police rookie is indoctrinated into what Erving Goffman terms "the total institution." Relationships to superiors, norms of friendship, dress, handling tools of his trade, and a thousand and one details of his new role are made to appear sufficiently new and different from all previous behaviors so that the outcome of training is a "new man," the rookie patrolman. Even the formula by which he must attend to his necessary functions is now dictated by the rule book.

Despite the training that emphasizes a simplified social science and public administration approach to law enforcement, the behavior of the typical police officer is usually in the "get tough first" mode.

The policeman and the teacher both meet two clienteles: the cooperative, responsive, minimally troublesome; and the uncooperative, extremely troublesome and physically dangerous. Teaching the teachable is enjoyable; teaching the recalcitrant is drudgery. Concurrently, patrolling a safe middle-class neighborhood is an act of public service; patrolling a lower-class neighborhood can be ugly, threatening, and dangerous.

"Because the application of the law depends to a large degree on the definition of the situation and the decision reached by the patrolman, he, in effect, makes the law; it is his decision that establishes the boundary between legal and illegal." The policeman is thus the most powerful of the three "dirty workers." The sense of power often compels him into a belief that he is "superior to the law. He may kill, destroy property, invade privacy, disregard traffic regulations, etc."

Neiderhoffer asserts that the modern urban police system produces two types of police: one predominantly authoritarian, less well educated, and relegated to lower rank, on the beat or just above; and the other class the command officers whose superior educational attainments are seemingly accompanied by less authoritarianism. Law enforcement thus oscillates from one philosophy to another. In any case, slum areas usually get the toughest and most cynical treatment by the police. This may be because of selection, or, alternatively, the ghetto may make any policeman into a tough.

Objective study of the police has been especially hampered by the institutional secrecy with which all of police work is surrounded. Much of this is undoubtedly justified, but significant paranoid reaction to outside intervention is caused by an extreme minority group syndrome. In fact, in may large cities typical police behavior is characterized by a feeling that outsiders, not only liberal types, but many judges and some college-educated police supervisors, are against law enforcement.

GOALS

The conflict between the academically trained police officer with a feel for professionalism and the "old-timer" with less formal education has produced significant strain within police ranks. To some degree this split coincides with differential treatment of civil-rights demonstrations and minority groups. Although this generalization is based upon data observed primarily in New York City, similar cleavages and associated behaviors have been observed in other large-city police departments.

Professionalization of police, increasingly urged as a means of improving police practice, may conflict with the desirability of recruiting individuals who may have encountered gang and street-corner society as youths. The college-trained population, it appears, has not been tested to a large extent in the milieu in which they will be expected to perform. Thus, the use of academic credentials to upgrade quality of police personnel may depend on the police science offerings in community colleges, which are most apt, because of propinquity, to attract ghetto or other inner-city residents.

It has been proposed that there should be three kinds of police: (1) community service officer; (2) police officer; and (3) police agent. A police agent will be a generalist, capable of almost any task in police work and will usually have at least two years of college with preferably an A.A. or B.A. The police officer would enforce law and investigate crimes that do not require laboratory or crime detective specialist intervention; regulate traffic, for example. He would work in a team with police agents and CSOs in given situations. Present educational qualifications would suffice. Community service officers, between 17 and 21 years of age, would be apprentice policemen. They would perform many of the service functions that inner-city residents need and that present law enforcement officers have so little time to perform. The CSOs could be accepted despite a minor offense record. They would be promoted as soon as they qualified, thus providing multiple entry into police work. The lack of multiple entry has been a major deterrent to attracting well-educated and effective personalities into police work, for each small force has tended to be the single unit within which advancement and promotion was attained. Under these circumstances, seniority and tenacity are more important to promotion than innovation and efficiency.

CONCEPTS FOR THE POLICE SYSTEM

Because the police enforce community beliefs concerning what is right and wrong, lawful and criminal, and because community norms are neither certain nor clearly stated, the beliefs that the police themselves have about their roles and the proper goals of their actions become most important. The first selections attempt this: The operative word here is "attempt" because the police themselves are influenced by many conflicting forces and so quite often behave differently at different times.

In "The 'Rotten Apple' View of Man," Skolnick proposes that the police in general accept a widespread American community belief system that deviant behavior such as burglary, rape, or rioting, is caused by certain "rotten apple" individuals. Deviance is therefore caused by inherent evil. These "rotten apple" individuals are the product of poor upbringing: They had parents who failed to instill in them, when they were children, respect for common morality, a proper deference to legal authority, and a belief in religion.

Riots, caused by agitators who are usually outsiders to the district, stir up both the "rotten apple" members of the community and the quiet citizens. This theory of riots leads to a continuous search for conspiracy, for outside agitators.

The social science theories that collective behavior and much individual deviant behavior can be changed if the social situation is changed are diametrically opposed to these police system theories. Neither hypothesis has thus far been adequately tested. The theory of police and others that social control needs changes in individuals has elements of truth in it. Visible actions are those of individuals. Nonetheless, the effort needed to persuade individuals to change their behavior would be so enormous that the opposing hypothesis would become persuasive. This hypothesis states that to improve individual behavior we must create changes in poverty, housing, jobs, and similar social conditions.

Police behavior on the patrol and in the ghetto is graphically described in the second selection. The belief in "wicked" individuals and the experience of general hostility do much to explain the discourtesy, the harassment, and the occasional brutality of the police officer. The wider issues of the effects of the automobile and radio, as well as specialization in records and laboratory work on the policeman on the beat and in face-to-face contacts between the police and community members, are described.

Finally two articles move away from description or issues to explain some aspects of police behavior. In "The Policeman as Philosopher, Guide and Friend," the isolation of police from social agencies and community organizations and the support given by policemen in daily emergencies faced by the poor and the ignorant are dealt with using new concepts. So, too, the hostility felt by policemen and policemen's own organizations toward a city authority that demands that the individual policeman behave with professional responsibility on a workman's pay packet is an additional factor to be considered in any explanation of police behavior. In the final theoretical article by Black and Reiss, the authors combine community norms, citizen behavior, police responses, and juvenile arrests into an elegant, if difficult, theoretical statement.

The black community

Writing in 1962, three years before the Watts riots and almost the distant past in this respect, James Baldwin vividly portrayed the social isolation of the policeman in the black ghetto:

> ... The only way to police a ghetto is to be oppressive. None of the Police Commissioner's men, even with the best will in the world, have any way of understanding the lives led by the people; they swagger about in twos and threes patrolling. Their very presence is an insult, and it would be, even if they spent their entire day feeding gumdrops to children. They represent the force of the white world, and that world's real intentions are, simply, for that world's criminal profit and ease, to keep the black man corralled up here, in his place. The badge, the gun in the holster, and the swinging club, make vivid what will happen should his rebellion become overt. ...
>
> It is hard, on the other hand, to blame the policeman, blank, good-natured, thoughtless, and insuperably innocent, for being such a perfect representative of the people he serves. He, too, believes in good intentions and is astounded and offended when they are not taken for the deed. He has never, himself, done anything for which to be hated—which of us has? And yet he is facing, daily and nightly, the people who would gladly see him dead, and he knows it. There is no way for him not to know it: There are few things under heaven more unnerving than the silent, accumulating contempt and hatred of a people. He moves through Harlem, therefore, like an occupying soldier in a bitterly hostile country; which is precisely what, and where he is, and is the reason he walks in twos and threes.

Today the situation is even more polarized. There have been riots, and both black Americans and police have been killed. Black anger has become more and more focused on the police: the Watts battle cry of "Get Whitey" has been replaced by the Black Panther slogan: "Off the pigs." The black community is virtually unanimous in demanding major reforms, including police review boards and local control of the police. According to the Kerner Commission and other studies, conflict with the police was one of the most important factors in pro-

Reprinted from *The Politics of Protest: Violent Aspects of Protest and Confrontation*, Staff Report No. 3, prepared by Jerome Skolnick, to the National Commission on the Causes and Prevention of Violence, Washington, D.C., U.S. Government Printing Office, 1969:183-185, 189-190, 194-201, 213-214. Footnotes omitted.

ducing black riots. In short, anger, hatred, and fear of the police are a major common denominator among black Americans at the present time.

The police return these sentiments in kind—they both fear the black community and openly express violent hostility and prejudice toward it. Our review of studies of the police revealed unanimity in findings on this point: the majority of rank and file policemen are hostile toward black people. Usually such hostility does not reflect official policy, although in isolated instances, as in the Miami Police Department under Chief Headley, official policy may encourage anti-black actions. Judging from these studies, there is no reason to suppose that anti-black hostility is a new development brought on by recent conflicts between the police and the black community. What appears to have changed is not police attitudes, but the fact that black people are fighting back.

The Harlem Riot Commission Report of 1935 reserved its most severe criticism for the police:

> The police of Harlem show too little regard for human rights and constantly violate their fundamental rights as citizens. . . . The insecurity of the individual in Harlem against police aggression is one of the most potent causes for the existing hostility to authority. . . . It is clearly the responsibility of the police to act in such a way as to win the confidence of the citizens of Harlem and to prove themselves the guardians of the rights and safety of the community rather than its enemies and oppressors.

And William A. Westley reported from his studies of police in the late forties:

> No white policeman with whom the author has had contact failed to mock the Negro, to use some type of stereotyped categorization, and to refer to interaction with the Negro in an exaggerated dialect, when the subject arose.

Students of police seem unanimous in agreeing that police attitudes have not changed much since those studies. In a study done under a grant from the Office of Law Enforcement Assistance of the United States Department of Justice, and submitted to the President's Commission on Law Enforcement and the Administration of Criminal Justice in 1966, Donald J. Black and Albert J. Reiss, Jr., found overwhelming evidence of widespread, virulent prejudice by police against Negroes. The study was based on field observations by thirty-six observers who accompanied police officers for a period of seven weeks in the summer of 1966 in Boston, Chicago, and Washington, D.C. It was found that 38 percent of the officers had expressed "extreme prejudice," while an additional 34 percent had expressed "considerable prejudice" in front of the observers. Thus, 72 percent of these policemen qualified as prejudiced against black Americans. It must be remembered that these views were not solicited, but were merely recorded when voluntarily expressed. And it seems fair to assume that some proportion of the remaining 28 percent were sophisticated enough to exercise a certain measure of restraint when in the presence of the observers. Also, examples presented by Black and Reiss make it clear that their observers found intense and bitter hatred toward blacks. Moreover, these are not rural Southern policemen, and our investigation has shown that their views are typical of those in most urban police forces.

Concrete examples of this prejudice are not hard to find. For example, the Commission's Cleveland Study Team found that prejudice had been festering in the Cleveland police force for a long time but suddenly bloomed into virulent bigotry following the July, 1968, shoot-out between police and black militants. When white police were withdrawn from the ghetto for one night to allow black community leaders to quell the rioting, racist abuse of Mayor Carl B. Stokes, a Negro, could be heard on the police radio. And posters with a picture of the Mayor under the words "WANTED FOR MURDER" hung in district stations for several weeks after the shoot-out. Elsewhere our interviews disclosed the fact that nightsticks and riot batons are at times referred to as "nigger knockers." Robert Conot writes that "LSMFT"—the old Lucky Strike slogan—has slipped into police argot as: "Let's Shoot a Mother-Fucker Tonight."

Police actions often reflect these attitudes. In recent years there have been numerous allegations by Negro and civil liberties groups of police insulting, abusing, mistreating, and even beating or murdering blacks. Studies of the police by independent bodies tend to support these allegations. For instance, the 1961 Report on Justice, by the United States Civil Rights Commission, concluded that "Police brutality . . . is a serious problem in the United States." Without presently recounting specific additional instances and varieties of misconduct, suffice it to say that this conclusion finds support throughout the literature on police.

The problem has become even more acute with the emergence of increased black militancy. Reports in numerous cities, including Detroit, San Francisco, New York, and Oakland, indicate that police officers have attacked or shot members of the black community, often Black Panthers, at offices, social events, and even courthouse halls. Indeed, it appears that such incidents are spreading and are not isolated in a few police departments.

Moreover, difficult to document, it seems clear that police prejudice impairs the capacity of the police to engage in impartial crowd control. If anything, the bahavior that typifies day-to-day policing is magnified in riot situations. The report of the Kerner Commission indicates that, for example, police violence was out of control during the 1967 riots, and similar findings are seen elsewhere, including the study of the Commission's Cleveland Study Team.

● ● ●

The policeman's job

The outlines of the growing demands upon the police are well known and require but brief review here. Increasingly, the police are required to cope with the problems that develop as conditions in the black community remain intolerable and as black anger and frustration grow. Yet all intelligent police observers recognize that the root causes of black violence and rebellion are beyond the means or authority of the police. As a former Superintendent of the Chicago Police Department, O. W. Wilson, commented on riots in a recent interview:

> I think there is a long-range answer—the correction of the inequities we're all aware of: higher educational standards, improved economic opportunities, a catching up on the cultural lag, a strengthening of spiritual values. All of these things in the long run must be brought to bear on the problem if it is to be solved permanently, and obviously it must be solved. It will be solved, but not overnight.

Since the publication of the Kerner Commission Report there is no longer much reason for anyone not to understand the nature of the social ills underlying the symptomatic violence of the black ghettos. But while we all know what needs to be done, it has not been done. The American policeman as well as the black American must therefore suffer daily from the consequence of inaction and indifference.

James Baldwin's characterization of the police as an army of occupation, quoted earlier, requires more and more urgent consideration. The police are set against the hatred and violence of the ghetto and are delegated to suppress it and keep it from seeping into white areas. Significantly, no one knows this better than the police who must try to perform this dangerous and increasingly unmanageable and thankless task. Throughout our interviews with members of major urban police forces, their despair and anger in the face of worsening violence and impending disaster were evident. No recent account about the police by scholars and journalists reports evidence to the contrary. As the *Saturday*

Reprinted from *The Politics of Protest: Violent Aspects of Protest and Confrontation*, Staff Report No. 3, prepared by Jerome Skolnick, to the National Commission on the Causes and Prevention of Violence, Washington, D.C., U.S. Government Printing Office, 1969:183-185, 189-190, 194-201, 213-214. Footnotes omitted.

Evening Post recently wrote of the police in St. Louis: "To many policemen, the very existence of [an emergency riot mobilization] plan implies that it will be used, and it is this sense of inevitability, this feeling that events have somehow slipped out of their control, that unnerves and frustrates them. . . ."

And, of course, the police are correct. Events are slipping out of their control and they must live, more than most people, with the threat of danger and disaster. As one patrolman told a *Post* reporter, "the first guys there [responding to the riot plan] —they've had it. I've thought of getting myself a little sign saying 'expendable' and hanging it around my neck." When the temperatures rise above 100 degrees in the ghetto and tenements overrun with people, rats, hopelessness, and anger, it is the police who are on the line; and any mistake can bring death. A New York policeman interviewed by our task force put the widespread apprehensions of the police simply: "Yeah, I'm scared. All the cops are. You never know what's going to happen out there. This place is a powder keg. You don't know if just putting your hand on a colored kid will cause a riot."

Similarly, the police can do little to ameliorate the reasons for student and political protest. Many demands of the protesters—moral political leadership, peace, and reform of the universities—lie outside the jurisdiction of the police. But when protesters are met with police, protest becomes a problem for the police.

Protest, moreover, poses an *unusual* problem for the policeman. Although policemen are characteristically referred to as law enforcement officers, more than one student of police has distinguished between the patrolman's role as a "peace officer" concerned with public order and the policeman's role as detective, concerned with enforcing the law. As a peace officer, the patrolman usually copes with his responsibilities by looking away from minor thefts, drunkenness, disturbances, assults, and malicious mischief. "[The] normal tendency of the police," writes James Q. Wilson, "is to underenforce the law."

In protest situations, however, the police are in the public eye, and frequently find themselves in the impossible position of acting as substitutes for necessary political and social reform. If they cope with their situation by venting their rage on the most apparent and available source of their predicament—blacks, students, and demonstrators—it should occasion no surprise. The professional restraint, compassion, and detachment oftentimes displayed by police are admirable. Under pressure and provocation, however, the police themselves can pose serious social problems.

The police view
of protest and protesters

Faced with the mounting pressures inherent in their job, the police have naturally sought to understand why things are as they are. Explanations which the police, with a few exceptions, have adopted constitute a relatively coherent view of current protests and their causes. The various propositions making up this view have nowhere been set out and made explicit, but they do permeate the police literature. We have tried to set them out as explicitly as possible.

As will be seen, this view functions to justify—indeed, it suggests—a strategy for dealing with protest and protesters. Like any coherent view of events, it helps the police plan what they should do and understand what they have done. But it must also be said that the police view makes it more difficult to keep the peace and increases the potential for violence. Furthermore, police attitudes toward protest and protesters often lead to conduct at odds with democratic ideals of freedom of speech and political expression. Thus the police often view protest as an intrusion rather than as a contribution to our political processes. In its extreme case, this may result in treating the fundamental political right of dissent as merely an unnecessary inconvenience to traffic, as subversive activity, or both.

THE "ROTTEN APPLE" VIEW OF MAN

What is the foundation of the police view? On the basis of our interviews with police and a systematic study of police publications, we have found that a significant underpinning is what can best be described as a "rotten apple" theory of human nature. Such a theory of human nature is hardly confined to the police, of course. It is widely shared in our society. Many of those to whom the police are responsible hold the "rotten apple" theory, and this complicates the problem in many ways.

Under this doctrine, crime and disorder are attributable mainly to the inten-

Reprinted from *The Politics of Protest: Violent Aspects of Protest and Confrontation,* Staff Report No. 3, prepared by Jerome Skolnick, to the National Commission on the Causes and Prevention of Violence, Washington, D.C., U.S. Government Printing Office, 1969:183-185, 189-190, 194-201, 213-214. Footnotes omitted.

tions of evil individuals; human behavior transcends past experience, culture, society, and other external forces and should be understood in terms of wrong choices, deliberately made. Significantly—and contrary to the teachings of all the behavioral sciences—social factors such as poverty, discrimination, inadequate housing, and the like are excluded from the analysis. As one policeman put it simply, "Poverty doesn't cause crime; people do." (And as we discuss later, the policeman's view of "crime" is extremely broad.)

The "rotten apple" view of human nature puts the policeman at odds with the goals and aspirations of many of the groups he is called upon to police. For example, police often relegate social reforms to the category of "coddling criminals" or, in the case of recent ghetto programs, to "selling out" to troublemakers. Moreover, while denying that social factors may contribute to the causes of criminal behavior, police and police publications, somewhat inconsistently, denounce welfare programs not as irrelevant *but as harmful* because they destroy human initiative. This negative view of the goals of policed communities can only make the situation of both police and policed more difficult and explosive. Thus, the black community sees the police not only as representing an alien white society but also as advocating positions fundamentally at odds with its own aspirations. A recent report by the Group for Research on Social Policy at Johns Hopkins University (commissioned by the National Advisory Commission on Civil Disorders) summarizes the police view of the black community:

> The police have wound up face to face with the social consequences of the problems in the ghetto created by the failure of other white institutions—though, as has been observed, they themselves have contributed to those problems in no small degree. The distant and gentlemanly white racism of employers, the discrimination of white parents who object to having their children go to school with Negroes, the disgruntlement of white taxpayers who deride the present welfare system as a sinkhole of public funds but are unwilling to see it replaced by anything more effective—the consequences of these and other forms of white racism have confronted the police with a massive control problem of the kind most evident in the riots.

> In our survey, we found that the police were inclined to see the riots as the long range result of faults in the Negro community—disrespect for law, crime, broken families, etc.—rather than as responses to the stance of the white community. Indeed, nearly one-third of the white police saw the riots as the result of what they considered the basic violence and disrespect of Negroes in general, while only one-fourth attributed the riots to the failure of white institutions. More than three-fourths also regarded the riots as the immediate result of agitators and criminals—a suggestion contradicted by all the evidence accumulated by the riot commission. The police, then share with the other groups—excepting the black politicians—a tendency to emphasize perceived defects in the black community as an explanation for the difficulties that they encounter in the ghetto.

A similar tension sometimes exists between the police and both higher civic officials and representatives of the media. To the extent that such persons recognize the role of social factors in crime and approve of social reforms, they are viewed by the police as "selling out" and not "supporting the police."

Several less central theories often accompany the "rotten apple" view. These theories, too, are widely shared in our society. First, the police widely blame the current rise in crime on a turn away from traditional religiousness, and they fear an impending moral breakdown. Yet the best recent evidence shows that people's religious beliefs and attendance neither reduce nor increase their propensity toward crime.

But perhaps the main target of current police thinking is permissive child-rearing, which many policemen interviewed by our task force view as having led to a generation "that thinks it can get what it yells for." Indeed, one officer interviewed justified the use of physical force on offenders as a corrective for lack of childhood discipline. "If their folks had beat 'em when they were kids, they'd be straight now. As it is, we have to shape 'em up." While much recent evidence, discussed elsewhere in this report, has shown that students most concerned with social issues and most active in protest movements have been reared in homes more "permissive," according to police standards, than those who are uninvolved in these matters, it does not follow that such "permissiveness" leads to criminality. In fact the evidence strongly suggests that persons who receive heavy corporal punishment as children are more likely to act aggressively in ensuing years.

The police also tend to view perfectly legal social deviance, such as long hair worn by men, not only with extreme distaste but as a ladder to potential criminality. At a luncheon meeting of the International Conference of Police Associations, for example, Los Angeles patrolman George Suber said:

> You know, the way it is today, women will be women—and so will men! I got in trouble with one of them. I stopped him on a freeway after a chase—95, 100 miles an hour. . . . He had that hair down to the shoulders.
>
> I said to him, "I have a son about your age, and if you were my son, I'd do two things." "Oh," he said, "what?" "I'd knock him on his ass, and I'd tell him to get a haircut."
>
> "Oh, you don't like my hair?" "No," I said, "you look like a fruit." At that he got very angry. I had to fight him to get him under control.

Nonconformity comes to be viewed with nearly as much suspicion as actual law violation; correspondingly, the police value the familiar, the ordinary, the status quo, rather than social change. These views both put the police at odds with the dissident communities with whom they have frequent contact and detract from their capacity to appreciate the reasons for dissent, change, or any form of innovative social behavior.

EXPLAINING MASS PROTEST

It is difficult to find police literature which recognizes that the imperfection of social institutions provides some basis for the discontent of large segments of

American society. In addition, organized protest tends to be viewed as the con-spiratorial product of authoritarian agitators—usually "Communists"—who mislead otherwise contented people. From a systematic sampling of police litera-ture and statements by law enforcement authorities—ranging from the Director of the Federal Bureau of Investigation to the patrolman on the beat—a common theme emerges in police analyses of mass protest: the search for such "leaders." Again, this is a view, and a search, that is widespread in our society.

Such an approach has serious consequences. The police are led to view protest as illegitimate misbehavior, rather than as legitimate dissent against policies and practices that might be wrong. The police are bound to be hostile to illegitimate misbehavior, and the reduction of protest tends to be seen as their principal goal. Such an attitude leads to more rather than less violence; and a cycle of greater and greater hostility continues.

The "agitational" theory of protest leads to certain characteristic conse-quences. The police are prone to underestimate both the protesters' numbers and depth of feeling. Again, this increases the likelihood of violence. Yet it is not only the police who believe in the "agitational" theory. Many author-ities do when challenged. For example, the Cox Commission found that one reason for the amount of violence when police cleared the buildings at Columbia was the inaccurate estimate of the number of demonstrators in the buildings:

> It seems to us, however, that the Administration's low estimate largely resulted from its inability to see that the seizure of the building was not simply the work of a few radicals but, by the end of the week, involved a significant portion of the student body who had become disenchanted with the operation of the university.

In line with the "agitational" theory of protest, particular significance is attached by police intelligence estimates to detection of leftists or outsiders of various sorts, as well as to indications of organization and prior planning and preparation. Moreover, similarities in tactics and expresses grievances in a num-ber of scattered places and situations are seen as indicative of common leadership.

Thus Mr. J. Edgar Hoover, in testimony before this commission on September 18, 1968, stated:

> Communists are in the forefront of civil rights, anti-war, and student demonstrations, many of which ultimately become disorderly and erupt into violence. As an example, Bettina Aptheker Kurzweil, twenty-four year old member of the Communist National Committee, was a leading organizer of the "Free Speech" demonstrations on the campus of the University of Cali-fornia at Berkeley in the fall of 1964.
>
> These protests, culminating in the arrest of more than 800 demonstrators during a massive sit-in, on December 3, 1964, were the forerunner of the cur-rent campus upheaval.
>
> In a press conference on July 4, 1968, the opening day of the Communist Party's Special National Convention, Gus Hall, the Party's General Secretary,

stated that there were communists on most of the major college campuses in the country and that they had been involved in the student protests.

Mr. Hoover's statement is significant not only because he is our nation's highest and most renowned law enforcement official, but also because his views are reflected and disseminated throughout the nation—by publicity in the news media and by FBI seminars, briefings, and training for local policemen.

Not surprisingly, then, views similar to Mr. Hoover's dominate the most influential police literature. For instance, a lengthy article in the April, 1965, issue of the *The Police Chief*, the official publication of the International Association of Chiefs of Police, concludes, referring to the Berkeley "Free Speech Movement":

> One of the more alarming aspects of these student demonstrations is the ever-present evidence that the guiding hand of communists and extreme leftists was involved.

By contrast, a "blue-ribbon" investigating committee appointed by the Regents of the University of California concluded:

> We found no evidence that the FSM was organized by the Communist Party, the Progressive Labor Movement, or any other outside group. Despite a number of suggestive coincidences, the evidence which we accumulated left us with no doubt that the Free Speech Movement was a response to the September 14th change in rules regarding political activity at Bancroft and Telegraph, not a pre-planned effort to embarrass or destroy the University on whatever pretext arose.

And more recently, the prestigious Cox Commission, which was headed by the former Solicitor General of the United States and investigated last spring's Columbia disturbances, reported:

> We reject the view that describes the April and May disturbances primarily to a conspiracy of student revolutionaries. That demonology is no less false than the naive radical doctrine that attributes all wars, racial injustices, and poverty to the machinations of a capitalist and militarist "Establishment."

One reason why police analysis so often finds "leftists" is that its criteria for characterizing persons as "leftists" are so broad as to be misleading. In practice, the police may not distinguish "dissent" from "subversion." For example, listed in *The Police Chief* article as a "Communist-linked" person is a "former U.S. government employee who, while so employed, participated in picketing the House Committee on Un-American Activities in 1960." Guilt by association is a central analytical tool, and information is culled from such ultraright publications as *Tocsin* and *Washington Report*. Hostility and suspicion toward the civil rights movement also serve as a major impetus for seeing Communist involvement and leadership. *The Police Chief* found it significant that black civil rights leaders such as James Farmer, Bayard Rustin, John Lewis, James Baldwin, and William McAdoo were among "the swarm of sympathizers" who sent messages of support to the FSM.

Some indication of how wide the "communist" net stretches is given by a December, 1968, story in the *Chicago Tribune*. The reporter asked police to comment on the Report of this commission's Chicago Study Team:

> While most district commanders spoke freely, many policemen declined to comment unless their names were withheld. The majority of these said the Walker report appeared to have been written by members of the United States Supreme Court or Communists.

Supplementing the problem of police definition and identification of leftists is a special vision of the role that such persons play. Just as the presence of police and newsmen at the scene of a protest does not mean they are leaders, so the presence of a handful of radicals should not necessarily lead one to conclude that they are leading the protest movement. Moreover, our chapter on student protest as well as other studies of student protest—including the Byrne Report on the Free Speech Movement and the Cox Report on the Columbia disturbances—indicate that "the leadership," leaving aside for the moment whether it is radical leadership, is able to lead only when events such as administration responses unite significant numbers of students or faculty. For example, the FSM extended over a number of months , and the leaders conducted a long conflict with the university administration and proposed many mass meetings and protests, but their appeals to "sit-in" were heeded by students only intermittently. Sometimes the students rallied by the thousands; at other times the leadership found its base shrunken to no more than several hundred. At these nadir points the leaders were unable to accomplish anything significant; on their own they were powerless. Renewal of mass support for the FSM after each of these pauses was not the work of the leadership, but only occurred when the school administration took actions that aroused mass student feelings of betrayal or inequity. The "leadership" remained relatively constant in its calls for support—and even then had serious internal disputes—but the students gave, withdrew, and renewed their support independently, based on events. Clearly, the leaders did not foment student protest on their own; and whatever the intentions or political designs of many FSM leaders, they never had the power to manufacture the protest movement.

One special reason for this kind of police analysis of student protest may derive from police unfamiliarity with the student culture in which such protests occur. When this culture is taken into account, one need not fall back upon theories of sinister outside organizers to explain the ability of students to organize, plan, and produce sophisticated leaders and techniques. Even at the time of the Free Speech Movement in 1964, many of the students, including campus leaders, had spent at least one summer in the South taking part in the civil right struggles. Moreover, everyone had read about or seen on television the "sit-ins" and other nonviolent tactics of the civil rights movement. Also, while the police in Berkeley saw the use of loudspeakers and walkie-talkies as evidence of outside leadership, the former had long been standard equipment at student rallies and meetings, and the latter were available in nearby children's toy stores (and were largely a "put-on" anyway). Finally, with the intellectual and human resources of thousands of undergraduates, graduate students, and faculty at one of the most honored universities in the world, one would hardly expect less competent organization and planning.

A similar analysis may be made of conspiracy arguments relying on similarities in issues and tactics in student protests throughout the nation; explanations more simple than an external organizing force can be found. There is no question that there has been considerable contact among student protesters from many campuses. For example, students who are undergraduates at one university often do graduate work at another. And television news coverage of protest, student newspapers, and books popular in the student culture have long articulated the grievances and tactics around which much unrest revolves. Thus, when it is also considered that students throughout the country do face similar circumstances, it is hardly surprising for similar events to occur widely and to follow a recognizable pattern. Interestingly, collective actions, such as panty raids, have spread through the student subculture in the past without producing sinister conspiracy theories.

A related problem for police is sorting among certain types of claims from and statements about radical movements. Chicago prior to and during the Democratic National Convention is a case in point. To quote from the report of the commission's Chicago Study Team:

> The threats to the City were varied. Provocative and inflammatory statements, made in connection with activities planned for convention week, were published and widely disseminated. There were also intelligence reports from informants.
> Some of this information was *absurd,* like the reported plan to contaminate the city's water supply with LSD. But some were *serious;* and both were strengthened by the authorities' *lack of any mechanism for distinguishing one from the other.*
> The second factor—*the city's response—matched in numbers and logistics, at least, the demonstrators' threats.*

Surely it is unsatisfactory not to distinguish the absurd from the serious. And just as surely, the incapacity to distinguish can only result in inadequate protection against real dangers, as well as an increased likelihood of unnecessary suppression and violence. Again, this illustrates some of the problems of the police view when confronted with modern mass protest. The police are more likely to believe that "anarchist" leaders are going to contaminate a city's water supply with LSD than they are to believe that a student anti-war or black protest is an expression of genuine, widespread dissatisfaction. Moreover, some radicals have increasingly learned to utilize and exploit the power of the media in order to stage events and create scenes, to provoke police into attacking peaceful protesters, and the police have played an important role in assuring their success.

An interesting footnote to this discussion of police ideas about protest may be added by noting that, if the standards used by leading police spokesmen to identify a conspiracy were applied to the police themselves, one would conclude that police in the United States constitute an ultra-right-wing conspiracy. For example, one would note the growing police militancy with its similar rhetoric and tactics throughout the nation, and the presence of such outside "agitators" as John Harrington, president of the Fraternal Order of Police, at the scene of particular outbursts of militancy. We hasten to add that we do not feel that this is an adequate analysis of the situation. Police, like students, share a common culture and are subject to similar pressures, problems, and inequities; the police across the country respond similarly to similar situations because they share common interests, not because they are a "fascist"-led conspiracy.

• • •

THE MILITARY ANALOGY

Political involvement of the police—even apart from its contribution to more radical forms of police militancy—raises serious problems. First, aside from the military, the police have a practical monopoly on the legal use of force in our society. For just such a reason our country has a tradition of wariness toward politicization of its armed forces, and thus both law and custom restrict the political activities of members of the military. Similar considerations obviously apply to the police.

In some senses the police are an even greater source of potential concern than the armed forces because of their closeness to the day-to-day workings of the political process and their frequent interaction with the population. These factors make police abuse of the political process a more immediate prospect. For example, bumper stickers on squad cars, political buttons on uniforms, selective ticketing, and similar contacts with citizens quickly impart a political message.

A second factor which has led to restrictions on members of the armed forces is the fear that unfettered political expression, if adopted as a principle, might in practice lead to political coercion *within* the military. Control over promotions and disciplinary action could make coercion possible, and pressure might be exerted on lower-ranking members to adopt, contribute to, or work for a particular political cause. Thus, again, regulation (and sometimes prohibition) of certain political activities has been undertaken. For example, superiors are prohibited from soliciting funds from inferiors, and many political activities are prohibited while in uniform or on duty. Such considerations, again, apply to the police.

THE JUDICIAL ANALOGY

Even where coercion of the populace (or fellow force members) does not exist in fact, politicization of the police may create both hostility toward the police and disrespect for the legal and political system.

Moreover, lobbying, campaigning, and the like, in and of themselves, tend to make the policing function itself appear politically motivated and nonneutral. Since the policing function is for so many people so central and important a part of our legal mechanisms, the actual or apparent politicization of policing would carry over to perceptions of the entire legal system. Such perceptions of politicization would be contrary to society's view that the system should be neutral and nonpolitical. And such a situation would, of course, have adverse consequences for confidence in and thus reliance on its legal system to resolve disputes peacefully. And this is most true of those groups—students, anti-war protesters, and blacks—who perceive the police political position as most hostile to their own aspirations and who are also among the most heavily policed. Moreover, the legal system would in turn be exposed to even greater political pressures than is presently the case.

So, while the police may be analogous to other government employees or to members of the armed forces, they are also, and perhaps more importantly, analogous to the judiciary. Each interprets the legal order to, and imposes the laws on, the population, and thus the actions of each are expected to be neutral and nonpolitical. In the case of the judiciary, there is a strong tradition of removing them from the partisan political arena lest their involvement impede the functioning of the system.

It may be useful in this connection to illustrate just how strong are our societal norms concerning judicial behavior and to note that these norms often demand standards of conduct higher than what is legally required. For example, even when judges run for reelection, it is widely understood that the election should not be political in the usual sense. Moreover, at various times in our history there has been public uneasiness about justices of the Supreme Court advising Presidents of the United States. Perhaps even more to the point, however, is the fact that whereas justices have from time to time informally advised Presidents, it is unthinkable that they would take to the stump or engage in overt political activity in their behalf.

● ● ●

Police conduct
and patrol practices

In an earlier era third-degree interrogations were widespread, indiscriminate arrests on suspicion were generally accepted, and "alley justice" dispensed with the nightstick was common.

Today, many disturbances studied by the Commission began with a police incident. But these incidents were not, for the most part, the crude acts of an earlier time. They were routine police actions such as stopping a motorist or raiding an illegal business. Indeed, many of the serious disturbances took place in cities whose police are among the best led, best organized, best trained and most professional in the country.

Yet some activities of even the most professional police department may heighten tension and enhance the potential for civil disorder. An increase in complaints of police misconduct, for example, may in fact be a reflection of professionalism; the department may simply be using law enforcement methods which increase the total volume of police contacts with the public. The number of charges of police misconduct may be greater simply because the volume of police-citizen contacts is higher.

Here we examine two aspects of police activities that have great tension-creating potential. Our objective is to provide recommendations to assist city and police officials in developing practices which can allay rather than contribute to tension.

POLICE CONDUCT

Negroes firmly believe that police brutality and harassment occur repeatedly in Negro neighborhoods. This belief is unquestionably one of the major reasons for intense Negro resentment against the police.

The extent of this belief is suggested by attitude surveys. In 1964, a New York Times study of Harlem showed that 43 percent of those questioned believed in the existence of police "brutality." In 1965, a nationwide Gallup Poll

Reprinted from *Report of the National Advisory Commission on Civil Disorders,* Washington, D.C., U. S. Government Printing Office, 1968:158-161. Footnotes omitted.

found that 35 percent of Negro men believe there was police brutality in their areas; 7 percent of white men thought so. In 1966, a survey conducted for the Senate Subcommittee on Executive Reorganization found that 60 percent of Watts Negroes aged 15 to 19 believed there was some police brutality. Half said they had witnessed such conduct. A University of California at Los Angeles study of the Watts area found that 79 percent of the Negro males believed police lack respect for or use insulting language to Negroes and 74 percent believed police use unnecessary force in making arrest. In 1967, an Urban League study of the Detroit riot area found that 82 percent believed there was some form of police brutality.

The true extent of excessive and unjustified use of force is difficult to determine. One survey done for the Crime Commission suggests that when police-citizen contacts are systematically observed, the vast majority are handled without antagonism or incident. Of 5,339 police-citizen contacts observed in slum precincts in three large cities, in the opinion of the observer, only 20—about three-tenths of 1 percent—involved excessive or unnecessary force. And although almost all of those subjected to such force were poor, more than half were white. Verbal discourtesy was more common—15 percent of all such contacts began with a "brusque or nasty command" on the part of the officer. Again, however, the objects of such commands were more likely to be white than Negro.

Such "observer" surveys may not fully reflect the normal pattern of police conduct. The Crime Commission Task Force concluded that although the study gave "no basis for stating the extent to which police officers used force, it did confirm that such conduct still exists in the cities where observations were made." Our investigators confirm this conclusion.

Physical abuse is only one source of aggravation in the ghetto. In nearly every city surveyed, the Commission heard complaints of harassment of interracial couples, dispersal of social street gatherings, and the stopping of Negroes on foot or in cars without obvious basis. These, together with contemptuous and degrading verbal abuse, have great impact in the ghetto. As one Commission witness said, these strip the Negro of the one thing that he may have left—his dignity, "the question of being a man."

Some conduct—breaking up of street groups, indiscriminate stops and searches—is frequently directed at youths, creating special tensions in the ghetto where the average age is generally under 21. Ghetto youths, often without work and with homes that may be nearly uninhabitable, particularly in the summer, commonly spend much time on the street. Characteristically, they are not only hostile to police, but eager to demonstrate their own masculinity and courage. The police, therefore, are often subject to taunts and provocations, testing their self-control and, probably, for some, reinforcing their hostility to Negroes in general. Because youths commit a large and increasing proportion of crime, police are under growing pressure from their supervisors—and from the community—to deal with them forcefully. "Harassment of youths" may therefore be viewed by some police departments—and members even of the Negro community—as a proper crime prevention technique.

In a number of cities the Commission heard complaints of abuse from Negro adults of all social and economic classes. Particular resentment is aroused by harassing Negro men in the company of white women—often their light-skinned Negro wives.

"Harassment" or discourtesy may not be the result of malicious or discriminatory intent of police officers. Many officers simply fail to understand the effects of their actions because of their limited knowledge of the Negro community. Calling a Negro teenager by his first name may arouse resentment because many whites still refuse to extend to adult Negroes the courtesy of the title, "Mister." A patrolman may take the arm of a person he is leading to the police car. Negroes are more likely to resent this than whites because the action implies that they are on the verge of flight and may degrade them in the eyes of friends or onlookers.

In assessing the impact of police misconduct we emphasize that the improper acts of a relatively few officers may create severe tensions between the department and the entire Negro community. Whatever the actual extent of such conduct, we concur in the Crime Commission's conclusion that:

> . . . all such behavior is obviously and totally reprehensible, and when it is directed against minority-group citizens it is particularly likely to lead, for quite obvious reasons, to bitterness in the community.

POLICE PATROL PRACTICES

Although police administrators may take steps to attempt to eliminate misconduct by individual police officers, many departments have adopted patrol practices which in the words of one commentator, have ". . . replaced harassment by individual patrolmen with harassment by entire departments."

These practices, sometimes known as "aggressive preventive patrol," take a number of forms, but invariably they involve a large number of police-citizen contacts initiated by police rather than in response to a call for help or service. One such practice utilizes a roving task force which moves into high-crime districts without prior notice, and conducts intensive, often indiscriminate, street stops and searches. A number of obviously suspicious persons are stopped. But so also are persons whom the beat patrolman would know are respected members of the community. Such task forces are often deliberately moved from place to place making it impossible for its members to know the people with whom they come in contact.

In some cities aggressive patrol is not limited to special task forces. The beat patrolman himself is expected to participate and to file a minimum number of "stop-and-frisk" or field interrogation reports for each tour of duty. This pressure to produce, or a lack of familiarity with the neighborhood and its people, may lead to widespread use of these techniques without adequate differentiation between genuinely suspicious behavior, and behavior which is suspicious to a particular officer merely because it is unfamiliar.

Police administrators, pressed by public concern about crime, have instituted such patrol practices often without weighing their tension-creating effects and the resulting relationship to civil disorder.

Motorization of police is another aspect of patrol that has affected law enforcement in the ghetto. The patrolman comes to see the city through a windshield and hear about it over a police radio. To him, the area increasingly comes to consist only of law breakers. To the ghetto resident, the policeman comes increasingly to be only an enforcer.

Loss of contact between the police officer and the community he serves adversely affects law enforcement. If an officer has never met, does not know, and cannot understand the language and habits of the people in the area he patrols, he cannot do an effective police job. His ability to detect truly suspicious behavior is impaired. He deprives himself of important sources of information. He fails to know those persons with an "equity" in the community—homeowners, small businessmen, professional men, persons who are anxious to support proper law enforcement—and thus sacrifices the contributions they can make to maintaining community order.

The problem
of police protection

The strength of ghetto feelings about hostile police conduct may even be exceeded by the conviction that ghetto neighborhoods are not given adequate police protection.

This belief is founded on two basic types of complaint. The first is that the police maintain a much less rigorous standard of law enforcement in the ghetto, tolerating there illegal activities like drug addiction, prostitution and street violence that they would not tolerate elsewhere. The second is that police treat complaints and calls for help from Negro areas much less urgently than from white areas. These perceptions are widespread. As David Hardy, of the staff of *The New York Daily News*, testified:

> To put it simply, for decades little if any law enforcement has prevailed among Negroes in America, particularly those in the ghettos. If a black man kills another black man, the law is generally enforced at its minimum. Violence of every type runs rampant in a ghetto.

A Crime Commission study found that Negroes in Philadelphia and San Diego are convinced that the police apply a different standard of law enforcement in the ghettos. Another Crime Commission study found that about one white person in two believes police provide very good protection in his community; for Negroes, the figure is one in five. Other surveys have reported that Negroes in Harlem and South Central Los Angeles mention inadequate protection more often than brutality or harassment as a reason for their resentment toward the police.

The report of a New Haven community group summarizes the complaints:

> The problem of the adequacy of current police protection ranked with "police misconduct" as the most serious sore points in police-community relations. . . . When calls for help are registered, it is all too frequent that police respond too slowly or not at all. . . . When they do come, [they] arrive with many more men and cars than are necessary . . . brandishing guns and adding to the confusion.

Reprinted from *Report of the National Advisory Commission on Civil Disorders*, Washington, D.C., U.S. Government Printing Office, 1968:158-161. Footnotes omitted.

There is evidence to suggest that the lack of protection does not necessarily result from different basic police attitudes but rather from a relative lack of police personnel for ghetto areas, considering the volume of calls for police. As a consequence, the police work according to priorities. Because of the need for attention to major crimes, little, if any, attention can be accorded to reports of a suspicious person, for example, or a noisy party, or a drunk. And attention even to major crimes may sometimes be routine or skeptical.

Ghetto residents, however, see a dual standard of law enforcement. Particularly because many work in other areas of the city and have seen the nature of police responsiveness there, they are keenly aware of the difference. They come to believe that an assault on a white victim produces one reaction and an assault on a Negro quite another. The police, heavily engaged in the ghetto, might assert that they cannot cover serious offenses and minor complaints at the same time—that they cannot be two places at once. The ghetto resident, however, often concludes that the police respond neither to serious offenses nor to minor complaints.

Recent studies have documented the inadequacies of police response in some ghetto areas. A Yale Law Journal study of Hartford, Connecticut, found that:

> The residents of a large area in the center of the Negro ghetto are victims of over one-third of the daylight residential burglaries in the city. Yet during the daytime only one of Hartford's eighteen patrol cars and none of its eleven foot patrolmen is assigned to this area. Sections in the white part of town about the same size as the central ghetto area receive slightly more intensive daytime patrol even though the citizens in the ghetto area summon the police about six times as often because of criminal acts.

In a United States Commission on Civil Rights study, a review of police communications records in Cleveland disclosed that police took almost four times as long to respond to calls concerning robbery from the Negro district as for the district where response was next slowest. The response time for some other crimes was at least twice as long.

Elaine and Ian Cumming
Laura Edell

The policeman
as an agent of control

We have adopted the convention of looking at social agents and agencies in terms of their relatively supportive or relatively controlling character. We have assumed that it is difficult for an agent to exercise both support and control at the same time and that any agent tends, therefore, to specialize in one or the other aspect of the integrative process. Even when he is specialized, such an agent may be considered controlling when he is compared with some agents, and supportive when compared with others. Thus, the probation officer is more on the client's side, that is, supportive to him, than the policeman, but less so than the psychiatrist. Furthermore, the agent may be seen as supportive by the layman but experienced as controlling by the client, and *vice versa.* For example, the prisoner remanded by the court for psychiatric treatment may well experience his hospitalization as incarceration. Conversely, a chronic alcoholic may be grateful, in mid-winter, for a night in prison.

There is another aspect to this duality in the handling of deviance. While it is probably impossible to perform acts of support and control simultaneously, support without control is overprotection and invites passivity and dependency, while control without support is tyranny and invites rebellion. While the agent may specialize in one aspect of social control of deviance, the other must, nevertheless, be part of his repertoire. Thus while physicians and clergymen are generally supportive of people in pain or trouble, such people are expected, in return, to perform appropriately the role of patient or parishioner. The support is overt, the control is latent. In general, the agent's training and professional ethics focus on the skills needed for the overt part of his role; the latent aspects are derived from and governed by general norms and values. Role conflict can be avoided in part by keeping the "contradictory" side of a role latent.

The policeman's role in an integrative system is, by definition and by law, explicitly concerned with control—keeping the law from being broken and apprehending those who break it—and only latently with support. For example, if you break the law, you can expect to be arrested, but if you go along quietly,

Reprinted in abridged form from Elaine and Ian Cumming and Laura Edell, "Policeman as Philosopher, Guide and Friend," *Social Problems,* 1965, 12(3):276-286, with permission of The Society for the Study of Social Problems. Footnotes omitted.

you can, unless there is a special circumstance, expect to be treated reasonably. In the course of controlling one member of society, moreover, the policeman often provides indirect support to another. For example, when he apprehends, and thus controls a wife-beating husband, he supports the wife, just as, in a reverse situation, the doctor controls the behavior of those attending a patient when he prescribes rest and sympathy. Finally, besides latent support, the policeman often gives direct help to people in certain kinds of trouble. When he does this, the balance between support and control has shifted, and he is acting overtly as a supportive agent and only latently in his controlling role. He has, at the same time, changed from a professional to an amateur. This paper reports a study of the requests for help received by a city police department and the policeman's response to them, with special attention to what is assumed here to be the latent side of his role.

METHOD OF STUDY

Because there seems to be no systematic account of the day-to-day activities of policemen, two specific questions were posed: (1) What kinds of calls for help do policemen get, and (2) How do they answer them? Two kinds of data were collected. First, a total of 801 incoming telephone calls at the police complaint desk in a metropolitan police department were observed over a total of 82 hours. These hours were not evenly distributed around the 24 hours, for reasons connected with the field worker, not with the Police Department. As each complaint was received and disposed of, a description was dictated into a tape recorder. Fourteen selected prowl car calls were then observed. At the end of this phase of the study, the worker submitted field notes concerned with the general culture of the police station. Secondly, interviews were conducted with detectives concerning their special assignments. A formulation of the nature of the policeman's supporting role was then constructed from these data.

RESULTS

The Complaint Desk

. . . The hourly distribution in the first part of the week differs from the last part of the week. The daily peak activity is between the evening hours of seven and eight o'clock excepting for Thursday, Friday and Saturday when it is between nine and ten. . . . The last part of the week also shows a greater volume of calls than the first. In general, the high rate of calls in the evening and on weekends suggests that problems arise when the social pulse is beating fast—when people are coming and going, regrouping, and, of course, engaging in informal rather than formal activities.

In order to interpret these rhythms further, the calls were classified according to their content, as Table I shows:

TABLE I   Classification of Calls to the Complaint Desk of a Metropolitan Police
Department During 82 Selected Hours in June and July 1961

Type of Call	Number of Calls	Percent of Total
Total	801	100.0
Calls included in analysis	652	81.4
1. Calls about "things"	255	31.8
2. Calls for support	397	49.6
Persistent personal problems	230	28.7
a. Health services	81	10.1
b. Children's problems	83	10.4
c. Incapacitated people	33	4.1
d. Nuisances	33	4.1
Periodic personal problems	167	20.9
a. Disputes	63	7.9
b. Violence	43	5.4
c. Protection	29	3.6
d. Missing persons	11	1.4
e. Youths' behavior	21	2.6
Calls excluded from analysis	149	18.6
Information only	33	4.1
Not police business	28	3.5
Feedback calls	88	11.0

. . . 652 calls were for service within the purview of these police. They are
treated as independent, but the unit of analysis is the call, and not the caller,
and results must be interpreted with this in mind.

The 652 calls included in the study were divided into two major groups: the
first included calls for service in connection with things or possessions, while the
second included calls for support or assistance with regard to problems of health,
safety or interpersonal relationships.

The first (nearly one-third of the total of 801 calls) include traffic violations,
reports of losses or thefts, calls about unlocked doors, fallen power wires and so
on. These are part of the regular controlling function of the police and are not
the main focus of this paper. The second major group (about one-half of all
calls) is concerned with personal problems and therefore may reasonably be
expected to include the need or desire for some form of support. These calls
were subdivided into two types: (1) persistent problems occuring throughout the
week; and (2) periodic problems occurring mainly on the weekend.

As Table I shows, the first type comprises 230 calls, of which about one-third
are requests for health services, that is, ambulance escorts, investigation of accidents, suicide attempts, and so on; another third are children's problems, usually

complaints about trespassing, or destructive behavior; and the remainder are divided equally between incapacitated people, usually described over the phone as drunk or "psycho," and nuisances, usually noisy behavior.

Periodic problems comprise 167 calls of which more than a third are about disputes and quarrels of all kinds, both in families and among unrelated people. Almost half are concerned with violence or protection from potential violence and the remainder are about missing persons or gangs of youths and hot-rodders.

Table II shows the distribution of the calls, by type, through the days of the week and the period of the day. It now appears that the heaping up of calls in the last part of the week is made up of two effects: first, routine police business

TABLE II Number of Calls to the Complaint Desk of a Metropolitan Police Department by Type of Problem,* Day of Week, Time of Day, and Hours of Observation During 82 Selected Hours in June and July 1961

Time of Day, Hours of Observation, and Type of Call	Total	Sun.	Mon.	Tue.	Wed.	Thurs.	Fri.	Sat.
All calls	652	50	69	55	76	95	54	253
(hours observed)	(82)	(8)	(14)	(9)	(9)	(9)	(6)	(27)
12:01 a.m.-5:00 a.m.	91	16	18					
(hours observed)	(14)	(2)	(5)	(0)	(0)	(0)	(0)	(7)
Routine	28	4	8					16
Persistent	21	4	4					13
Periodic	42	8	6					28
5:01 a.m.-noon	52		9	19		17		7
(hours observed)	(13)	(0)	(4)	(3)	(0)	(3)	(0)	(3)
Routine	36		6	11		15		4
Persistent	10		2	4		2		2
Periodic	6		1	4		0		1
12:01 p.m.-6:00 p.m.	187	18		36	38	38	31	26
(hours observed)	(26)	(4)	(0)	(6)	(5)	(3)	(4)	(4)
Routine	88	9		12	18	18	16	15
Persistent	68	6		17	11	16	12	6
Periodic	31	3		7	9	4	3	5
6:01 p.m.-midnight	322	16	42		38	40	23	163
(hours observed)	(29)	(2)	(5)	(0)	(4)	(3)	(2)	(13)
Routine	103	4	13		17	15	2	52
Persistent	131	5	22		18	17	7	62
Periodic	88	7	7		3	8	14	49

*Departures from uniformity:

1. Periodic interpersonal calls occur more often than chance would indicate on Friday evening (χ^2 = 24.1, d.f. = 5, P < .01) and the early hours of Saturday (χ^2 = 8.4, d.f. = 2, P = .02).

2. Both routine police calls and persistent interpersonal calls occur more frequently than chance would indicate on Thursday, the former in the morning (χ^2 = 12.3, d.f. = 3, P < .01) and the latter in the afternoon (χ^2 = 13.1, d.f. = 5, P = .05).

and persistent interpersonal calls occur most frequently on Thursday, while periodic interpersonal problems heap up on Friday night. The meaning of this finding is not clear, but it may be that the tensions associated with the instrumental activity of the working week are increasing by Thursday and are then let go on Friday—payday—and on the weekend, when formal constraints are fewer. Because fewer of the other agents are available at these times, the policeman takes over many emergency health and welfare services, a kind of division of labor through time.

Almost three quarters of all 652 calls were answered by dispatch of a patrolman in a squad car to the scene, while about eight percent received various kinds of advice or information, and about four-and-one-half percent were referred to another source of help. Of the 29 referrals, one was to a medical service, one to a social service, 19 to other legal services and the remaining eight to commercial concerns, such as the Telephone Company. Almost 15 percent of the calls were terminated—that is, service was withheld for reasons not determined, occasionally because no car was available. . . .

. . . Table III (omitted). The probability of a car being sent out is inversely related to the rate at which calls are coming in. During the six time periods in which a total of 235 calls were received at a rate of fewer than eight calls per hour, 78 percent of them were responded to with cars. During the five time periods in which 417 calls were received at a rate of more than eight calls per hour, cars were sent only 68 percent of the time. This difference is highly significant ($x^2 = 7.54$, d.f. $= 1$), and suggests that cars are sent on a simple supply-and-demand basis. Furthermore, there is no difference among the three major categories with regard to the likelihood of a car being sent. Nevertheless, certain sub-categories of complaint are more likely to get service than others. As Table IV shows, calls regarding violence (control), children and youths (support and

TABLE IV   Disposition of 397 Calls to the Complaint Desk of a Metropolitan Police
Department Regarding Interpersonal Problems, by Sub-Category of
Complaint, 82 Selected Hours in June and July 1961

Type of Call	Total Calls	Percent Car-Sent
Total calls	397	76.8
Persistent problems	230	79.1
a. Health services	81	86.4
b. Children's problems	83	85.5
c. Incapacitated people	33	75.8
d. Nuisances	33	48.5
Periodic problems	167	73.7
a. Disputes	63	50.8
b. Violence	43	95.3
c. Protection	29	79.3
d. Missing persons	11	81.8
e. Youths' behavior	21	85.7

control), and illness (support) are the most likely to be responded to with a car, although the likelihood of the law being broken—which defines the police mandate—is greater for some of these complaints than for others.

When the complainant reports a nuisance or a dispute, he has only one chance in two of getting more than advice—albeit philosophical advice. Thus, a man calls to say that he has had a fight with his girl and she hasn't come to see him, although he knows she is off duty from the hospital; the policeman says he can't make her come to his house—perhaps she doesn't want to—and goes on to advise the man that that's the way life is sometimes.

It is possible that some of the calls about violence are later stages of these unanswered dispute calls. For example, to one complaint, "My boyfriend is mad at me and is going to beat me up," the answer was, "Call us again when he does."

It is quite apparent that the policeman must often exercise a kind of clinical judgement about these complaints, and that this judgement reflects his own values. The field notes suggest, for example, that policemen are sincerely, if sentimentally, concerned about children, and that negligent parents are likely to find the police at their most truculent. The following example is taken from the notes:

> A call came from a very kindly-sounding Italian man at about 11 o'clock in the evening. He was reporting that he had found a little boy from next door wandering in the street . . . and he thought the police ought to know about the situation. A car was dispatched and reported that there was nobody home, and in fact, there were three smaller children in the house. . . . The captain dispatched a camera crew, child placement was notified and the children were immediately placed in a temporary placement home. A state-out was set for the parents. Meanwhile the pictures had been developed and they showed four under-nourished, under-clothed little children lying in their own feces on a mattress on the floor. The refrigerator contained two cans of condensed milk and some rotten vegetables; the place was filthy and unheated. As the time went by, anger began to rise and when at about four o'clock in the morning the parents were brought in to the station everybody was in an ugly mood. . . . Had they been the least bit smart, glib, or said almost anything other than "yes" or "no" while they were issued tickets, they would have gotten poked.

All-out support for the children is accompanied by the barest minimum of support to the parents in the form of approval for appropriately docile behavior.

The Squad Car

Certain calls are considered serious enough to warrant a captain following the squad car to the scene. The following thumb-nail summaries represent 14 calls made by the captains in a 23-hour period. Half of them were not considered serious, but the field worker asked the captain to go to the scene.

(1) A man, reported by his ex-wife as dangerous and perhaps mentally ill, is found asleep; his ex-wife and her mother are in an agitated state. They report that when the ex-wife came to the home the husband shook his fist under her nose and said, "I have divorced you, I want you out of this goddam house by morning." The police officer woke up the man who once again threatened his ex-wife, and the officer then told her that since it was his house and she was legally divorced from him, she and her mother should "please leave, and not cause any more trouble."

(2) A car accident severely injures a woman and the police supervise her removal to hospital.

(3) A bartender asks for, and receives, help in closing up so that there will be no problems—a routine "preventive" police service usually given by the car on the beat.

(4) A man has beaten up his female neighbor earlier in the day and she has called the police and preferred charges. At the time of this call, the man's wife had threatened this woman with a knife. All are drunk and are taken to the station for further investigation.

(5) A call from a woman about neighborhood children bullying a small boy who wears glasses. The field notes read, "There was a lot of argument and a lot of screaming back and forth, nothing was particularly accomplished, the three policemen (captain and two officers from a squad car) stood around for awhile, questioned people, did a little shouting, got shouted at, then the whole thing sort of dissolved and was resolved in a manner that I don't understand."

(6) A woman complains that her husband doesn't bring home enough of his money to feed the kids. She is advised to go to Children's Court.

(7) Field notes read: "Husband destroying property at his house. He's drunk and he and his wife got in an argument over the children . . . the wife smashed the gift he had given her for Mothers' Day. This set the incident off. He fought the officers, they handcuffed him, and is taken to the station—a psycho."

(8) A slightly drunk man is an unwelcome visitor in his ex-wife's home. Police send him home in a cab.

(9) An ex-patient from a mental hospital is missing from her relative's home. They will broadcast a missing persons call.

(10) A drunk man claims he has been slugged, but cannot amplify so no action is taken. "This is a low IQ street," says the policeman.

(11) A woman in her pajamas and covered with mud says her husband threw her out. He is at home drunk with the children. As he has a police record, two cars are dispatched, one with a tear-gas gun. The house is found in a shambles. The wife is taken to hospital, children to a shelter, and the husband is booked for investigation and possible psychiatric treatment.

(12) Fight in a third floor apartment between a man and his wife. Policeman settles it is some undiscernible fashion.

(13) A man has "gone out of his mind over a girl" and has gone beserk with a gun. The man is shipped to hospital and witnesses are taken in because the gun makes the affair a felony.

(14) The call is "see if an ambulance is needed." A young Negro in a filthy, crowded house appears to be in agony. Police examine him for knife wounds and being satisfied that he has not been stabbed, and that no further investigation is needed, send him to hospital in an ambulance.

There seem to be three types of cases here. In the first, the police act as guides or conveyors to the courts and hospitals, giving indirect support meanwhile. In the second, they appear to resolve problems by giving concrete information and guidance about what is and is not possible under the law. Here both indirect and overt support are given. In the third type, they appear to settle problems through some consensual method based on mutual understanding between the police and the people involved. Here support is fairly overt but control is, of course, latent because of the policeman's representation of law and order. Occasionally, the police give outright friendly support, as in the following incident from the field notes:

> Sitting in the police station is an old man, a citizen wanderer who is on his way to Oregon, and has become dissatisfied with the Rescue Mission and walked out. He's going to spend the night out of the rain until the morning when he's going over to the Salvation Army.

It is of course, not possible to say what proportion of the policeman's responses to citizens fall into these three types, nor indeed, to know what other types there may be, because of the method of selecting the squad car calls.

Detectives

Four detectives of the twenty in the department, selected only because they were on duty at the time of the field worker's visit, were asked to describe their ten most recent cases. It was felt that they might be assigned the more "professional" and hence controlling tasks. Two of them were specialists in theft and forgery and so their cases were, indeed, of this character. However, fifteen out of twenty cases described by the two general detectives fell into our two personal-problem categories, and were similar to the complaint calls except that they were being further investigated because of more serious breaches of the law.

Another detective, in charge of services to alcoholics, reported that in 1956 the police department sent him to Yale for training in the handling of alcoholics. He says, "As a police officer I saw people being arrested for drunk and re-arrested for drunk and I thought it was a pretty medieval way of going about trying to help a person with a basic problem and illness that the public was just kicking in the corner and that's how I wound up here." This officer handles about 900 alcoholics a year. Of these, he takes about 150 charged persons on suspended sentence from the court and tries to arrange for some agency to carry them—an outright supportive service.

Missing persons: The sergeant in charge of this service estimates that he locates about 600 missing people from this area in a year, about half of them children. He further estimates that from three to five percent are mentally disturbed adults. This particular officer says that he sometimes counsels with children that he has traced after they have been returned home. At the same time, he complains to the interviewer that children don't respect police officers the way they did when he was young.

Detectives in charge of homicide and those on duty with the vice squad were not interviewed, so it is impossible to say what proportion of all detective work is supportive. These data suggest that it is similar to the patrolman's.

Police Culture

The field worker reports several impressions that are relevant to our interests. Although they cannot be demonstrated from these data, some of them are similar to findings from other studies. First, poor, uneducated people appear to use the police in the way that middle-class people use family doctors and clergymen—that is, as the first port of call in time of trouble. Second, the policeman must often enforce unpopular laws among these poor people at the same time that he sees these laws being flouted by those in positions of power. Third, many policemen are themselves recruited from, and sympathetic to, the class of people from whom most of the "interpersonal" calls for assistance come.

Fourth, the police have little knowledge of, and liason with, social or even medical agencies, and seem to feel that these agencies' activities are irrelevant to the problems they, themselves, face.

Fifth, the police appear to have a concern not only for children but also for those they define as disturbed and ill. They are tolerant, for example, about many crank calls, and will, if a car is available, help a paranoid old lady search her house for the malignant intruder she feels sure is hiding there. Nevertheless, it is possible to see, both in episodes of prejudice against minorities, and in less dramatic ways, how their own values transcend the individual's rights. A field note says, for example, "A woman wants protection from her doctor who is trying to commit her to a mental institution; the officer replies, 'That's not police business, lady. The police cannot go against any doctor.'"

Finally, many policemen are bitter about their low pay, the label "punitive" applied to them in a world that values "warmth," the conflicting demands of their jobs, and the ingratitude of the public. This bitterness is reflected, in this police force, in a catch phrase, "I hate citizens."

SUMMARY AND DISCUSSION

We return now to our starting questions: What calls are made on the police and how do they respond? More than one-half of the calls coming routinely to the police complaint desk, and perhaps to detectives, appear to involve calls for help and some form of support for personal or interpersonal problems. To about three-quarters of these appeals, a car is sent. When the policeman reaches the scene, the data suggest that he either guides the complainant to someone who can solve his problem or tries to solve it himself. To do this, he must often provide support, either by friendly sympathy, by feeding authoritative information into the troubled situation, or by helping consensual resolution to take place. We started with the assumption that these activities belonged to the latent aspect of his role, and he is certainly an amateur—these policemen have no training for this kind of service. Why, then, are they called upon to exercise their amateur talents half of the time?

The reasons are probably complex. First, the policeman has to do much of what he does because he is on duty at times of the day when no other agent is available. Second, he deals with the problems of a group of people—the poor and the ignorant—that studies of our own and others have shown no other agent to be anxious to serve and, third, he has knowledge of, and access to, very few other agents. In other words, he is part of an integrative system in which the labor is divided not so much on the basis of function as on the basis of the time of day and the nature of the target population. All citizens can count on emergency help from the police when there is sudden illness at night, but only a certain kind of citizen takes his marital troubles to them.

The policeman's supportive acts are not only the latent and hence amateur part of his role, they are also latent in not being recognized and legitimated by the other agents in the integrative system. These others, our own studies show, prefer to recognize the policeman's professional controlling function, which they both need and often call upon. Thus, it is as an agent of control that the policeman participates in a divided labor with social workers, doctors, clergymen, lawyers and teachers in maintaining social integration. The problems he faces appear to be a *failure of integration within the integrative system*, so that he cannot mobilize the other agents when he needs them.

Some modern advocates of "professionalization" of police work recognize that the policeman of the beat spends about half his time as an amateur social worker and they hope, instead of improving the referral process, to equip him with the skills of a professional. The policeman will then have a role containing both overtly supportive and overtly controlling elements. If our assumption that these are incompatible activities is correct, this development would lead to a division of labor within police work that would tend once more to segregate these elements. This, in turn, would result in a basic shift in the relationship of the police to the rest of the integrative system. All of this might remove the policeman's present reasons for hating citizens, but it would not guarantee that they would not be replaced with others.

Donald J. Black
Albert J. Reiss, Jr.

Police control
of juveniles

The findings reported here derive from systematic observation of police-citizen transactions conducted during the summer of 1966. Thirty-six observers—persons with law, law enforcement, and social science backgrounds—recorded observations of routine patrol work in Boston, Chicago, and Washington, D.C. The observer training period comprised one week and was identical across the three cities. The daily supervision system also was similar across the cities. The observers rode in scout cars or, less frequently, walked with patrolmen on all shifts on all days of the week for seven weeks in each city. To assure the inclusion of a large number of police-citizen encounters, we gave added weight to the times when police activity is comparatively high (evening watches, particularly weekend evenings).

No attempt was made to survey police-citizen encounters in all localities within the three cities. Instead, police precincts in each city were chosen as observation sites. The precincts were selected so as to maximize observation in lower socio-economic, high crime rate, racially homogeneous residential areas. This was accomplished through the selection of two precincts each in Boston and Chicago and four precincts in Washington, D.C. The findings pertain to the behavior of uniformed patrolmen rather than to that of policemen in specialized divisions such as juvenile bureaus or detective units.

The data were recorded by the observers in "incident booklets," forms much like interview schedules. One booklet was filled out for every incident that the police were requested to handle or that they themselves noticed while on patrol. A total of 5,713 of these incidents were observed and recorded. This paper concerns only those 281 encounters that include one or more juvenile suspects among the participants.

THE CONTEXT

Although large police departments invariably have specialized divisions for handling incidents that involve juveniles, the great majority of juvenile encounters

Reprinted in slightly abridged form from Donald J. Black and Albert J. Reiss, Jr., "Police Control of Juveniles," *American Sociological Review,* 1970, 35(1):63-77. Footnotes omitted.

with policemen occur with general duty, uniformed patrolmen, rather than with "youth officers." Youth officers receive most of their cases on a referral basis from members of the uniformed patrol division. Usually these referrals enter the police system as arrests of juveniles by uniformed patrolmen. It will be seen, however, that uniformed patrolmen arrest only a small fraction of the legally liable juvenile suspects with whom they have encounters in the field. Youth bureau officers, then, determine what proportion of those arrested will be referred to juvenile court. The outputs of the patrol division thus become the inputs for the youth bureau, which in turn forwards its outputs as inputs to the court. By the time a juvenile is institutionalized, therefore, he has been judged a delinquent at several stages. Correspondingly, sanctions are levied at several stages; institutionalization is the final stage of a sanctioning *process*, rather than *the* sanction for juvenile deviance.

After the commission of a deviant act by a juvenile, the first stage in the elaborate process by which official rates of delinquency are produced is detection. For the police, as for most well-differentiated systems of social control, detection is largely a matter of organizational mobilization. Mobilization is the process by which incidents come to the initial attention of agents of the police organization. There are two basic types of mobilization of the police: *citizen-initiated*, or "reactive" mobilization, and *police-initiated*, or "proactive" mobilization, depending upon who makes the original decision that police action is appropriate. An example of a citizen-initiated mobilization occurs when a citizen phones the police to report an event and the radio dispatcher sends a patrol car to handle the call. A typical police-initiated mobilization takes place when a policeman observes and acts upon what he regards as a law violation or, as in the case of a "stop-and-frisk," a "suspicious" person or situation.

Popular and even sociological conceptions of the police err through an overreliance on proactive imagery to characterize police operations. Although some specialized divisions of municipal police departments, such as traffic bureaus and vice units, do depend primarily upon proactive mobilization for their input of cases, in routine patrol work the great majority of incidents come to police attention through the citizen-initiated form of mobilization. The crime detection function is lodged mainly in the citizenry rather than in the police. Moreover, most police work with juveniles also arises through the initiative of citizen complainants. In this sense, the citizen population in good part draws the boundaries of its own official rate of juvenile delinquency.

DETECTION OF JUVENILE DEVIANCE

Observation of police encounters with citizens netted 281 encounters with suspects under 18 years of age, here treated as juveniles The great majority of the juveniles were from blue-collar families. Of the 281 police-juvenile encounters, 72% were citizen-initiated (by phone) and 28% were initiated by policemen on patrol. Excluding traffic violations, these proportions become 78% and 22%, respectively. The mobilization of police control of juveniles is then overwhelmingly a reactive rather than a proactive process. Hence it would seem that the moral standards of the citizenry have more to do with the definition of juvenile deviance than do the standards of policemen on patrol.

Moreover, the incidents the police handle in citizen-initiated encounters differ somewhat from those in encounters they bring into being on their own initiative. (See Table 1.) This does not mean, however, that the standards of citizens and

TABLE 1   Percent of Police Encounters with Juvenile Suspects According to Type of Mobilization and Race of Suspect, by Type of Incident

	Type of Mobilization and Race of Suspect						
	Citizen-Initiated		Police-Initiated		All Citizen-Initiated	All Police-Initiated	All Encounters
Type of Incident	Negro	White	Negro	White			
Felony	10	—	10	—	5	5	5
Misdemeanor, except rowdiness	18	11	5	14	15	9	13
Misdemeanor, rowdiness	62	77	40	33	69	37	60
Traffic violation	1	—	26	28	*	27	8
Suspicious person	—	1	17	22	*	19	6
Noncriminal dispute	8	12	2	3	10	3	8
Total percent	99	101	100	100	99	100	100
Total number	(109)	(94)	(42)	(36)	(203)	(78)	(281)

*.5 percent or less.

policemen necessarily differ; the differences between incidents in reactive and proactive police work seem to result in large part from differences in detection opportunities, since the police are limited to the surveillance of public places. For example, non-criminal disputes are more likely to occur in private than in public places; they account for 10% of the police-juvenile contacts in citizen-initiated work but for only 3% of the proactive encounters. On the other hand, the "suspicious person" is nearly always a police-initiated encounter. Traffic violations, too, are almost totally in the police-initiated category; it is simply not effective or feasible for a citizen to call the police about a "moving" traffic violation (and nearly all of these cases were "moving" rather than "standing" violations). In short, there are a number of contingencies that affect the detection of juvenile deviance in routine policing.

A broader pattern in the occasions for police-juvenile transactions is the overwhelming predominance of incidents of minor legal significance. Only 5% of the police encounters with juveniles involve alleged felonies; the remainder are less serious from a legal standpoint. Sixty percent involve nothing more serious than juvenile rowdiness or mischievous behavior, the juvenile counterpart of "disorderly conduct" or "breach of the peace" by adults. This does not mean that the social significance of juvenile deviance is minor for the citizens who call the police or for the police themselves. It should be noted, moreover, that these incidents do not necessarily represent the larger universe of juvenile deviance, since (1) in many cases the juvenile offender is not apprehended by the police, and (2) an unknown number of delinquent acts go undetected. Nonetheless, these incidents represent the inputs from which uniformed patrolmen produce juvenile arrests and thus are the relevant base for analyzing the conditions under which juveniles are sanctioned in police encounters.

Another pattern lies in the differences between Negro and white encounters with policemen. In the aggregate, police encounters with Negro juveniles pertain to legally more serious incidents, owing primarily to the differential in felony encounters (see Table 1). None of the encounters with white juveniles involved the allegation of a felony, though this was true of 10% of the transactions with Negro juveniles in both citizen- and police-initiated encounters. Apart from this difference between the races, however, the occasions for encounters with Negro and white juveniles have many similarities.

It might be noted that the data on the occasions for police-juvenile encounters do not in themselves provide evidence of racial discrimination in the selection of juveniles for police attention. Of course, the citizen-initiated encounters cannot speak to the issue of discriminatory *police* selection. On the other hand, if the police tend to stop a disproportionate number of Negroes on the street in minor incident situations, we might infer the presence of discrimination. But the findings in Table 1 do not provide such evidence. Likewise, we might infer police discrimination if a higher proportion of the total Negro encounters is police-initiated than that of the total white encounters. Again the evidence is lacking: police-initiated encounters account for 28% of the total for both Negro and white juveniles. More data would be needed to assess adequately the issue of police selectivity by race.

INCIDENTS AND ARREST

Of the encounters patrol officers have with juvenile suspects, only 15% result in arrest. Hence it is apparent that by a large margin most police-juvenile contacts are concluded in the field settings where they arise. These field contacts, 85% of the total, generally are not included in official police statistics on reported cases of juvenile delinquency, and thus they represent the major invisible portion of the delinquency control process. In other words, if these sample data are reasonably representative, the probability is less than one-in-seven that a policeman confronting a juvenile suspect will exercise his discretion to produce an official case of juvenile delinquency. A high level of selectivity enters into the arrest of juveniles. This and subsequent sections of the paper seek to identify some of the conditions which contribute to that selection process.

A differential in police dispositions that appears at the outset of the analysis

TABLE 2 Percent of Police Encounters with Juvenile Suspects According to Type of Incident and Race of Suspect, by Field Disposition

Field Disposition	Type of Incident and Race of Suspect														
	Felony		Misdemeanor; Except Rowdiness		Misdemeanor; Rowdiness		Traffic Violation		Suspicious Person		Non-Criminal Dispute		All Negro	All White	All Encounters
	N	W	N	W	N	W	N	W	N	W	N	W			
Arrest	73	—	36	20	13	8	8	—	—	(1)	—	—	21	8	15
Release-in-Field	27	—	64	80	87	92	92	100	(7)	(8)	100	100	80	92	85
Total Percent	100	—	100	100	100	100	100	100	—	—	100	100	101	100	100
Total Number	(15)	—	(22)	(15)	(85)	(84)	(12)	(10)	(7)	(9)	(10)	(12)	(151)	(130)	(281)

is that between Negroes and whites. The overall arrest rate for police-Negro
encounters is 21%, while the rate for police-white encounters is only 8%. This
difference immediately raises the question of whether or not racial discrimination determines the disposition of juvenile suspects. Moreover, Table 2 shows
that the arrest rate for Negroes is also higher within specific incident categories
where comparisons are possible. The race difference, therefore, is not merely a
consequence of the larger number of legally serious incidents that occasion
police-Negro contacts.

Apart from the race differnce, Table 2 reveals that patrol officers make proportionately more arrests when the incident is relatively serious from a legal
standpoint. The arrest rate for Negro encounters is twice as high for felonies as it
is for the more serious misdemeanors, and for encounters with both races the
arrest rate for serious misdemeanors doubles the rate for juvenile rowdiness. On
the other hand, policemen rarely make arrests of either race for traffic violations
or for suspicious person situations. Arrest appears even less likely when the incident is a noncriminal dispute. The disposition pattern for juvenile suspects
clearly follows the hierarchy of offenses found in the criminal law, the law for
adults.

It is quite possible that the legal seriousness of incidents is more important in
encounters between *patrol* officers and juveniles than in those between *youth*
officers and juveniles. As a rule, the patrol officer's major sanction is arrest,
arrest being the major formal product of patrol work. By contrast, the youth
officer has the power to refer cases to juvenile court, a prosecutorial discretion
with respect to juveniles that patrolmen in large departments usually do not
have. Whether he is in the field or in his office, the juvenile officer plays a role
different from that of the patrolman in the system of juvenile justice. For this
reason alone, the factors relating to the disposition of juveniles may differ
between the two. The youth officer may, for example, be more concerned with
the juvenile's past record, a kind of information that usually is not accessible to
the patrolman in the field setting. Furthermore, past records may have little
relevance to a patrol officer who is seeking primarily to order a field situation
with as little trouble as possible. His organizational responsibility ends there. For
his purposes, the age status of a suspect may even be irrelevant in the field. Conversely, the youth officer may find that the juvenile court or his supervisor
expects him to pay more attention to the juvenile's record than to the legal
status of a particular incident. In short, the contingencies that affect the sanctioning of juveniles may vary with the organizational sources of the discretion of
sanction.

SITUATIONAL ORGANIZATION AND ARREST

Apart from the substance of police encounters—the kinds of incidents they
involve—these encounters have a social structure. One element in this structure is

the distribution of situational roles played by the participants in the encounter. Major situational roles that arise in police encounters are those of suspect or offender, complainant, victim, informant, and bystander. None of these roles necessarily occurs in every police encounter.

In police encounters with suspects, which account for only about 50% of all police-citizen contacts, particularly important is the matter of whether or not a citizen complainant participates in the situational action. A complainant in search of justice can make direct demands on a policeman with which he must comply. Likewise a complainant is a witness of the police officer's behavior; thus he has the ability to contest the officer's version of an encounter or even to bring an official complaint against the officer himself. In these respects as well as others, the complainant injects constraints into police-suspect confrontations. This is not to deny that the complainant often may be an asset to a policeman who enters a pre-existing conflict situation in the field. The complainant can provide what may be otherwise unavailable information to a situationally ignorant patrolman. The patrol officer is a major intelligence arm of modern police systems, but he, like other policemen, must live with a continual dependence upon citizens for the information that is his allotted responsibility to gather. Furthermore, when a suspect is present in the field situation, the information provided by a complainant, along with his willingness to stand on his word by signing a formal complaint, may be critical to an arrest in the absence of a police witness.

The relationship between arrest and the presence of a complainant in police-juvenile encounters is shown in Table 3. It is apparent that this relation between situational organization and disposition differs according to the suspect's race. Particularly interesting is the finding that when there is no citizen complainant in the encounter the race difference in arrest rates narrows to the point of being negligible—14% versus 10% for encounters with Negro and white juveniles

TABLE 3   Percent of Police Encounters with Juvenile Suspects According to Situational Organization and Race of Suspect, by Field Disposition. (Table Excludes Felonies, Traffic Violations, and Non-Criminal Disputes.)

Field Disposition	Situational Organization and Race of Suspect				All Suspect Only	All Complainant and Suspect	All Encounters
	Suspect Only		Complainant and Suspect				
	Negro	White	Negro	White			
Arrest	14	10	21	8	11	16	13
Release-in-Field	86	90	79	92	89	84	87
Total Percent	100	100	100	100	100	100	100
Total Number	(66)	(93)	(48)	(26)	(159)	(74)	(233)

respectively. By contrast, when a complainant participates, this difference widens considerably to 21% versus 8%. This latter difference is all the more striking since felony situations and traffic and noncriminal dispute situations, which may be regarded as confounding factors, are excluded from the tabulation.

It also should be noted that as far as the major citizen participants are concerned, each of these encounters is racially homogeneous. The comparatively rare, mixed race encounters are excluded from these computations. Thus the citizen complainants who oversee the relatively severe dispositions of Negro juveniles are themselves Negro. The great majority of the police officers are white in the police precincts investigated, yet they seem somewhat more lenient when they confront Negro juveniles alone than when a Negro complainant is involved. Likewise, it will be recalled (Table 3) that the arrest difference between Negro and white juveniles all but disappears when no complainant is involved. These patterns complicate the question of racial discrimination in the production of juvenile arrests, given that a hypothesis of discrimination would predict opposite patterns. Indeed, during the observation period a strong majority of the policemen expressed anti-Negro attitudes in the presence of observers. It might be expected that if the police were expressing their racial prejudices in discriminatory arrest practices, this would be more noticeable in police-initated encounters than in those initiated by citizens. But the opposite is the case. All of the encounters involving a citizen complainant in this sample were citizen-initiated typically by the complainants themselves. Proactive police operations rarely involve complainants. To recapitualte: the police are particularly likely to arrest a Negro juvenile when a citizen enjoins them to handle the incident and participates as a complainant in the situational action, but this is not characteristic of police encounters with white juveniles. Finally, it is noteworthy that Negro juveniles find themselves in encounters that involve a complainant proportionately more than do white juveniles. Hence, the pattern discussed above has all the more impact on the overall arrest rate for Negro juveniles. Accordingly, the next section examines the role of the complainant in more detail.

THE COMPLAINANT'S PREFERENCE AND ARREST

If the presence of a citizen complainant increases the production of Negro arrests, then the question arises as to whether this pattern occurs as a function of the complainant's mere presence, his situational behavior, or something else. In part, this issue can be broached by inquiring into the relationship between the complainant's behavioral preference for police action in a particular field situation and the kind of disposition the police in fact make.

Before examining this relationship, however, it should be noted that a rather large proportion of complainants do not express clear preferences for police action such that a field observer can make an accurate classification. Moreover, there is a race differential in this respect. Considering only the misdemeanor

TABLE 4   Percent of Police Encounters with Juvenile Suspects that Involve a Citizen Complainant According to Race of Suspect and Complainant's Preference, by Field Disposition. (Table Excludes Felonies, Traffic Violations, and Non-Criminal Disputes.)

| Field Disposition | Race of Suspect and Complainant's Preference | | | | | | All Negro Encounters | All White Encounters | All Encounters |
| | Negro | | | White | | | | | |
	Prefers Arrest	Prefers Informal Disposition	Preference Unclear	Prefers Arrest	Prefers Informal Disposition	Preference Unclear			
Arrest	60	—	17	(1)	—	(1)	8	8	16
Release-in-Field	40	100	83	(3)	100	(6)	92	92	84
Total Percent	100	100	100	—	100	—	100	100	100
Total Number	(10)	(15)	(23)	(4)	(15)	(7)	(26)	(26)	(74)

situations, the Negro complainant's preference for action is unclear in 48% of the police encounters with Negro juveniles, whereas the comparable proportion drops to 27% for the encounters with white complainants and juveniles. Nevertheless, a slightly larger proportion of the Negro complainants express a preference for arrest of their juvenile adversaries—21%, versus 15% for whites. Finally, the complainant prefers an informal disposition in 31% of the Negro cases and in 58% of the white cases. Thus white complainants more readily express a preference for police leniency toward juvenile suspects than do Negro complainants.

Table 4 suggests that white juveniles benefit from this greater leniency, since the police show a quite dramatic pattern of compliance with the expressed preferences of complainants. This pattern seems clear even though the number of cases necessitates caution in interpretation. In not one instance did the police arrest a juvenile when the complainant lobbied for leniency. When a complainant explicitly expresses a preference for an arrest, however, the tendency of the police to comply is also quite strong. Table 4 includes only the two types of misdemeanor, yet the Negro arrest rate when the complainant's preference is arrest (60%) climbs toward the rate of arrest for felonies (73%, Table 2). In no other tabulation does the arrest rate for misdemeanors rise so high. Lastly, it is notable that when the complainant's preference is unclear, the arrest rate falls between the rate for complainants who prefer arrest and those who prefer an informal disposition.

These patterns have several implications. First, it is evident that the higher arrest rate for Negro juveniles in encounters with complainants and suspects is largely a consequence of the tendency of the police to comply with the preferences of complainants. This tendency is costly for Negro juveniles, since Negro complainants are relatively severe in their expressed preferences when they are compared to white complainants vis-à-vis white juveniles. Furthermore, it will be remembered that it is in encounters with this situational organization rather than in those with suspects alone that the race differential is most apparent. Given the prominent role of the Negro complainant in the race differential, then, it may be inappropriate to consider this pattern an instance of discrimination on the part of the policemen. While police behavior follows the same *patterns* for Negro and white juveniles, differential *outcomes* arise from differences in *citizen* behavior.

Another implication of these findings is more general, namely, that the citizen complainant frequently performs an adjudicatory function in police encounters with juveniles. In an important sense the patrol officer abdicates his discretionary power to the complainant. At least this seems true of the encounters that include an expressive or relatively aggressive complainant among the participants. To say that the complainant often can play the role of judge in police encounters is tantamount to saying that the moral standards of citizens often can affect the fate of juvenile suspects. Assuming that the moral standards of citizens vary across social space, i.e., that there are moral subcultures, then it follows that police dispositions of juvenile suspects in part reflect that moral diversity. To this degree policemen become the unwitting custodians of those moral subcultures and thereby perpetuate moral diversity in the larger community. Assuming the persistence of this pattern of police compliance, then it would seem that police behavior is geared, again unwittingly, to moral change. As the moral interests of the citizenry change, so will the pattern of police control. Earlier it was noted that most police encounters with juveniles come into being at the beckoning of citizens. Now it is seen that even the handling of those encounters often directly serves the moral interests of citizens.

SITUATIONAL EVIDENCE AND ARREST

Another variable that might be expected to affect the probability of arrest is the nature of the evidence that links a juvenile suspect to an incident. In patrol work there are two major means by which suspects are initially connected with the commission of crimes: the observation of the act itself by a policeman and the testimony by a citizen against a suspect. The primary evidence can take other forms, such as a bloodstain on a suspect's clothing or some other kind of physical "clue," but this is very unusual in routine patrol work. In fact, the legally minor incidents that typically occasion police-juvenile contacts seldom provide even the possibility of non-testimonial evidence. If there is neither a policeman who witnesses the incident nor a citizen who gives testimony concerning it, then ordinarily there is no evidence whatever in the field setting. Lastly, it should be emphasized that the concept of evidence as used here refers to "situational evidence" rather than to "legal evidence." Thus it refers to the kind of information that appears relevant to an observer in a field setting rather than to what might be acceptable as evidence in a court of law.

In about 50% of the situations a police officer observes the juvenile offense, excluding felonies and traffic violations. Hence, even though citizens initially detect most juvenile deviance, the police often respond in time to witness the behavior in question. In roughly 25% of the situations the policeman arrives too late to see the offense committed but a citizen gives testimonial evidence. The remaining cases, composed primarily of non-criminal disputes and suspicious person situations, bear no evidence of criminal conduct. In a heavy majority of routine police-juvenile encounters, the juvenile suspect finds himself with incriminating evidence of some sort. The low arrest rate should be understood in this context.

On the other hand, it should not be forgotten that these proportions pertain to misdemeanor situations and that the arrests are all arrests without a formal warrant. The law of criminal procedure requires that the officer witness the offense before he may make a misdemeanor arrest without warrant. If the officer does not observe the offense, he must have a signed complaint from a citizen. Such is the procedural law for adults. The law for juveniles, however, is in flux as far as questions of procedure are concerned. It is not at all clear that

TABLE 5 Percent of Police Encounters with Juvenile Suspects According to Major Situational Evidence and Race of Suspect, by Field Disposition. (Table Excludes Felonies and Traffic Violations.)

Field Disposition	Major Situational Evidence and Race of Suspect								All Negro Encounters	All White Encounters	All Encounters
	Police Witness		Citizen Testimony		No Evidence		Not Ascertained				
	N	W	N	W	N	W	N	W			
Arrest	16	10	22	14	—	4	(2)	—	15	9	12
Release-in-Field	84	90	78	86	100	96	(7)	(2)	85	91	88
Total Percent	100	100	100	100	100	100	—	—	100	100	100
Total Number	(57)	(69)	(36)	(21)	(22)	(28)	(9)	(2)	(124)	(120)	(244)

an appellate court would decide on a juvenile's behalf if he were to appeal his case on the grounds that he was arrested for a misdemeanor even though the arresting officer neither witnessed the act nor acquired a formal complaint from a citizen. Even so, it might be expected that the rate of arrest would be higher in encounters where the act is witnessed by a policeman, if only because these would seem to be the situations where the juvenile suspect is maximally and unambiguously liable. But this expectation is not supported by the observation data (see Table 5).

In Table 5 it is shown that in "police witness" situations the arrest rate is no higher but is even slightly, though insignificantly, lower than the rate in "citizen testimony" situations. It is possible that some or all of these arrests where the major situational evidence lies with the testimony of a citizen would be viewed as "false" arrests if they involved adult suspects, though this legal judgment cannot be made with certainty. It is conceivable, for example, that some citizen complainants signed formal complaints at the police station subsequent to the field encounters.

The low arrest rate in "police witness" situations is striking in itself. It documents the enormous extent to which patrolmen use their discretion to release juvenile deviants without official sanction and without making an official report of the incident. Official statistics on juvenile delinquency vastly underestimate even the delinquent acts that policemen witness while on patrol. In this sense the police keep down the official delinquency rate. One other implication of the low arrest rate should be noted. Because the vast majority of police-juvenile contacts are concluded in field settings, judicial control of police conduct through the exclusion of evidence in juvenile courts is potentially emasculated. Police control of juveniles—like that of adults—may be less prosecution-oriented than the law assumes. In other words, much about the policing of juveniles follows an informal-processing or harassment model rather than a formal-processing model of control. From a behavioral standpoint, law enforcement generally is not a legal duty of policemen.

On the other hand, the importance of situational evidence should not be analytically underestimated. Table 5 also shows that the police very rarely arrest juveniles when there is no evidence. In only one case was a juvenile arrested when there was no situational evidence in the observer's judgment; this was a suspicious person situation. In sum, then, even when the police have very persuasive situational evidence, they generally release juveniles in the field; but, when they do arrest juveniles, they almost always have evidence of some kind. When there is strong evidence against a suspect, formal enforcement becomes a privilege of the police officer. This privilege provides an opportunity for discriminatory practices.

THE SUSPECT'S DEFERENCE AND ARREST

A final factor that can be considered in its relation to the situational production of juvenile arrests is the suspect's degree of deference toward the police.

Earlier research on police work suggests a strong association between situational outcomes and the degree of respect extended to policemen by suspects, namely, the less respectful the suspect, the harsher the sanction. In this section it is shown that the observation data on police-juvenile contacts draw a somewhat more complex profile of this relationship than might have been anticipated.

Before the findings on this relationship are examined, however, it should be noted that the potential impact of the suspect's deference on juvenile dispositions in the aggregate is necessarily limited. Only a small minority of juveniles behave at the extremes of a continuum going from very deferential or very respectful at one end to antagonistic or disrespectful at the other. In most encounters with patrolmen the outward behavior of juvenile suspects falls between these two extremes: the typical juvenile is civil toward police officers, neither strikingly respectful nor disrespectful. The juvenile suspect is civil toward the police in 57% of the encounters, a rather high proportion in view of the fact that the degree of deference was not ascertained in 16% of the 281 cases. The juvenile is very deferential in 11% and antagonistic in 16% of the encounters. Thus if disrespectful juveniles are processed with stronger sanctions, the sub-population affected is fairly small. The majority of juvenile arrests occur when the suspect is civil toward the police. It remains to be seen, however, how great the differences are in the probability of arrest among juveniles who display varying degrees of deference.

The relationship between a juvenile suspect's deference and his liability to arrest is relatively weak and does not appear to be unidirectional. Considering all of the cases, the arrest rate for encounters where the suspect is civil is 16%. When the suspect behaves antagonistically toward the police, the rate is higher— 22%. Although this difference is not wide, it is in the expected direction. What was not anticipated, however, is that the arrest rate for encounters involving very deferential suspects is also 22%, the same as that for the antagonistic group. At the two extremes, then, the arrest rate is somewhat higher.

Table 6 shows the arrest rates of suspects, excluding felony situations, accord-

TABLE 6   Percent of Police Encounters with Juvenile Suspects According to the Suspect's R_. and Degree of Deference Toward the Police, by Field Disposition. (Table Excludes Felonies.)

| Field Disposition | Race and Suspect's Degree of Deference | | | | | | | | |
| | Negro | | | | White | | | | |
	Very Deferen- tial	Civil	Antago- nistic	Not Ascer- tained	Very Deferen- tial	Civil	Antago- nistic	Not Ascer- tained	All Enc ters
Arrest	20	15	24	—	10	9	13	12	1:
Release-in-Field	80	85	76	100	90	91	87	100	8:
Total Percent	100	100	100	100	100	100	100	100	10(
Total Number	(20)	(72)	(21)	(23)	(10)	(76)	(23)	(21)	(26(

ing to their race and degree of deference toward police. The bipolar pattern appears in the encounters with Negro juveniles, though in the encounters with white juveniles it does not. In fact, the number of cases where a white juvenile is extreme at one end or the other, particularly where he is very deferential, is so small as to render the differences insignificant. Likewise there is a case problem with the Negro encounters, but there the differences are a little wider, especially between the encounters where the suspect is civil as against those where the suspect is antagonistic. Overall, again, the differences are not dramatic for either race.

Because of the paucity of cases in the "very deferential" and "antagonistic" categories, the various offenses, with one exception, cannot be held constant. It is possible to examine only the juvenile rowdiness cases separately. In those encounters the arrest rates follow the bipolar pattern: 16% for very deferential juveniles, 11% for civil juveniles, and 17% for the encounters where a juvenile suspect is antagonistic or disrespectful. When felony, serious misdemeanor, and rowdiness cases are combined into one statistical base, the pattern is again bipolar: 26%, 18%, and 29% for the very deferential, civil, and antagonistic cases respectively.

● ● ●

OVERVIEW

This paper examines findings on the official detection and sanctioning of juvenile deviance. It begins with a conception of deviance that emphasizes sanctioning *probabilities*, thereby linking the empirical operation of social control systems to the analytical definition of deviant behavior itself. In the present investigation, the central concern is to specify situational conditions that affect the probability of sanction by arrest subsequent to the mobilization of policemen in field settings. It is a control approach to juvenile deviance. Simultaneously it is a study of interaction between representatives of the legal system and juveniles—a study of law-in-action.

Several major patterns appear in the finding from the observation research. It would seem wise to conclude with a statement of these patterns in propositional form. Observation of police work in natural settings, after all, is hardly beyond an exploratory phase.

I: Most police encounters with juveniles arise in direct response to citizens who take the initiative to mobilize the police to action.
II: The great bulk of police encounters with juveniles pertain to matters of minor legal significance.
III: The probability of sanction by arrest is very low for juveniles who have encounters with police.
IV: The probability of arrest increases with the legal seriousness of alleged

juvenile offenses, as that legal seriousness is defined in the criminal law for adults.

V: Police sanctioning of juveniles strongly reflects the manifest preferences of citizen complainants in field encounters.

VI: The arrest rate for Negro juveniles is higher than that for white juveniles, but evidence that the police behaviorally orient themselves to race as such is absent.

VII: The presence of situational evidence linking a juvenile to a deviant act is an important factor in the probability of arrest.

VIII: The probability of arrest is higher for juveniles who are unusually respectful toward the police and for those who are unusually disrespectful.

Collectively the eight propositions, along with the corollary implications suggested in the body of the analysis, provide the beginning of an empirical portrait of the policing of juveniles. At some point, however, a descriptive portrait of this kind informs theory. This paper proceeds from a definition of deviance as any class of behavior for which there is a probability of negative sanction subsequent to its detection. From there it inquires into factors that differentially relate to the detection and particularly the official sanctioning of juveniles. Hence it inquires into properties that generate a control response. This strategy assumes that sanctioning probabilities are contingent upon properties of social situations besides rule-violative behavior. Since deviance is defined here in terms of the probability of sanction, it should now be apparent that the referent of the concept of deviance may include whatever else, besides rule-violative behavior, generates sanctioning. The present analysis suggests that sanctioning is usually contingent upon a configuration of situational properties. Perhaps, then, deviance itself should be treated theoretically as a configuration of properties rather than as a unidimensional behavioral event. A critical aspect of the sociology of deviance and control consists in the discovery of these configurations. More broadly, the aim is to discover the social organization of deviance and control.

The topic at hand embraces a good deal more than police encounters with juveniles. There is a need for information about other contexts of social control, studies of other detection and sanctioning processes. There is a need for comparative analysis. What is the role of the complainant upon comparable occasions? Is a complainant before a policeman analogous to an interest group before a legislature? Little is known about the differences and similarities between legal and nonlegal systems of social control. What is the effect of evidence in nonlegal contexts? How is a policeman before a suspect like a psychiatrist before a patient or a pimp before a whore? Are there varieties of procedural control over the sanctioning process in nonlegal contexts? To what extent are other legal processes responsive to moral diversity in the citizen population? The intricacies of social control generally are slighted in sociology. Correspondingly the state of the general theory of deviance and control is primitive.

SELECTED BIBLIOGRAPHY

American Behavioral Scientist, 2, 4 (March-April 1968), 1-55. Whole issue deals with urban violence and disorder.

Banton, Michael. *The Policeman in the Community.* New York: Basic Books, 1964.

Besag, Frank. *The Anatomy of a Riot.* Buffalo: State University at Buffalo Press, 1967.

Bittner, Egon. "Police on Skid-Row: A Study of Peace-Keeping," *American Sociological Review,* 32 (October 1967), 699-715.

Black, Algernon D. *The Police and the People.* New York: McGraw-Hill, 1969.

Blum, Richard (ed.). *Police Selection.* Springfield, Ill.: C. C Thomas, 1964.

Bordua, David (ed.). *The Police: Six Sociological Essays.* New York: Wiley, 1967.

Bordua, David, and Reiss, Albert J., Jr. "Command, Control, and Charisma," *American Journal of Sociology,* 72 (July 1966), 68-76.

Chevigny, Paul. *Police Power.* New York: Pantheon, 1969.

Clark, John P. "Isolation of the Police: A Comparison of the British and American Situations," *Journal of Criminal Law, Criminology, and Police Science,* 56 (September, 1965).

Cray, Edward. "Annotated Bibliography on Police Review Boards," *Law in Transition Quarterly,* 3 (Summer 1966), 197-205.

Cray, Edward. *The Big Blue Line: Police Power Against Human Rights.* New York: Coward-McCann, 1967.

Day, Frank D. "Police Professionalism," *Municipal Yearbook,* 1967, 433-438.

Fogelson, Robert M. "From Resentment to Confrontation: The Police, the Negroes, and the Outbreak of the 1960's Riots," *Political Science Quarterly,* 83 (June 1968), 217-247.

Fox, V. "Sociological and Political Aspects of Police Administration," *Sociology and Social Research,* 51 (October 1966), 39-48.

Gellhorn, Walter. "Police Review Boards: Hoax or Hope?" *Columbia University Forum,* 9 (Summer 1966), 4-10.

Haurek, E. W., and Clark, J. P. "Variants of the Integration of Social Control Agencies," *Social Problems,* 15 (Summer 1967), 46-60.

Havlick, Robert. "Police Recruit Training," *Municipal Yearbook,* 1968, 339-350.

Hoffman, P. "Police Birchites: The Blue Backlash," *Nation,* CIC (December 7, 1964), 425 ff.

Jeffery, C. Ray. "The Sociology of the Police." In Joseph S. Roucek (ed.), *Sociology of Crime.* New York: Philosophical Library, 1961.

Kates, Solis L. "Rorshach Responses, Strong Black Scales and Job Satisfaction Among Policeman," *Journal of Applied Psychology,* 34 (1950), 249-254.

LaFave, Wayne. *Arrest: The Decision to Take a Subject into Custody.* Boston: Little, Brown, 1965.

Matarazzo, Joseph. "Characteristics of Successful Policemen and Firemen Applicants," *Journal of Applied Psychology,* 48 (1964), 123-133.

Neiderhoffer, Arthur. *Behind the Shield: Police in the Urban Society.* New York: Doubleday, 1967.

Osterburg, James. "Cadet Programs: An Innovative Change," *Journal of Criminal Law,* 58 (March 1967), 112-118.

Piliavin, Irving, and Briar, Scott. "Police Encounters with Juveniles," *American Journal of Sociology,* 70 (September 1964), 206-214.

Preiss, Jack, and Erlich, Howard. *An Examination of Role Theory: The Case of the State Police.* Topeka: University of Kansas Press, 1966.

President's Commission on Law Enforcement and the Administration of Justice. *Task Force Report: The Police.* Washington, D.C.: U.S. Government Printing Office, 1967.

Reiss, Albert J., Jr. "How Common Is Police Brutality?" *Trans*-action, 8, 5 (July-August 1968), 10-19.

Sayre, N. "College for Policemen," *New Statesman*, 73 (May 5, 1967), 608.

Shekow, R., and Roemer, D.V. "Riot That Did Not Happen," *Social Problems*, 14 (Fall 1966), 221-233.

Skolnick, Jerome. *Justice Without Trial*. New York: Wiley, 1966.

Smith, Ralph. *The Tarnished Badge*. New York: Crowell, 1965.

Stern, Mort, "What Makes Policemen Go Wrong," *Journal of Criminal Law, Criminology, and Police Science*, 52 (March 1962).

Stinchcombe, A. L. "Institutions of Privacy in the Determination of Police Administrative Practices," *American Journal of Sociology*, 69 (1963), 150-160.

Terris, Bruce, "The Role of the Police." *Annals*, 374 (November 1967), 58-69.

Walker Report, *Rights in Conflict*. New York: Bantom, 1968.

Webster, John. "Police and the Community," *Issues in Criminology*, 3 (Summer 1967), 1-81.

Westley, William, "Violence and the Police," *American Journal of Sociology*, 59 (1953), 34-41.

Westley, William. "Secrecy and the Police," *Social Forces*, 34 (1956), 254-257.

Whittemore, L. H. *Cop: A Close-up of Violence and Tragedy*. New York: Holt, Rinehart & Winston, 1969.

Wilson, James Q. "The Police and Their Problems: A Theory," *Public Policy* 12 (1963), 189-216.

Wilson, James Q. "Generational and Ethnic Differences Among Career Police Officers," *American Journal of Sociology* 69 (March 1964), 522-528.

Wilson, James Q. *Varieties of Police Behavior*. Cambridge, Mass.: Harvard University Press, 1968.

Wilson, O. W. "Police Authority in a Free Society," *Journal of Criminal Law, Criminology, and Police Science*, 54, (June 1963), 175-177.

Wood, S. M. "Uniform—Its Significance as a Factor in Role Relationships." *Sociological Review*, n.s. 14 (June 1966), 139-151.

The Welfare System

Social welfare as a means of dealing with the needs of the helpless and the indigent is under massive scrutiny and attack by its clients, by the professional workers within the service, and by social reformers speaking in the name of the society as a whole. As a bureaucracy, it is easily, in the eyes of the gainfully employed, the least defensible of the three urban bureaucracies, because its clients are the most depressed and dejected of the urban population. Further, unlike education and the police, welfare deals exclusively with the impoverished sector of the society. Furthermore, some of the most explosive issues in domestic politics arise over the spiralling costs of welfare. In 1969, many informal observers credited the blue-collar revolt against rising taxes, violence in the streets, and the laws that promise equality in housing as responsible for the defeat at the polls of those liberal mayors and city politicians who were identi-fied with the cause of the Negro, that is, the major inner-city welfare recipient.

Welfare as a right, not a charity, is championed by liberal politicians, by those concerned with social welfare, and now by some conservative economists and the Nixon Administration. This awareness is also due to the activities of the national organizations of welfare clients. Although it is a long step from aware-ness to acceptance by local councillors, or by judges on the bench, the process of change has begun. The Nixon Administration's Family Assistance System may be the beginning of an irreversible process. These events are creating turbulence within the ranks of professional social workers and organizations concerned with social welfare policies. Jane Addams, with her goal of reforming society, is now seen as a more suitable role model of activism. Many see it as more appropriate for the present era than the clinical, person-to-person, Freudian model that has inspired schools of social work for decades. Social work as a profession is now in conflict; its dominant forces insist that social work has become a handmaiden to a social process that causes its clients distress and degradation.

Not so long ago clients receiving public funds were called "paupers." Now the demand is heard that welfare recipients, in official communications at least, be called something more dignified. The idea, still so new as to be almost revolutionary to many, is that welfare clients be considered as citizens with social rights equal to those of all others. Some maintain that such an idea will have strong appeal in a country like the United States where equality is an important social goal and part of our ethos: Others hold that where success is concerned, equality is forgotten as a goal of the society.

CONCEPTS FOR PUBLIC WELFARE

Each selection on welfare chosen for this book has a stronger application to social policy than selections on education and the police.

Barr (1965), in a series of transcripts from tape recordings, uses the words of the poor to describe the social world as they see it and move about in it. The reversal of attitudes toward approved standards of behavior such as earning and saving when a family begins to receive public welfare is surprising. Difficulties in having welfare clients treated like the remainder of the population are outlined in the second descriptive selection, which concentrates on interaction between welfare workers and their clients. As in the case of the policemen, the welfare field worker has to make decisions in particular situations and can create the "law" in many instances. The powers of welfare workers are given by the rules of the public welfare bureaucracies: In cases where client and worker disagree on the meaning of any particular rule, the worker usually wins. The duty of the welfare worker to save the public purse from the hordes of the needy is clearly supported by the bureaucracy and the community.

The next two selections turn to the problems of the origins of the poor. The concepts of public dependency and individual responsibility are shown to be largely responsible. Complementing "The Strange Case of Public Dependency," is the discussion of family dependency by Spencer. This is the beginning of a theory for welfare that classifies dependency into five different types.

In a society such as ours, where individual equality is believed to be possible, and where differences are believed to be due to individual choice, the persistence of welfare and of poverty are puzzling. Because neither political scientists, economists, sociologists, nor psychologists have any comprehensive theory, the discusssion by Coser of the meaning and stigma of poverty is valuable. Rein describes how industrial organizations that select workers through tests for excellence in performance create a group of rejects who are dependents: So, too, he described how technical progress and other institutional practices create dependency. Any complex society will have many different social levels: Any society that values achievement and success will create a group of nonachievers and unsuccessful persons.

The community model of a successful society produces more goods and creates more middle and high income people. The United States is such a society, but it also is a society with a bottom layer of poverty. The existence of large numbers of alientated, poor, nonachievers does not fit the dynamic model of the society. These people are not ignored; they are stigmatized. Bernard Beck sees this as a response to conflicts in the value system. Productivity and success are rewarded, but nonsuccess and poverty do not disappear; they must be morally stigmatized. These theories are interesting but disturbing to many intelligent thinkers. They fit into this selection because they discuss welfare as part of morals or values of a community social system.

Sherman Barr

Budgeting and the poor:
a view from the bottom

The materials on which this paper is based are excerpts taken from over 200 taped interviews with poor persons residing in the Lower East Side of Manhattan. Almost all are receiving funds from the New York City Department of Welfare. These interviews were the major efforts of the Project on Poverty, a project of the Research Center of the Columbia University School of Social Work for Mobilization for Youth.

LIFE STYLE OF THE POOR

The study, wholly impressionistic, engaged in three major lines of inquiry. The first sought information in regard to the life style of the poor. In this connection we were concerned with the management of such day to day activities as washing, shopping, housekeeping, child care, budgeting, and the like. A second line of inquiry was related to how the poor perceive and use the public and private services on which they are almost completely dependent. The third dimension of the study obtained information about poor persons' perceptions and insights into the various individuals and groups which comprise the social, economic and political structures.

First, I will quote literally from several taped interviews and summarize other quotes that are particularly relevant to how the poor view what is called "budgeting." Time permits me to note only a portion of the most revealing interviews.

I will present some implications for services and programs which arise from the material.

Mr. P. is 67 years old and blind. In one interview he related how he uses surplus food. "Well, here's what I do with the surplus food. I don't use the lard and they give you so much cheese that it's impossible to use. So I sell some things to my neighbors and with this money I buy myself an extra chicken. When I cook up the chicken I take off the fat first. I make good chicken fat and sell it back to

Reprinted in abridged form from *Public Welfare*, October 1965:246-250, with the permission of the American Public Welfare Association.

the butcher. I make a few cents, my neighbors a few cents and so does the butcher."

An eight-year-old boy in a nearby park responded as follows in regard to questions about savings. "Maybe one of these days I'll be able to save. But, if I had money, I would first buy two knives, two guns, and a holster, and then I'd kill the people who rob my apartment. And then I'd buy a hat and new pants for my father so he could look for a job. And then I'd buy cake, cookies, candy, toys, and furniture so we would have something to sit on in the living room."

A young pregnant mother said, "I'd wear a girdle to the unemployment office and as soon as I'd sign for the check, I'd run to the ladies room and take it off and thank God I had another check stacked away. What did I lie for? I'll tell you—to be able to buy my child's crib."

Another elderly gentleman had this to say: "What can you do if we are not lucky enough in the richest city in the world? We've got to go on Welfare and have the Welfare worker come up to see us and tell us how to live and then she looks in the ice box at what we have. They want to know what kind of clothes you have and when they see a telephone they want to know who is paying for it and why that money isn't being used for food. They try every way to get you. They make it hard for you and they don't want to know from nothing. But *they* get a big salary every week. Before you get the first check, you wait three or four weeks and when you get it you don't know what to do first. They should have on their bones how much they give you. But you've got to make the best of it. One of these days I'll go up to the top of the Brooklyn Bridge, yell 'Here I go' and then jump off. And you know what? Nobody will know! Nobody will care! Nobody will miss me. Maybe the Welfare would be happy because they wouldn't have to give me money any more. Who are you going to fight? City Hall? You've got to have pull and, if you don't have it, it's no good. If only people who get together would organize and put up a fight, maybe there would be something for them so they wouldn't have to suffer so much, so they won't be cranky."

Mrs. C. raises three energetic boys on AFDC funds. Three brief incidents tell us something about how she budgets. During one interview when we discussed what she read, she pointed out that the afternoon paper was delivered daily. When I questioned the expense of this method, she said that the delivery was the way she manipulated not having five cents to make a daily purchase. By having it delivered, she was assured of semi-monthly billing and thus was able to pay for it when the semi-monthly public assistance checks came. Mrs. C. was creative in other ways. When she received a used television set from her son's god-mother, she no longer had the need to spend money for a clock. To know the time, she turns on the television. Finally, Mrs. C. told me of her failure to obtain funds for a communion suit from the Welfare Department after several weeks of frustrating negotiation. She finally got together seven dollars by asking many friends for small loans of ten to twenty-five cents each. Being without proper clothes for herself, she did not attend the communion. When her son returned home, he was proud of how he looked and asked permission to visit old friends in the neighborhood. She understood and agreed. He came back many hours later with over one dollar in change. When she pressed him for an explanation, he volunteered that when he arrived at his old haunts, he met the grocery man who offered him a commission for selling frozen fuit ices. Of course he agreed. And Mrs. C's last words for that interview were these: "And can you picture my little sweet Alex standing there in his communion suit selling ices to make some money. What a picture." She began to laugh. And she laughed and laughed and laughed, and as she looked at me, her cheek bones twitched, her lips trembled, and her tears of laughter dissolved into tears of weeping.

The F. family perceived the following ten choices they were faced with over a short period of time. Seven of the ten were related to budgeting.

1. Complain to the landlord and face the possibility of being evicted or accept poor service.
2. Complain to Welfare and possibly be cut off or insist on a revised budget.
3. Leave lights burning all night to keep away rats and then have large utility bills or take a chance with the rats.
4. Take a feverish child to clinic with inadequate clothes or stay home and hope for the best.
5. Take the five children to a clinic and spend the carfare or stay home and hope for good health.
6. Go to clinic for personal reasons and lose one-half day's pay or not go at all.
7. Report a salary increase to the Housing Authority or pay off some debts and then notify them.
8. Send the children to school with inadequate clothing or keep them home and face the embarrassemnt of answering notes from the attendance officers.
9. Ask DW for camp clothing again so that the children can go to camp or, in the mother's words, "keep them home during the summer and have them drive me crazy."
10. Tell the investigator that her parents in Puerto Rico are dead or tell the truth and let her parents find out that she never "made it" in the United States.

Mr. J. works and is out of the home from 8:00 a.m. to 6:00 p.m. Mrs. J. works and is out of the home from 5:00 p.m. to 11:00 p.m. From 5:00 p.m. to 6:00 p.m. the eight children are scheduled in Mrs. J.'s words, "like the Marine Corps." The rest of her life, particularly budgeting, is just as disciplined. She knows exactly which door to use in which department store on which day for which purpose. She travels from Manhattan to the Bronx to save a few pennies on meat. She knows personally the owner of every good second-hand clothing store on the Lower East Side. Her sons get their haircuts at the Bowery barber schools where she saves one dollar over the regular price. She would never move from her overcrowded apartment in a low-income project to a different project because she is now living adjacent to a middle-income development populated largely by Jews because where Jews are, you can find better schools, better police protection, better shopping, better recreation and better support for various civic improvements. She knows which police station to go to for Christmas toys, which social agency for money, and which church to belong to because it offers more clothing than other churches. In short, she is everything some people in our society want poor people to be—thrifty, disciplined, and organized. However, after the seventh interview, she blurted out that all wasn't what it appeared to be. Occasionally, she and her husband engage in violent physical battles which sometimes result in the police being called in. "Something has to give," she said. "Something just has to give."

Mrs. G. is a mother of seven and after much negotiation was able to secure a washing machine in place of the regular laundry allowance. The machine is required to be a hand wringer type and after three weeks of use, she said: "I guess it makes no difference how you get a heart attack—bringing the clothes up and down the stairs or wringing until your guts come out. Maybe, if I had a heart attack, they'd get me an automatic."

Mrs. M. is a spry, energetic young mother of two. In telling us how she shopped wisely for a new bed for which she was granted $24.00, she pointed out the following:

1. she vistied four different second-hand stores covering a distance of ten miles;
2. she spent $1.20 for fares;
3. she antagonized both her children whom she had to take with her on this expedition;
4. the shopping trip took two days to complete;
5. and finally, she said, and I quote, "And you can bet your life I got that receipt to show the investigator. She'd never believe I got such a good buy. Without that receipt she'd start asking all kinds of questions and then 'pop,' I get mad at her and I'm in trouble again."

WHAT POOR PERSONS TOLD US

More of the significant material is summarized. May I remind you that these statements are not presented as facts, but simply as a report on what poor persons have told us.

1. Poor persons see themselves as vicitimzed by society and do not see themselves to blame for the variety of financial difficulties in which they find themselves. They believe that the affluent society can never know or understand the

world of the poor, particularly the suffering and relentless recurrence of financial crisis.

2. Service agencies are seen as systems which must be manipulated if decent service is to be obtained. Similarly, personnel employed by these agencies are seen as "welfare adjusters," that is, persons who help you to adjust to the *status quo*. It is this feeling that dealing with the Welfare Department in particular requires power and a level of knowledge and sophistication which is impossible for them to obtain, learn and employ. Adhering to present budgeting procedures and standards requires a level of planning, coordination, and education which they feel is not within their ability, experience or life style. Many welfare recipients employ some small "illegitimate" means to obtain additional funds, services, or goods. In the welfare system is the embodiment of all of society's injustice, callousness, insensitivity, cruelty and illogicalness. This perception is quickly incorporated by even the youngest member of the family. Thus, as we know, the welfare system bears the blame for all of society's ills.

3. Some semblance of a broad prevailing pattern of budgeting seems to exist in that food is given top priority and rent lowest. There is a generalized belief that the city will "get you off the hook" so to speak and issue a duplicate check for rent, but not for food. Social pressures for jewelry, television set, clothing for special occasions and the like are so great that many families, who would be regarded as not budgeting adequately by present criteria, do amazingly well in regard to purchasing these items from their recurring allotments. Of course, these purchases are made at the expense of other important needs. All interviewees reported that they never receive any instructions in regard to budgeting requirements, allowances, and procedures. Many of them did not have budgets.

4. A constantly recurring theme which our interviewees provided was that society in a sense evaluates them negatively by giving them inadequate grants to purchase monotonous, shabby clothing and worn furniture. Soon, the poor, too, begin to think this way negatively about themselves.

5. While money is considered as the most vital element in their lives, the interviewees do not necessarily equate the possession of money with personal qualitites of intelligence or industry. As a matter of fact, there is a tendency to regard wealthy persons as people who have gotten their wealth through illegitimate means or at the expense of others, namely, the poor.

If these observations made by the poor have any merit, and I think they do, they have implications for how we deal with the specific problems of budgeting and the related larger problems of welfare services. How might our programs and practices be made more effective and responsive to the needs of the poor?

Richard A. Cloward

Frances Fox Piven

We've got rights!
the no-longer silent welfare poor

Nearly eight million Americans depend on public assistance checks for their sustenance, including 4.4 million children, 2.1 million aged persons, and 700,000 of the blind or otherwise incapacitated. And this nearly eight million are less than a quarter of the poor (urban families of four with an annual income under $3,100, or rural families of comparable size with no more than $1,860 a year). So the public welfare system today leaves millions of the poor unaided. It may, however, be made to do considerably more. Favorable rulings in test cases now before the courts or in preparation could double or treble the number of people on welfare rolls.

On June 10, a three-judge federal court in Connecticut rendered a historic decision, declaring unconstitutional the state's residency requirements for welfare assistance. These requirements, some variation of which exists in every state, generally restrict welfare payments to people who can prove that they have lived in the jurisdiction for anywhere from six months to six years. The plaintiff in the Connecticut case had been receiving public aid in Boston, moved to Hartford to be with her mother, applied for welfare and was turned down. The majority of the court held that "the right of interstate travel also encompasses the right to be free of discouragement of interstate movement. Denying . . . even a gratuitous benefit because of her constitutional right effectively impedes the exercise of that right."

Nor is this the only instance in which constitutional issues have been raised in public welfare. New York's highest court has ruled that social welfare laws do not authorize the jailing of male welfare recipients who refuse to work under terms dictated by a welfare department. Any other interpretation, said the court, might result in violation of the Thirteenth Amendment and the Federal Anti-Peonage Act, which prohibit involuntary servitude.

In situations where fraud is suspected, welfare recipients are often told that if they refuse to answer questions which might incriminate them, their benefits will be cut off. Cases now being prepared in several jurisdictions charge that this threat—frequently carried out—is a violation of the Fifth Amendment. Mass searches without warrants (e.g., midnight raids) have recently been declared unconstitutional by the California Supreme Court.

This new concern for developing a rule of law in programs of the welfare state owes much to the legal scholarship of Jacobus tenBroek, a blind professor of political science at the University of California in Berkeley, and more recently to Charles Reich, a Yale law professor. TenBroek has spent the better part of his career exposing America's dual system of justice—one for the affluent, another for the poor.

A leading strategist in the current assault against "poor law" agencies is Edward Sparer, director of the Center on Social Welfare Policy and Law, sponsored by the Columbia University School of Social Work and financed by both the Stern Family Fund and OEO. Sparer and his six-man legal staff give advice on tactics and help to prepare briefs for other organizations taking test cases. Representation in the courts is being performed by the Neighborhood Legal Service agencies sponsored by the Office of Economic Opportunity (one of which handled the Connecticut case), the NAACP Legal Defense Fund, the Scholarship Education and Defense Fund for Racial Equality (formerly affiliated with CORE), the American Civil Liberties Union (and its special division, the Lawyers Constitutional Defense Committee), as well as the Lawyers Committee for Civil Rights Under Law. Here and there, lawyers affiliated with the more traditional legal aid societies are also becoming active. The Law Students Civil Rights Research Council recruits law-student volunteers to provide information on legal rights and subsidizes reserarch for attorneys representing recipients.

The growing number of court challenges deal with two areas of grievance: violations of the civil liberites of welfare recipients, and arbitrary denials of benefits. Our discussion focuses on the second area.

Many state laws work to the disadvantage of the very poor. A prime example is the requirement that every new resident wait one year before applying for benefits. In a few states, like New York, there is no specific waiting period, but a test of "motive" can be applied. If welfare officials believe that the applicant came in order to obtain welfare, they may deny benefits and issue a bus ticket to get the applicant out of the state. In practice the applicant must disprove the allegation to the satisfaction of welfare officials, which is usually impossible. The Connecticut decision casts doubt on the constitutionality of both types of residue laws. Similar cases are pending in federal courts in half a dozen states.

If the Connecticut decision is upheld, the consequences will go far beyond affirming a constitutional right of indigents to travel. The effect of residence laws has been to deny aid to the most economically depressed, such as rural people driven into urban ghettos by rapid agricultural mechanization and by federal agricultural subsidies which favor large landholders. One sizable group— 2.5 million migrant workers—remain untouched by the Connecticut decision, for the court did not extend the protection of its ruling to persons who do not intend to establish permanent residence in the state. So long as welfare aid remains unavailable to migrant workers, they will be compelled to accept jobs on terms dictated by farmers in each locality.

WHAT MOTHERS MUST DO

Then too, there is some form of "employable mother" rule in about half the states, designed partly to keep taxes low and to ensure a labor supply which can be driven by the threat of starvation to do any kind of work at any wages. For instance, a Georgia regulation requires that to be eligible for Aid to the Families of Dependent Children—a program intended to help needy youngsters—mothers whose children are over three years old must accept "suitable" employment when it is deemed to be "available." The rule also prohibits county welfare departments from paying supplementary benefits to mothers who are employed at wages lower than what they would normally receive on public assistance. Finally, it directs county welfare boards to deny *all* applications and close *all* existing cases of AFDC mothers who are deemed able to work during what the board calls "full-time employment" periods in communities with seasonal employment (*e.g.*, cotton chopping). A group of mothers are now bringing suit in Georgia, claiming racial discrimination because the rule is used to exlude Negro mothers far more frequently than white mothers (picking cotton is not deemed "suitable" work for white women). They also claim that denying supplementary benefits to mothers who are employed for less money than they would get on welfare is contrary to the purpose of the program. The fact that a mother works, they contend, is an arbitrary basis for classifying the beneficiaries of federal aid, in violation of the equal-protection provisions of the Fourteenth Amendment.

These Georgia AFDC mothers are also asking for the right to rebut the presumption that they can get jobs merely because a welfare official says they are employable. They base their challenge on a prior ruling of the US Supreme Court, "that a statute creating a presumption which operates to deny a fair opportunity to rebut it violates the due process clauses of the Fourteenth Amendment." A panel of three judges has been appointed, and trial is pending. It is estimated that AFDC rolls in Georgia will double if the employable mother rule is struck down.

Traditionally, benefits have been denied to families if the husband is present and "employable" (whether or not he can get a job). Unemployed husbands therefore "desert," and mothers may then get on relief (if they agree to sue for nonsupport). But often the men remain near their families, despite the danger of being apprehended and jailed for nonsupport. Welfare departments maintain squads of investigators who track down these men, sometimes by invading homes between midnight and dawn without warrants.

Not content with driving husbands away, the system has also traditionally

disqualified mothers who appear, on investigation, to have a conjugal relationship with a man. In Alabama, for example, children can be denied assistance if
their mother "appears" to have a relationship with a "substitute father," defined
as a man who either (1) lives in the home, (2) "visits frequently for the purpose
of cohabitation," or (3) "does not frequent the home but cohabits with the
child's natural or adoptive mother elsewhere." (Cohabitation is defined by the
Alabama welfare department as sexual relations.) These rules, attorneys believe,
violate the equal-protection clauses of the Constitution by establishing an arbitrary and unreasonable basis for distinguishing among children: whether their
mothers do or do not have intercourse. In a case now being taken in the federal
district court, the plaintiff is an Alabama widow with several children whose
benefits were terminated after she admitted that a male friend visits in her home.

An especially vicious feature of these rules is that if a caseworker judges that
such a man "appears" to exist, the burden of proving that he is not a "substitute
father" falls on the mother. A Texas woman and her five children lost their
benefits because of the mother's alleged association with a man who was not the
children's father and was not helping to support them. A state hearing officer
reversed the local departmental decision on the ground that the evidence concerning the man's presence in the home was insufficient. However, the administrative appeals board reversed the decision again: the reason it gave was that the
mother had failed to *disprove* the allegation.

The welfare applicant who is not excluded by statutes and rules does not
automatically get on the rolls, or then stay on. Far from it. According to a *New
York Times* editorial of May 18: "New York City Welfare Commissioner
Mitchell I. Ginsberg reports that there are nearly as many eligible families *off* the
relief rolls as there are on. The welfare budget for the year starting July 1 is estimated at $913 million, up to $207 million over the outlay for this year; yet that
staggering amount will take care of only half of those who could qualify for aid
if every eligible applied."

This vast discrepancy results from the fact that welfare functionaries everywhere, responding to community pressures to hold costs down, try to keep
people off public assistance. If information about eligibility were widely disseminated, claims would rise precipitously, and so welfare departments do
nothing to advertise the availability of benefits; indeed, they try to keep
potential recipients in ignorance. A survey in Detroit uncovered many families in
dire need, but more than half did not know about public welfare or erroneously
believed that they were ineligible. To remedy this situation, groups of recipients
are preparing to sue for access to welfare manuals, on the ground that these are
public documents.

Those who do know about public welfare must run a grueling bureaucratic
obstacle course in order to qualify. In effect, the applicant must prove his
poverty to functionaries who are at best skeptical. HEW, having surveyed procedures in a number of cities, reports that applicants are "being required to assume

too much responsibility for substantiating their own eligibility." Several cities require that applicants produce documents to support information on birth, past places of residence and employment, income and the like. Frequently they are forced to answer questions about their sexual behavior, open their closets to inspection and permit their children to be interrogated. To resist any of these procedures is to risk rejection for "failure to comply with departmental regulations." Rather than submit many withdraw or do not apply.

To overcome this pattern of intimidation, some applicants are demanding the right to bring an advocate to the intake cubicles—a friend, a representative of a welfare recipients' organization or a lawyer. A recent suit established this right in New York, but elsewhere welfare administrators still resist, claiming that they have a legal obligation to "protect applicants" by holding transactions "confidential."

Furthermore, many of those who do apply and endure all of the investigatory procedures are turned down. In Philadelphia, for example, half of the applications are rejected, and lawyers estimate that half of the rejections are not expressly justified under existing statutes. In 1962, the Moreland Commission of the New York State legislature noted that a great many "rejections are arbitrary," for only 35 percent of the denials were based on the contention that the family had "sufficient income."

Perhaps the cruelest exercise of discretion by welfare department functionaries is the arbitrary suspension or termination of benefits. Taking a sample of poor families headed by women, the New York City Community Council found that only 12 percent had received assistance continuously for 18 months following childbirth. Some 29 percent had had their cases closed and reopened at least once during that period despite continual financial need. Some investigators close as a disciplinary measure, knowing that when the affected families ask to have their cases reopened, as they usually do, they are likely to be more compliant. Other cases are closed because the investigator has noticed a new item of clothing or furniture and has not received what he regards as a satisfactory explanation as to where the money was found to make the purchase. Still other terminations are the result of administrative errors in a system burdened by fantastic paperwork and haphazard procedures.

The practice of summarily terminating people from the rolls without a written reason or an opportunity for a hearing led Boston recipients to stage a sit-in. When the police beat them, the demonstrators screamed out the windows of the welfare department, and rioting erupted in the streets for three nights.

NO RIGHTS IF YOU'RE ON RELIEF

What makes these practices possible is the absence of any tradition of legal rights for welfare beneficiaries, as is illustrated by a recent court ruling in the nation's capital. When a group of AFDC mothers sued for declaratory and injunctive relief against unreasonable searches, harassing surveillance, eavesdropping and interrogation concerning their sexual activities, the district court not only ruled against them but rendered the astonishing opinion that welfare benefits are a gratuity, that statutes governing welfare agencies merely define who is *not* eligible for benefits and do not impose the obligation to grant benefits to all those who meet eligibility requirements. Which of the eligibles are actually to get benefits is, the court held, within the absolute discretion of administrative functionaries and therefore is not a proper subject of judicial review. During the courtroom argument, the judge commented on an allegation regarding illegal search: "Any recipient has a perfect right to slam the door in the face of the investigator. Of course, he runs the risk then of being cut off the rolls." In other words, the welfare system can treat people as it sees fit; if people don't like it, they don't have to take the money. (On appeal, however, a higher court directed that the welfare department hold a full hearing on the mothers' charges preliminary to further court review.)

The main thrust of the legal attack on arbitrary terminations of benefits is in public housing. In two cases now in the federal district courts, tenants allege that public housing authorities violated their rights under the due-process clause of the Fourteenth Amendment by evicting them without a written reason or an opportunity for a hearing. In a third case, taken against the public housing authority in Durham, N.C., the U.S. Supreme Court had agreed to a review. Before the case could be argued, however, officials of the federal public housing agency issued a bulletin stating that local authorities must inform tenants of the reasons for evictions and give them opportunity to rebut. The Supreme Court ordered the case back to the state courts.

An important challenge is also developing in Mississippi, where, in early April, a beneficiary under the Aid to the Permanent and Totally Disabled program was abruptly notified that he was no longer medically qualified for assistance. No specific reasons were given, nor was a hearing offered prior to the termination. The client, a 30-year-old Negro father, secured affidavits from prominent doctors confirming that his right hand had been amputated and that he had both pulmonary tuberculosis and sickle-cell disease (a type of anemia which leads to progressive weakening and, in this case, to a short life expectancy). The day before the court hearing, welfare officials visited the plaintiff to say that a mistake had been made and would be rectified. Nevertheless, the plaintiff insisted that a hearing be held, arguing that his benefits might be arbitrarily terminated at some later time unless the constitutional issues raised by welfare procedures were ruled upon. Despite protests by attorneys for the state, the judge agreed that serious questions of due process were involved and held the matter over for trial.

The number of people who would be affected by successful court challenges to termination procedures is suggested by experience in the District of Columbia. There, under the iron rule of Senators Robert Byrd (D, W.Va.), chairman of the Senate subcommittee on appropriations for the District of Columbia, the department of welfare has been forced to acquire nearly as many "fraud investigators," bent upon cutting people off relief, as "social investigators," who are responsible for passing on initial eligibility. In speeches on the floor of the Senate, Byrd has reported that under his aegis AFDC case loads fell from a peak of 5,628 in November 1961, to 3,823 by October 1963. His request for appropriations with which to hire additional investigators was struck out on a technicality in a House-Senate conference. As a result, he says, "the AFDC case load has gradually crept back up, and by August 1966 had recorded a total of 4,767 cases." Bad though he believes this is, he observes that without the investigators who were available, the case loads would have reached 9,600—double the present rolls. (The Senator reacted to the recent tide of legal appeals with these remarks: "I'm not against fair hearings, but I'm not going to sit by and watch our agency attacked. What business do [these lawyers] have to question [the Department's] regualtions?")

AND WHAT DO THEY GET?

Once on the rolls, recipients get very little. In large part this is because of the low grant levels set by state legislatures; annual AFDC payments to a family of four range from an average of $388 in Mississippi to $2,700 in New York, or about $1,800 nationally. More than half the states do not even appropriate enough to meet their own "minimum standards" for welfare payments. Some limit the amount that can be given to any one family, to discourage the poor from having large numbers of children. (The notion persists that the poor have children in order to obtain additional welfare allotments—an extraordinary idea considering the size of the increments.) As a result, a child in a large family may get less to eat than a child in a small family. The constitutionality of this arbitrary and discriminatory classification is being challenged by the parents of 10 AFDC children in Maryland, where the law increases aid only up to seven family members. In this case, the complaint follows an earlier and successful suit taken in Iowa.

It is characteristic of the American way of public welfare that people on the rolls are regularly cheated out of such benefits as the law provides. As a consequence of the high turnover among welfare employees, many of them never learn the complex regulations governing allowances or master the equally complex administrative procedures. And recipients, as we have noted, are rarely permitted to examine the regulations. The result is underbudgeting, which is estimated to deprive recipients of about 20 percent of what the law says should be included in their regular biweekly or monthly checks.

In addition to these regular checks, public assistance recipients in many places are entitled to receive special allowances, as needed, for clothing, household equipment and furniture. A study in central Harlem found that two-thirds of the

AFDC mothers interviewed had never been informed by their investigators of the availability of such funds. There are 650,000 recipients in New York City. Informed observers estimate that it would cost an average of $100 to bring each recipient up to standard. In other words, the department has saved a total of $65 million in this fiscal year by not providing grants to which people are lawfully entitled.

Groups of recipients in New York City have become alert to these deprivations and have been circulating check lists of the items which welfare regulations define as entitlements. The completed check lists are submitted to the welfare department in bulk. As a result of this tactic many families have received special allotments, although sometimes after the long delay, and sometimes for only a few of the items requested. The client groups are now beginning to back up requests that the department meet "minimum standards" with applications for "fair hearings." This is likely to compel far more expeditious handling of the original requests, if only because of the expense and travail "fair hearing" procedures involve for government. In Washington, D.C., the chief of the welfare department's investigative arm recently protested the rising volume of appeals against the department's decision: "Our costs have gone up at least 25 percent because of this type of activity." The true purpose of these challenges he said, "is to increase the cost to the point where it is better to leave clients on the rolls."

LIVE ALONE AND LIKE IT

Recipients are also cheated by techniques of computing other sources of income which are presumed to be available to them. Even where state law permits fathers to remain with their families without disqualifying them for benefits, the traditional "man-in-the-house" mentality persists: if a man is about, even though he is not a legal spouse, and even though he is not the father of the children, the presumption is often made that his income is available to the family, and their welfare payments are correspondingly reduced. If the man refuses to disclose his income, the mother and children can be dropped from the rolls.

One such case was recently heard by the New York State Department of Social Welfare. A 66-yar-old recipient of Old-Age Assistance allowed a man of similar age to live in her home. Her benefits were terminated when the man refused to disclose his income. The state hearing officer agreed with the recipient that the mere fact that the man lived in her house did not demonstrate support, and that her grant should be reduced only by the amount of the man's actual contribution to the household expenses. As a result of another case recently heard in New York, the state acknowledged that the "man-in-the-house" regulations are ambiguous, and that local welfare departments have exploited this ambiguity to impose an unlawful obligation upon men to support children not their own.

A more fundamental challenge is now in the federal courts in California. At issue is the constitutionality of a state provision which requires that the income of a stepfather be considered available to his stepchildren in computing the mother's AFDC benefits. But a man has no legal obligation ot support his wife's children by a previous union; therfore, an AFDC mother deprived of a portion of her grant because of the stepfather's income cannot sue to compel him to contribute his income. This case is of more than passing interest to AFDC mothers, for welfare regulations in effect make them ineligible for marriage unless they can find a mate who is both able and willing to take over the support of their children. Such men are not in abundant supply, especially among the poor. In the California stepfather case, the desperate mother instituted divorce proceedings, and thereupon became eligible for AFDC again.

Recipients also lose funds because of the general reluctance of welfare departments to make any form of retroactive payment, even when they admit that benefits were unlawfully denied. A court action is pending in the District of Columbia, where an applicant for Aid to the Disabled was forced to wait 85 days for a decision, and then was not given retroactive payment although the department's regulations appear to authorize it.

As a consequence of the laws and practices we have described, only one in four of America's 32 million poor are now receiving public welfare—their aggregate benefits represent a mere .7 percent of national personal income. One reason is that federal enabling legislation leaves great power to the states and localities, which are typically harsh in dealings with the poor. Since most welfare laws and regulations are made by the states, or under the authority of state officials, they are designed to keep expenditures down—usually by seeing to it that as few people as possible obtain as few beneifts as possible. Successful attacks in the courts could do much to alter welfare practices and to increase the volume of benefits available to people, provided that welfare departments comply with new regulations. Pressure to compel compliance is now beginning to be exerted by recipients' organizations springing up all over the country, as part of a new National Welfare Rights Movement which staged a series of demonstrations June 30 in more than 40 cities.

The growing legal assault is also helping to build a case for some new and federally administered income programs. Each legal challenge reveals new abuses by the present system of locally administered public assistance. It thus adds to pressure for a federally administered income program (such as family allowances or a guaranteed income), which would provide uniform and decent grant levels based on need as the sole criterion for eligibility. The "poor law" still stands, but its foundation is beginning to crumble.

Martin Rein

The strange case
of public dependency

A famous violinist once told Groucho Marx that he had supported himself
since the age of five. "What were you before that," Groucho demanded to know,
"a bum?"

All of us, even concert violinists, are dependent during major and important
periods of our lives. No one finds this strange or reprehensible. What does cause
great, and rising, concern is *public* dependency—even though it may apply to the
same periods, and even sometimes to the same persons.

This conception of dependency as a social evil is in part the legacy inherited
from the early English Victorians. It is deeply ingrained in our philosophy of
individualism and our commitment to industrialism. The critical social problem
in the early 19th century was "pauperism," a condition defined as individual
weakness of character which "poor relief" only encouraged. Nor have we today
resolved the moral dilemma posed in the Victorian era. The fear that economic
security robs intitiative and promotes dependency is an abiding and disturbing
issue in contemporary social policy.

In a period of unprecedented prosperity, with the predicted Gross National
Product for 1965 almost 660 billion dollars, three very different factors
intensify public concern over dependency: rising welfare costs. obtrusiveness
of the urban poor, and rising unemployment.

The Social Security Administration estimates that the total spent on health,
welfare, and education during fiscal 1963-64 was 71 billion dollars. This exceeds
the total outlay for national defense. Today about 12 percent of the Gross
National Product is spent on social welfare. When public and private costs are
taken together, expenditures exceed 108 *billion* dollars. The unrelenting *rise* in
public assistance expenditures (which in the public mind is identified with the
dole) worries critics even more than the total cost. Expenditures for public aid
(including medical payments and other programs) more than doubled in the past
decade and a half, rising from approximately two-and-a-half billion dollars in
1949-50 to more than five-and-a-half billion in 1963-64. But the critics seldom
note that public aid expenditures as a percentage of Gross National Product

Reprinted with permission from *Trans*-action, 1965, 2(3):16-23.

remained unchanged at .9 percent, and the per capita cost increased less than almost every other kind of social welfare expenditure.

More than 220,000 families have been displaced by "urban renewal" in the last fourteen years. This does not include those moved for "public improvements"—public housing, parks, highways, public buildings, code reinforcement. It is estimated—and estimates are usually conservative—that the next decade will see close to a million persons displaced.

Two-thirds of those uprooted by renewals have been Negro. Their ability to move in the city and to find suitable low cost homes is limited. Their plight has been graphically described as a black neck caught in a white suburban noose. Uprooted and transported, they have suddenly become prominent and visible.

They have been wrenched from their protective sub-cultures and exposed to the standards of a more demanding society. Chester Hartman, research fellow at the MIT—Harvard Joint Center for Urban Studies, after an extensive review of the literature on relocation concludes that "the deleterious effects of the uprooting experience, the loss of familiar places and persons, and the difficulties of adjusting to and accepting new living environments may be far more serious issues than are changes in housing status." Those who are relocated may experience a greater sense of personal failure and have less ability to cope with their environment. A program intended to aid the poor may unintentionally serve to increase their dependency.

Unemployment continues high. Recovery from each recession finds it at a higher level than the preceding recession. Our traditional institutions seem unable to cope with our growing labor force and the technologically displaced. The private sector of the economy has had in the past five years a growth rate which has absorbed less than half of the increase in the labor force. Some critics believe that we are in danger of producing in the future a social underclass, displaced victims of a society which no longer requires their labor and rejects them as useless.

Like our Victorian predecessors we want to reduce dependency (pauperism), and like them we tend to see it in individual and personal terms, a form of social pathology. We prescribe social services for those receiving public financial aid; rehabilitation to make slum dwellers more acceptable tenants; and training programs to make them more employable. But in our attempts to reduce these dependencies we neglect the idea that those receiving public aid have a *right* to adequate and decent levels of assistance. We tend to ignore the amount of low income housing actually available to the poor; and we neglect the development of policies to expand industries and services which can contribute jobs for the unskilled.

But what actually is dependency? What assumptions do we hold about it?

We believe that the dependents among us can be isolated and identified as somehow morally and socially, if not physically, less adequate human beings than the rest of us.

We believe dependency would disappear if only we would eliminate the personal inadequacies of the dependents themselves.

We believe dependency is bad. We must work to reduce it.

Here is the popular dichotomy: those who give and those who recive; those who take out of our economic system more than they put into it, and those who pay the difference. Broadly speaking, those who work or have wealth are considered to contribute more than they get. If these ideas shed light on little else, they do illustrate how our social thinking is tied to the ethic that the "improvident" poor have somehow brought their ills upon themselves.

Each of these assumptions warrants re-examination.

I believe it far more profitable to view economic dependence as biologists view ecologic dependence: we are all involved with one another. Life is interdependent—and the most fruitful understanding of it can come from examining degrees and conditions of interdependency, rather than from isolating debits and credits in a ledger which draws a dichotomy between the dependent and the independent.

UNIVERSAL DEPENDENCY

Over time, as well as at any moment, man is both dependent and independent. The two states are closely related. After an age when most mammals have passed into senility or death, man is still dependent, still undergoing the long training in education, socialization, and skills he needs to function adequately; and as society grows more complex the process of maturation takes longer and longer.

We all experience dependency at some time. Childhood, schooling, illness, old age, pregnancy, child-birth, and early child-rearing all include periods of dependency. Few people now believe that these dependencies are undesirable. Few argue that we don't need more well-trained physicians, scientists, and humanists, even though this means that many adults will not "produce" until they are thirty. We belive that the social benefits—the "total production"—are well worth the temporary costs. Obviously then, not all dependency can be bad.

Generally, we are trying to extend socially desirable dependency to more and more people. Barbara Wootton has perceptively observed that economists make dizzy leaps between two rival assumptions about social dependency:

First, the doctrines of scarcity economics (which have the merit of being agreeable to common sense) teach that thrift and work are the keys to prosperity: the longer and the harder everyone works, the better will it be for all. Then, with the swing to economics of depression, common sense is abandoned in favor of the paradox that it is not saving but spending, not working but withdrawal from work, which conduces to economic health.

Many professionals believe that if we only knew what bothered the individual, and applied the right remedy to him, then we might be able to take him completly out of dependency and make him a right thinking, wealth-producing, tax-paying (rather than tax-eating) citizen, to use President Johnson's recent terminology.

No two schools agree on the exact composition of that elixir. Some favor a get-tough policy (Newburgh, New York), others prefer a more humanistic and thereapeutic approach, stressing individual rehabilitation (1962 amendments to the Social Security Act). Both views share a common assumption, that the dependent has an inadequate personality—a position which has been correctly described by Peter Marris as "fundamentally arrogant." This approach has, nevertheless, been made virtually the sole basis of many therapeutic professions. Dependency as well as poverty may not be the result of personal inadequacy nearly so much as it is the result of the structure of society.

If dependency is a fault of individual personality, and the dependent is a less adequate person, then the third common assumption follows inevitably: dependency is bad—let's get rid of it. However, if we view dependency in terms of social organization rather than individual pathology, we arrive at different social judgments and treatments.

Dependency is fundamental to life, part of its basic fabric. We must concentrate on its patterning and expansion, not regard it merely as an area of rot which must be cut out or at least "contained." It has long term causes and long term effects, and they must be analyzed. We need to devlop a language of social growth and social costs, comparable to the concepts of individual growth and individual pathology.

No act is, after all, without its consequences, no social act without its social costs. We often pay dearly for what seemed like a good policy at the time—and may even have been a necessity. Such socially unanticipated consequences—or "disservices"—greatly affect the amount and direction of dependency. They are the costs of progress.

According to William K. Knapp, writing on *The Social Costs of Private Enterprise*, economic disservices include "all direct and indirect losses suffered by persons or the general public as a result of economic activities." The costs of extra washing and of respiratory troubles from industrially polluted air are such disservices as are other hazards to health and safety caused by business and industry. Often the organization of the market does not require a business to pay the economic cost to others of its actions. In the same way, the social costs of technological change are not borne by those who benefit most directly.

We neglect these disservices partly because we tend to regard industrialization in a society much as we regard puberty in a youth—we assume that once it is technically past it is all over, and growing up and adjusting is finished. Actually the tensions and problems associated with growth continue at each stage of development.

In the early stage of industrialization almost all other interests of our society were subordinated to it. It left a toll of human suffering so severe and wide-spread that, according to Karl Polanyi, if unchecked, it could have wiped out civilization. With the movement from farm to industrial town came overcrowded slums, gross exploitation of labor, the brutalization of work, a declining standard of living (at least in the short run), and the incalculable psychological suffering as the centuries' old way of life broke down. Richard Titmuss notes: "Most of the long-industrialized countries of the West are still burdened by the as yet uncompensated disservices of the early stage of their economic growth."

THE TROUBLE WITH PROGRESS

We are hindered by the new adjustments rising from what George Friedman calls "making industrial man into an object of rationalized production." Close to a quarter billion tests are given annually to determine how well we can be made to fit into the increasingly specialized tasks of business and industry. All this testing and adjusting is going ahead despite the fact that, as a recent Russell Sage Foundation report says, "virtually nothing is known at present about the impact the testing movement is having on the society as a whole . . . (or) the individuals . . . directly affected."

Tests increase "rationality" and "objectivity." Many executives and educators welcome the chance to reduce the unpredictability of personality to scores on a profile or holes in a card.

But those tested are not as enthusiastic. As one passes through the sorting process, his chances for work, education, status, fulfillment, and even social benefits are determined by a new form of social discrimination, most potent against those already disadvantaged. The reject will likely respond by retreating—turning his back on what he is not "fit" to obtain. A recent proposal has urged a United States Supreme Court test of the constitutionality of determining the educational future of children of underprivileged backgrounds through the use of intelligence and aptitude tests. *"Selection for excellence"* is therefore *becoming an increasingly effective way to create dependents.*

Another potent multiplier of dependency is automation. This is becoming an old, much documented story. In the last decade the population of the United States increased by 20 percent, production increased 43 percent, but the number of factory workers decreased 10 percent. We will need twelve million new jobs in the next decade—at present rates, which may decline, we supply six.

It is not because our economy is not working well (as during the depression) that these people become dependent—but because it *is* working well. Efficiency has made them superfluous or branded them incompetent. They did not pass the tests; they had the wrong skills or backgrounds; they were too old; they were in the wrong place; they could not adapt quickly enough. They no longer fit and are rejected. *Technical progress increases dependency.*

While industry often informs a man that he is too old to be hired at forty, medicine informs him that he can expect to live past seventy. A white girl born in 1959 has a better chance of reaching age sixty than her grandmother, born in 1900, had of reaching age five. Should that grandmother, however, still be alive, she can look forward to another sixteen years. The aged population is increasing rapidly.

The young, too, are fruitful and multiply. Prosperity breeds optimism; prosperous women breed babies. More people marry, they marry younger, they have children earlier. Enough babies are born each year in the United States (and live past infancy) to populate Chicago, plus a couple of its suburbs. The young and old make up our two largest and most rapidly growing groups of dependents. Like the universe we are exploding in all directions.

And not only are the traditional killers of the very old and very young being overcome; we provide sheltered environments in which the deprived, rejected, handicapped, weak, and sick survive longer. We seldom make them well and competent (our illness patterns have shifted from acute to chronic)—we merely help them live longer. If anything, it has made them more dependent than before. *Medical progress increases dependency.*

Social disservices also occur in education and welfare—where social consequences are supposed to be anticipated. For instance, many believe that the best way to "anticipate" and "prevent" trouble is by early diagnosis and intensive treatment, but individuals singled out for such treatment often find themselves stigmatized and discriminated against—precisely what the treatments were supposed to prevent—and the programs boomerang. In England, epileptics avoid treatment for this reason—employable before "help" which labels them, they are often not employable after. In New York *potential* delinquents may find themselves bearing the onus of *actual* delinquents—and react accordingly. We are affected in what we are by the way others see us. Human behavior comes to conform with the assumptions we make about it. *Labelling increases dependency.*

We rehabilitate and retrain ex-convicts, ex-mental patients, and the unemployed to be able to hold jobs and fit into our society. We do not retrain industry, unions, government, or people generally to accept them. We run the risk of not delivering what we promise. Programs aimed solely at changing individuals and which neglect institutional reforms must encounter this difficulty.

The Job Corps as organized remains a splintered and isolated program; unless positive steps are taken to assume that its graduates really get more jobs or education or social and health services, it will have little effect. Established programs tend to stubbornly resist integration with new resources, and this contributes to one of the gravest deficiencies in these community programs. There is danger in starting a cycle of social change for which we provide no closure.

The higher the expectation, the greater and more complete the disappointment and feelings of hopelessness, worthlessness, and cynicism so characteristic of the American poor. The greater the leap between aspiration and reality, the more inevitable that fall. We may succeed in imbuing lower-class people with middle-class standards of success; and thereby do little more than deprive them of the supports of lower-class life.

The Job Corps, like all retraining programs, must decide whom to take and whom to reject. To assure the success and continued congressional support of this controversial program, a substantial amount of "creaming" may be unavoidable—accepting those who need the program least, but are most likely to succeed. But what will be the meaning for those who are turned away? What explanations will be offered to those not accepted? Titmuss has recently suggested that rejection from the Job Corps may mean ultimate rejection from the world of work, and this may prove to be more important than rejection by the armed forces, the colleges, or employers in business and government. And if we fail to provide those who have been rejected with physical and mental health services, we also exclude them from the world of clinical help. We thus assign them to a form of social death—scrap them as "social junk," to use Park's graphic term.

We give capital depletion allowances and pursue other policies resulting in the use of labor saving devices and the reduction of low skilled jobs. But, for the most part we do not create national policies which encourage the development of labor-intensive industries such as health, nursing, education, recreation, and welfare—vital to the poor themselves as services. Shortages in these fields could be partly met if those jobs which needed less training were filled by those who had less training. But the people who take such jobs must feel that they have futures and can rise eventually to professional status. Little organized effort is being made to reduce the rigidities of procedure which block this upward mobility. Professional associations, as well as labor unions, attack it as a threat to "quality of service" and to professional privilege and position. *Retraining and professionalism themselves contribute to dependency.*

THE ODDS ON FAILURE

Since success is increasingly determined by who can get, or has, an education, future failures are being created earlier and earlier—and with less and less chance of reprieve. This trend is intensifying.

Not all failures come from lack of ability; a very great many are socially determined. Some persons never get adequate opportunities for education or training; others do not want—or do not know how—to take advantage of them. Alfred J. Kahn, professor at the New York School of Social work, sums up:

> Of every one hundred children of high school age, eighty-seven enter high school and sixty-seven graduate . . . only thirty enter college and fifteen are graduated. . . . Of school drop-outs, one of three leaves during the eighth grade or before. . . . .

More than two-thirds of *all* children complete high school, but only 45 percent of *poor* children; 30 percent of youth on Aid to Families of Dependent Children (age 18-24) had not completed high school. Nor is the situation improving. A recent national survey dismally notes: "Little, if any, gain has been realized in the proportions of ADC children finishing high school since (a comparable) 1950 study was completed." Eighty-nine percent of the bright sons of the well-to-do expect to go to college, but only 29 percent of the brightest sons of the poor. Among dullards (those with lowest quintile I.Q. scores) 56 percent of all the prosperous expect college, but only 9 percent of the poor even hope for it. Intentions must be distinguished from action. When actual enrollments rather than expectations are examined, the picture is even worse. Moreover, there is a strong and continuous trend downward—almost 1 in 4 heads of poor families have even *less* education than their parents, if those parents had nine grades or more—despite the urgent necessity for more education than the previous generation. The final grim shadow for the future is cast by the 1965 report of the Council of Economic Advisers:

> Many individuals fail to develop their talent fully, often for economic reasons. In 1960, one third of the top 25 percent of youth did not go on to college; 5 percent did not even finish high school. This is a serious waste.

The uneducated are even more handicapped in the search for jobs today than they were two decades ago. Since the median educational level of the entire male labor force has risen by more than 50 percent, the dramatic and disturbing results are clear. Today one third of all Negro youths age 16-21 who are out of school are also out of work.

A dropout who finds a job is, of course, "independent" early, and some might rejoice at this fact. But as a national survey shows, dependency increases soon, and greatly: 57 percent of dropouts under twenty-five were unemployed during the last five years, compared to 4 percent of college graduates.

The much-heralded theory of the poverty cycle assumes that poverty is self-perpetuating because deprivation in one generation leads, through cultural impoverishment, to family breakdown and indifference to educational achievement of children, to poverty in the next generation. A valid alternative analysis would focus not on personal defects but on institutional rejection, and the indifference which leads to development of protective sub-cultures which wall people off from the threatened destruction of their personalities.

Economic poverty begéts educational poverty which begets economic poverty which begets dependency which begets economic and educational poverty—in a continuous closed circle of "begets." Children of poor parents study in larger classes with more difficult students in schools with less money under teachers who are paid less and are less well trained. Their education is inferior and they are little motivated or encouraged.

The rejects from our various selection processes form an army of outcasts, the socially disaffiliated. England has its "teddy boys," Russia its "hoodlums," and we our delinquents and skid row bums. All countries have "problem families."

Our rising affluence increases the army of those who prosper and belong; it also creates a permanent underclass who suffer from deprivation, failure, and loss of status.

What happens to the "socially disaffiliated?" According to sociologist Erving Goffman in his article, "Cooling the Mark Out," we create social ghettos where,

> . . . . persons who have died in important ways come gradually to be brought together into a common grave-yard that is separated ecologically from the living community. . . . Jails and mental institutions . . . certain regions and towns in California (set aside) as asylums for those who have died in their capacity as workers and as parents, but . . . still alive financially. For the old in America who have also died financially . . . old folks homes and rooming house areas . . .

During a depression a "failure" can blame his plight on the "system"; during prosperity it is much more difficult to avoid blaming himself, and becoming hopeless and apathetic. The ethic of the prosperous—that their welfare is due entirely to their own virtuous efforts—is infecting the poor, in reverse.

How does a society respond to its socially deprived? Some writers, like Talcott Parsons and Bronislaw Malinowski, believe that social systems have built-in equilibrium mechanisms that make automatic adjustments to severe threat.

But they tend to ignore the time lag—the years during which much suffering and misery is endured, before "natural counter-forces" can deflect or gear them to useful purposes—if they ever do so.

As we examine the mechanism of response—the social services provided in America's Welfare State—it becomes apparent that there is a curious disregard for those dependents whose plight is most desperate. Two crucial policy questions must be examined: who gets what services? What is the quality of those services? Even a cursory examination of these questions led Gunnar Myrdal to conclude that there is "a perverted tendency" in American social policy so that those who need help most do not get it.

So pervasive has been our failure to cope with poverty and dependency that this tendency can be called the Iron Law of Social Welfare.

Medical Care

James N. Morgan and his colleagues found in a national study that only one-third of poor families have hospital insurance of minimal adequacy, and three-fifths have no insurance at all. Using disability as a measure of need, only 24 percent of families with a person disabled were covered, compared to 76 percent with no one disabled.

A recent report on the quality of medical care in New York City found that accredited specialists provide different care in different hospital settings. Ability and training alone do not assure quality services. How services are organized and, we expect, to whom they are offered, also affect the quality of care. Physicians consider out-patient clinics the Siberias of hospitals, and serve grudgingly; students and interns are seldom adequately supervised. There are too few physicians, too many sick, too little time, not enough concern for the patient.

Welfare

Welfare programs are supposed to add to the incomes of those who do not have enough to live decently. But a University of Michigan study showed that half of the families in poverty did not receive any form of transfer payments, including social security. Daniel P. Moynihan, Assistant Secretary of Labor, has recently quipped that "social security is for winners, not losers." meaning those who have won some economic stability. Pensions help even fewer; only 11 percent of the poor had private pension help, compared to 40 percent of all families. Finally, only 23 percent of the poor receive public assistance.

Child Care

The iron law does not make exceptions for the young and weak. Alfred Kahn has recently documented the nature and scope of what he calls our "urban-child care crisis." He calls attention to the long term and sometimes unnecessary institutionalization of children; long term waiting in temporary shelters; frequent shifting of children from foster home to foster home. The handicapped, emotionally damaged, and non-white children are those most disadvantaged. The long term consequences of their neglect will be paid in the next generations.

Education and Housing

These have already been discussed. Education is the path upwards—and the poor, down farthest, get the worst, and have least motivation to use what they have. In housing the very large families and the "socially unacceptable" (those with unwed mothers, for instance) are hardest to place.

Mental Health

The most skilled psychiatrists and psychologists have always worked with the least distrubed patients. Treating middle- and upper-class neurotics generally yields better results—and income—than treating lower-class psychotics. One of the reports of the Joint Commission on Mental Health and Illness notes: "Usually the most difficult social and psychological problems fall in the area of no one's responsibility. The psychotics, sexual psychopaths, persons with suicidal or homicidal impulses, and persons presenting acute somatic symptoms are the groups left without any help short of commitment."

Is the Iron Law of Social Welfare really iron—that is, inevitable? If so, why?

REPEALING THE IRON LAW

I believe that the three chief factors that lead to denial of services to those in greatest need are professionalization, the rejection or inability of the needy to use the services, and the logical consequences of our social philosophy.

Professionals want to get satisfaction, pleasure, prestige, status, and income for their work. They want their efforts to succeed and to be acknowledged and appreciated. The most difficult, suspicious, recalcitrant, ignorant, impoverished, and hopeless cases afford little opportunities for such satisfactions.

We need more knowledge about the professions which are "increasingly becoming the arbiters of our welfare fate." Titmuss notes that, "We have to ask . . . questions about the ways in which professional people (doctors, teachers, social workers, and many others) discharge their roles in diagnosing need and in selecting and rejecting patients, clients, and students for this or that service."

Professional associations will not readily pose these questions because they are organized by professionals themselves to serve their own interests. Change usually must come from outside, but often in cooperation with insurgent insiders. The public health movement rose over the vigorous opposition of physicians; and the juvenile courts developed in spite of lawyers, not because of them.

The poor and the dependent may be even less eager to work with professionals than the professionals are to work with them. Despite their physical presence in our cities they live in a far country with its own iron laws, which we must learn. As voluntary consumers of social services they will not willingly do things merely because respectable people think they should, nor deliberately seek out what looks like trouble or embarrassment. The barriers they create to social reformers are, as Herbert Gans has pointed out, "reaction(s) to the threat of humiliation."

Professional and organizational commitment must precede the demand for responsiblity, cooperation, motivation, and trust. Consumer rejection is most likely to be overcome only when we offer authentic programs with assured delivery, rather than promissory notes.

Our social philosophy states strongly that the greatest rewards should go to the most productive. "Who does not work, neither shall he eat." Those who do not produce are by implication, inferior. Our humanitarian values (no one should starve in the midst of plenty) may seem to be contradicted; nevertheless we increasingly demand of the needy that they be willing to conform and be "rehabilitated" from the sin of dependency to qualify for financial aid.

Many so-called welfare payments, like social security, are in fact rewards or delayed payments for productivity, not really welfare at all. Returns are related to earned salary; benefits are channeled through the wage system; the marginal groups follow the iron law and are excluded. When liens on property are required to qualify for public assistance, aid really becomes a temporary loan. One early reason given was ease of administration: the stable and employed are easy to handle and find. Another is the "foot in the door" tactic: it is felt to be politically sounder to establish a welfare principle with socially acceptable groups, and then hope coverage and benefits trickle down. But the trickle-down system has not always worked. For example, from its very inception workman's compensation was restricted to the aristocracy of the manual workers—the skilled laborer. Even today, 20 percent of workers, concentrated among the unskilled, are not covered. We often find it inexpedient to accept our social services for what they are. For instance educational programs of great national benefit appear coyly—and with inadequate coverage—behind the fig leaves of "GI BILLS" for veterans or national defense scholarships.

In broad summary:

Our present welfare policy is not really designed to reach the neediest.

The poor have their own defenses against imputations of inferiority, and they resist assimilation.

Professionalization has hindered work with the poor.

To repeal the iron law we must develop social philosophy and techniques specifically designed for that purpose. We have the choice—the dilemma is one of ideology not technology.

Social welfare is a means to an end—and it is within our power and privilege to choose both the means and the end. Bismarck used social welfare to perpetuate an empire; in the thirties the United States used it to preserve the middle-class ethic of rewarding the industrious.

We can continue along this path, or we can make welfare serve social justice and humanitarianism by using the criterion of *common citizenship*, in which need, not virtue, determines aid. If we choose the former, we had better think seriously about whether we really want to end the problems of dependency at all.

If we really mean to attack dependency:

Redistribution of income and benefits must be the fundamental principle which informs our social policy. We must invest much more work and money, absolutely and relatively, for the underprivileged. Post-hospital care, expanded job and educational opportunities—such services must be available to all of the poor.

Teachers, social workers, doctors, and others who choose to work with the poor, instead of being in effect penalized financially for their choice, should be given special rewards and incentives—including much more recognition.

When we think of the dependency of the poor, our attention is rigidly fixed on those who should be working and are not. We neglect the student preparing for a socially useful occupation, the mother caring for children, the aged who have earned retirement, the workers who are forced out of the labor force by technological change. We do not reject dependency—*only dependency of the poor.*

We need to extend the principles of socially accepted dependency to the poor. We also need to raise the "acceptable" school-leaving age, lower retirement age, and provide for periodic retraining. Dependency must become a social right which can expand freedom, and increase the range of human choice. Such a policy could well decrease future dependency and make old age less terrifying.

In the 20th century, we may witness as dramatic a change in social policy direction as the shift from pauperism to poverty in the preceding centry. We must in the next era develop policies based on: socially accepted forms of dependency; adequate rather than minimum services; compensation for those disadvantaged by rapid technological change. Such policies must be informed by a philosophy of redistributive social justice.

What would such a program look like? *The Economist,* a pragmatic scholarly journal in England, has proposed programs for the *radical reform* of the social services. *The Economist* divided social services into two distinct objectives: 1) generous compensation for those damaged by rapid economic change; 2) a separate program for the relief of need. In specifics:

Unemployment pay should be increased so substantially that, for a short time, a man thrown out of a job should actually get more than he did while on the job to compensate for the pain in looking for a new job.

Mustering out pay (or pension) for men displaced by technological change, to be drawn for short periods (five years) even after they accept other jobs.

Housing subsidies to be attached to tenants rather than to houses—that is, a redistribution of subsidies to people rather than to structures.

Income guarantees unrelated to previous wages earned, so that the retired can maintain a standard of living much higher than known during their working years; an income consistent with the changing standard of living resulting from economic growth which will permit the poorest section of the old-age population to maintain a decent and adequate standard of living without recourse to public assistance.

A graduated social security tax which would be sharply progressive and have an income redistributive effect.

Higher family allowances, even above the guaranteed income level (or the prevailing wage scale), for poor parents with very large families.

The politics of who gets what and how, outside of the market, will become the salient issue of our vast social services in the generations to come. Solutions to the problem of dependency will be found only as we develop a social calculus which acknowledges our social costs and a constituency which can, in this new political game, make its weight felt to help pay them. We must search out, as Titmuss has recently suggested, "ways of extending the welfare state to the poor."

Family dependency
and welfare

FROM ISSUE TO THEORY

To summarize, the major functions that a family performs for itself are:

1. the production of income for the meeting of instrumental needs
2. provision of emotional support to its members
3. contribution to early child rearing with the emphasis upon values, attitudes, and goals
4. linking of family members to the larger society

Families are dependent upon other social institutions for most everything else. This is a social fact of our highly industrialized, urbanized, and bureaucratized societal system. The important point is that this dependency is defined as normative, not as a social problem. Used in this way, an independent functioning family is not synonymous with a self-sufficient family. An independent family performs those functions normatively ascribed to it, but it is still dependent upon other systems for the meeting of many of its needs. The meeting of these other needs are no longer seen as functions that the family should be performing. They have been transferred to other social institutions upon which the family is now dependent.

THE ROLE OF SOCIAL WELFARE

What happens when a family does not for some reason perform those functions which are normatively ascribed to it? One possibility is that it will be thrown into a state of disorganization. The family which does not perform functions normatively ascribed to it does not meet the needs of individual family members, nor does it adequately perform in relationship to the larger society. Failure to perform internal functions—meeting of instrumental and integrative needs—will bring about the social disorganization and possible collapse of

Reprinted in abridged form from Gary Spencer, *A Comparative Study of the Reduction of Dependency in Four Low-Income Housing Projects,* Boston, Northeastern University Studies in Vocational Rehabilitation, No. 4, 1967:21-31, with permission of the author.

the family as an effective social system. Failure to perform its external function—the placement of individuals in social positions of other societal systems—means simply that the family is an isolated and powerless unit. However, the failure of a sufficiently large numer of families to perform their external function would bring about the disorganization of the larger system. This certainly accounts for the fact that some segments of the society lack an effective voice in many community and societal affairs. They quite simply are not participants in those systems. Lack of access to legitimate sources of power is a major problem among the poor.

As an alternative to disorganization when the family does not perform those functions normatively ascribed to it, other social systems may take over those functions and perform them for the family. Insofar as these are functions ascribed to the family, according to some normative definition, then this dependency comes to be defined as a social problem. Implicit in this dependency relationship is the assumption that when a system external to the family performs one of the functions which the family is not performing for itself, the stability of the family will be maintained enabling it to perform its other functions. Thus for example a program of income maintenance might still allow the family to perform its integrative functions.

Who performs the functions for the family when they do not perform them for themselves? In some instances relatives and friends help out when the family function is upset. At one time various ethnic groups had mutual aid societies. Religious and private organizations have also developed some types of structures for helping families in crisis.

Increasingly, however, the role of acting as family surrogate when the family does not perform for itself has fallen to the public social welfare institutions. Basically this role has fallen to the social welfare institutions by default. Other patterns for helping families in crisis have slowly gone out of existence or have lost their effectiveness. Ethnic groups become assimilated; the extended family system has given way to isolated nuclear families; and private organizations have become highly specialized and social class based, often steering clear of low-income poverty groups. The alternative to family disorganization thus becomes a dependency upon public social welfare institutions.

In relationship to dependent families, the two goals of social welfare institutions are:

1. maintenance of the family system by taking over those functions which the family does not perform for itself
2. seeking to restore those functions back to the internal family system

These goals are contiguous. The family is kept from reaching a stage of disorganization by its dependency upon the health and welfare system. At the same time, the health and welfare system is attempting to break this dependency pattern by restoring functions to the internal family system. *Programs of welfare maintenance without a program of rehabilitation create a new set of social definitions where dependency becomes a permanent institution.*

Maintenace centers around the performance of instrumental functions. When the family is not producing a level of income adequate to meet instrumental needs, the social welfare system is likely to provide an income allowance, public housing, food stamps, health care, or similar programs. Rehabilitation takes into account both instrumental and integrative functioning. Any rehabilitation effort that results in vocational training is instrumental since it prepares the family to take over the income producing function. Health and welfare programs that have to do with household management, child rearing, and family counseling are designed to help a family perform its integrative functions. In this sense, family casework can be said to be dealing with problems of the internal integration of the family. Programs which have to do with community organization are dealing with the function of external integration, tying the family into the community system so that it can begin to influence its own life chances rather than merely being acted upon. In short, we are suggesting that various health and welfare programs can be categorized as they relate to the major dimensions of family functioning:

Family System Problem	*Appropriate Social Welfare Functions*
instrumental functioning	income maintenance and vocational rehabilitation
internal integrative functioning	family casework
external integrative functioning	community organization

This simplified model provides a conceptual framework for studying the relationship between dependent families and the health and welfare institutions upon which they are dependent and identifies those functions which the family is not performing for itself. The functions that health and welfare instititions perform can now be examined both from the point of view of what function they are performing for the family and what efforts are being made to restore that function to the internal family system. At this level of generalization one can encompass a wide gamut of specific family tasks that are not being performed along with a wide variety of health and welfare services which can be categorized within the above paradigm.

● ● ●

SOCIAL DEPENDENCY—A MODEL OF CLIENT PARTICIPATION

When individuals or groups are expected to play certain social roles but do not, either because they cannot or will not, this is a social disability from the point of view of those who have the expectations. When other individuals or groups must expend time and resources in performing the roles for the "disabled," then the disability is one of *social dependency*.

The mainstream values of our society define independent functioning as an important goal. If an individual in the ghetto is *dependent*, it is the mainstream that labels him *disabled*. The individual himself accepts this definition only if he also accepts the mainstream values and goals. Even if he accepts them, he must also have an opportunity structure that will allow for their achievement. The inability of a "typical" middle-class person to know how to find a "fence" in order to get rid of some "hot" (stolen) goods represents a social disability on his part for survival in the criminal sub-culture. Even if he accepts the values and goals of the criminal, he must still have access to the opportunity structures and agencies of socialization that will allow their achievement. To the middle-class individual, the person in the ghetto is socially disabled. To members of the criminal sub-culture, the middle-class individual trying to sell his stolen goods is also socially disabled. The sub-culture of the criminal world and that of the mainstream of society are alike in that both make it quite difficult for a "non-member" to gain access to their social resources. It is further true that by the time entrance into a particular system has been made available, the individual may have already entered and internalized the values and goals of an alternative structure. The middle-class individual remains in the mainstream, but the Negro remains in the ghetto.

Social disability is a result of a combination of the following: (1) *failure to internalize normative values and goals;* (2) *blocked opportunity structures for achieving normative goals; and* (3) *the existence of alternative structures for learning alternative values or goals.* Individuals are socialized so as to find certain *life styles* (cultural goals) desirable. Given these life styles, individuals have varying *life chances* (structural opportunities) for their realization. Merton was the first sociologist to identify this incongruity between cultural goals and structural opportunities. He went on to describe a series of regular responses to the conflict situation: conformity, innovation, ritualism, retreatism, and rebellion. Cloward extended Merton's theory by pointing out that when approved structures are blocked, the individual must gain access to deviant structures in order to participate. Levinson was the first in the social welfare field to suggest a typology of "chronic dependents." He identified three types of welfare clients: moral, calculative, and alienative. The following represents a synthesis and application of these basic ideas of Merton, Cloward, and Levinson.

Using the criteria of *independent functioning* as the goal and *participation in approved structures* as the means, it is possible to construct a typology of social dependency. This dependency becomes a means for predicting client involvement in the rehabilitation program in that the formal goal of the program is to restore individuals and families to independent functioning by preparing them for employment in occupations that are part of the approved, social structure. While these are the goals of the rehabilitation agency, they may not be the reason for the client's participation. The following combinations of means and goals are therefore possible:

	Participation in Approved Normative Structures (means)	Independent Functioning (goal)
Types of Social Dependency		
1. normative dependency	+	+
2. calculative dependency	-	+
3. ritual dependency	+	-
4. anomic dependency	-	-
5. alienative dependency	(∓)	(∓)

Notes + signifies the client has the means, or accepts the goal
   − signifies the client does not have the means, or does not accept the goal

Normative dependency is the category of clients who accept the goal of independent functioning and see participation in acceptable societal structures as the appropriate means for achieving this goal. These individuals have internalized the goal of independent functioning and will be highly motivated to break their dependency relationship and become employed in a job that will allow them to realize this. This is the "ideal-type" of participant. The organization's goals are the client's goals. The implication for the rehabilitation program is this individual will be highly motivated to achieve rehabilitation success. His limiting factors, if they exist, would be the existence of a physical disability or a lack of skill potential. The client is determined to achieve independent functioning through legitimate means providing that opportunity structures for jobs and job training are available. The latter is a factor external to the client and is a primary responsibility of the agency and the larger community which the agency is supposed to represent.

Calculative dependency typifies yet another type of participant. Those who fall into this category value the goal of independent functioning, but they reject the idea of participation in the normative systems of society. Calculative dependents see themselves as *earning their living*, at least in part, through participation in the rehabilitation program. For this type of client, participation is for a reason other than returning to work in normative structures. It is likely that this pattern of calculative dependency is multiplied in such a way that the individual will eventually achieve his desired life style pattern.

Clients in this category may be participants in other systems while they are also in the rehabilitation program. They may be receiving funds from several agencies who are unaware of each other, they may be dabbling in the rackets and other illegitimate structures. It is not uncommon for welfare recipients, rehabilitation clients, etc. to moonlight in jobs while they are receiving public funds which forbid this practice. It is important to keep in mind that this type of cal-culative behavior is not necessarily a characteristic of personality, but is a response to the social structural circumstance in which the individual finds him-self. Given the fact that the calculative individual has internalized the goal of independent functioning, it is the failure of the social structure to provide legiti-mate opportunities that open the way for the use of illegitimate means. The desired life style pattern is normative, but with life chances in the normative structure blocked, alternative illegitimate structures are chosen. Stated more pragmatically, when legitimate jobs are not available, deviant means for produc-ing an income are chosen.

What further exists in the urban ghetto is a situation where individuals have a better chance for entree into illegitimate structures than into legitimate ones; and their chances for success in the illegitimate structures are greater. Normative values thus become meaningless since adherance to them will not bring the realization of goals. These values may be discarded, or, as Rodman suggests, they may be stretched to include both legitimate and illegitimate means. The point is that chances to gain access to deviant agencies of socialization and the chances for success in these deviant structures are greater than chances for success in the normative system.

The implication for the rehabilitation program is an important one. The rehabilitation agencies are offering opportunities for entrance into normative occupational structures, but they are in competition with the non-normative street system. Given the same goal of material success and independence, it seems quite logical for an incumbent to carefully weigh his chances for success in each system. In the reality of the urban ghetto, the normative system has less to offer. The potential client must be convinced that his opportunities for success in the normative system are within his grasp, and this must be a reality. The rehabilitation counselor should keep in mind that this is indeed a variant from the middle-class pattern. The middle-class individual, while he may also value independent functioning, has a higher degree of access to normative structures and a lesser degree of access to deviant structures.

● ● ●

Lewis A. Coser

The sociology
of poverty

Discussions of the extent of poverty in a given society usually have been dog-
ged by definitional problems. One man's poverty is another's wealth; minimal
standards in a developed industrial society may be viewed as Utopian goals in an
underdeveloped one. What may be felt to constitute unendurable deprivation in
a society where the underprivileged compare their lot with that of others more
favorably placed in regard to the distribution of income and wealth, may be accepted as legitimate in societies where no such comparisons are socially available
or culturally sanctioned.

One may argue that a poor man is one whose economic means are not com-
mensurate with the economic ends he seeks; yet this does not stand up under
scrutiny. In societies that exhibit a strain toward anomy, a disjunction between
the ends that are striven for and the means available for attaining them, bound-
less appetites forever create new dissatisfactions at every level reached. This
seems to be typical not only of the deprived but of very large strata of the population. The economies of such societies are geared precisely to the creation of
ever new needs.

Rather than taking as a point of departure the condition or felt condition of
those presumed to be poor, this paper will attempt to provide a different perspective. Following Simmel's lead, poverty will be dealt with as a social category
that emerges through societal definition. Just as in Durkheim's view crime can
best be defined as consisting in acts having "the external characteristic that they
evoke from society the particular reaction called punishment," so I shall argue
here that the poor are men who have been so defined by society and have
evoked particular reactions from it. From this perspective, the poor have not always been with us. In Oriental societies, for example, deprivation was not socially visible and not within the focus of social awareness. The modern observer
might have discerned there a great prevalence of want and misery, yet the members of the society themselves did not perceive poverty and were unaware of its
prevalence. In such societies, the condition of those who were deprived did not
seem to touch the sensibilities of the upper strata; and it is, after all, they who

Reprinted in abridged form from Lewis A. Coser, "The Sociology of Poverty," *Social
Problems,* 1965, 13(2): 140-148, with permission of the Society for the Study of Social
Problems. Footnotes omitted.

determine the conscience and consciousness of the society. The deprived, insofar as they were recognized at all, were simply put into the same category as, say,
the victims of disease or natural disaster. They did not exist phenomenologically
as a separate category.

Historically, the poor emerge when society elects to recognize poverty as a
special status and assigns specific persons to that category. The fact that some
people may privately consider themselves poor is sociologically irrelevant. What
is sociologically relevant is poverty as a socially recognized condition, as a social
status. We are concerned with poverty as a property of the social structure.

In medieval society, the poor had the function of affording the rich the opportunity for socially prescribed "good deeds." In the Catholic injunction to give
alms the concern was not essentially with the physical condition of the poor but
primarily with the moral condition of the rich. The giver rather than the recipient tended to be the moral center of attention. The good works of the Christian
man were considered a major avenue to salvation. Giving alms hence was meant
to increase the chances of the giver in the next world and not primarily to improve the chances of the poor in this. The poor were not considered in their own
right but mainly as a means toward the other-worldly ends of the rich. This peculiar function of the poor was, however, of some consequence for the society
for it helped to unify the Christian community.

The medieval status of the poor was very different from that assigned to the
poor in Puritan England. Here they were given the social position of the "eter-
nally damned"—confirming to the righteous the fitness of their survival. To the
Puritan conscience, the poor, having no calling, were not considered a part of
the society. . . . The poor, like Indian untouchables, are assigned a status which
marks their exclusion from the social order.

In modern societies the deprived are assigned to the core category of the poor
only when they receive assistance. It might be objected that the category of the
economically deprived is presently much larger than that of the assisted poor.
Whereas the latter englobes around 8 million persons in contemporary America,
between 40 and 50 million fall into the former category. However, the point is
precisely that the current widespread discussion of the problems of poverty can
be seen in large part as an effort to broaden the core category of the poor by insisting that millions not heretofore included deserve societal assistance. If I
understand Michael Harrington and his co-thinkers aright, they argue in effect
that a redefinition of the problem of poverty is required so that the very large
number of deprived who have so far not received assistance can be included
among the poor receiving societal help of one kind or another.

It is not a person's lack of economic means that makes him belong to the core
category of the poor. As long as a man continues to be defined primarily in terms
of his occupational status, he is not so classified. Doctors, farmers, or plumbers
who have suffered financial reverses or strains are still typically called doctors,
farmers, or plumbers. "The acceptance of assistance," argues Georg Simmel,
"removes the man who has received it from the precondition of the previous

status; it symbolized his formal declassification." From that point on his private trouble becomes a public issue. In individual psychological terms the sequence of events leads from the experience of deprivation to a quest for assistance; the matter is reversed however in sociological perspective: those who receive assistance are defined as being poor. Hence, poverty cannot be understood sociologically in terms of low income or deprivation but rather in terms of the social response to such deprivations.

The modern poor are a stratum that is recruited from heterogeneous origins, and individual members of this stratum have a great number of differing attributes. They come to belong to the common category of the poor by virtue of an essentially passive trait, namely that society reacts to them in a particular manner. The poor come to be viewed and classified not in terms of criteria ordinarily used in social categorization, that is, not by virtue of what they do, but by virtue of what is done to them. To quote Simmel again: "Poverty hence presents a unique sociological constellation: a number of individuals occupy a specific organic position within the social whole through purely personal fate; but it is not personal destiny or personal conditions which determine the position but rather the fact that others—individuals, associations, or social totalities—attempt to correct this state of affairs. Hence it is not personal need which makes for poverty; rather, the sociological category of poverty emerges only when those who suffer from want are receiving assistance."

Though the poor are recognized as having a special status in modern societies, it is still a status that is marked only by negative attributes, that is, by what the status-holder does *not* have. This distinguishes him from any other status-holder in that it does not carry with it the expectation of a social contribution. This lack of expectation of a social contribution by the poor is symbolized by their lack of social visibility. Those who are assigned to the status of the poor offend the moral sensibilities of other members of the society who, unwittingly, or wittingly, keep them out of their sight. What is at issue here is not only physical segregation into special areas and districts that right-minded citizens would not normally care to visit and that are typically not shown to tourists, but also a kind of moral invisibility. The Gradgrinds and Bounderbys of Victorian England held views of the poor that were not very far removed from those of their Puritan ancestors. They consequently repressed awareness of the facts of deprivation. Only the persistent agitation of a host of reformers finally led to the horrified discovery by proper Victorian gentlemen that Britain was in fact split into "two nations." This accounts for the fact that, though general well being and standards of living clearly increased in England during the nineteenth century, perceived deprivation increased throughout the century as human misery gained at least some visibility.

Lest it be believed that we deal here only with the more remote past it may be well to remind us of a very similar trend in the recent history of the United States. John K. Galbraith remarked upon this a few years ago when he wrote:

"In the United States, the survival of poverty is remarkable. We ignore it because we share with all societies at all times the capacity for not seeing what we do not wish to see. Anciently this has enabled the nobleman to enjoy his dinner while remaining oblivious to the beggars around his door. In our own day it enables us to travel in comfort throughout South Chicago and the South." At the present moment, when poverty is suddenly receiving frontline attention among politicians, scholars and the mass media, it is difficult to remember that only recently it seemed hardly visible at all. . . . The editors of *Fortune* magazine published a volume, *America in the Sixties*, in which they attempted to forecast the major social and economic trends of the next decade. They concluded that soon deprivation would no longer be with us at all. They announced with self-congratulatory flourish that "only" 3,600,000 families have incomes under $2,000 and that if a family makes over $2,000 it cannot be considered deprived at all. Two years later Michael Harrington's *The Other America*, followed by a spate of other books and articles, suddenly helped to picture deprivation as the central domestic issue in the United States and led to the emergence of a new social definition of poverty. The deprived in America now were seen as constituting about 25 percent of the population all of whom deserved assistance. The number of objectively deprived is not likely to have changed appreciably between the complacent fifties and the self-critical sixties, but the extent of perceived deprivation changed drastically. As a consequence, what appeard as a peripheral problem only a few years ago suddenly assumes considerable national salience.

[I should like to point out here that it will not do to argue that the statistics indicating the extent of deprivation were available all along. In the first place it is not the availability of statistics but their use which is of social significance. Furthermore, it can be argued that a society bothers to keep accurate statistics mainly of those phenomena it deems worthy of attention. Some extreme cases from totalitarian societies come readily to mind. As Everett Hughes has reminded us in his examination of German Statistical Yearbooks, in the Nazi and pre-Nazi period, "From earlier work with German official statistics, I was practically certain that the pre-Nazi German had a religion, but not a race. The statistical German was the opposite of the statistical American, who had a race but no religion. . . . Race in the pre-Nazi Yearbooks was a characteristic of stallions." But all Yearbooks under the Nazi regime contained, among others, a category "Racial Classification of People who Married in X Year." A characteristic which was hitherto officially unnoticed was suddenly made visible through statistics. Or, to give another example, "In Lebanon there has not been a census since 1932 for fear that taking one would reveal such changes in the religious composition of the population as to make the marvelously intricate political arrangements designed to balance sectarian interests unviable." Finally, in the 1941 Indian census there were 25 million tribal peoples, but in 1951, after independence was attained, the number had shrunk through what has been called "genocide by definition" to 1.7 million.

No such drastic surgery was, of course, performed on American statistics. Yet one cannot help but be struck by the fact that, to give one example, the number of underprivileged will vary greatly depending on where you fix the income line. Thus the aforementioned *Fortune* study defined deprivation as a family income under $2,000 and concluded that there were only 3,600,000 poor families. Robert Lampman used the $2,500 cutoff for an urban family of four and on this basis came to the conclusion that 19 percent of the American population, 32,000,000 people, were underprivileged. In the same period, the AFL-CIO, using a slightly higher definition of what constituted low income, found that 41,500,000 Americans—24 percent of the total population—have substandard incomes. After all these studies were published, the Bureau of Labor Statistics issued a report containing newly calculated budgets for urban families of four which showed that previous calculations had underestimated minimal budgetary requirements. Harrington concludes on the basis of these new figures that the deprived number is more nearly 50,000,000.]

Enough has been said to indicate the extent to which objective misery and perceived deprivation may diverge. We can now return to the initial statement that, in modern societies, persons are assigned a position in the status category of the poor when they receive assistance. Receipt of such assistance is predicated upon the society's willingness to assume a measure of responsibility for the poor and upon its recognition of the fact that they are effectively a part of the community. But what are the terms upon which such assistance is granted and what are the consequences for the recipient?

Here I would like to contend that the very granting of relief, the very assignment of the person to the category of the poor, is forthcoming only at the price of a degradation of the person who is so assigned.

To receive assistance means to be stigmatized and to be removed from the ordinary run of men. It is a status degradation through which, in Harold Garfinkel's words, "the public identity of an actor is transformed into something looked on as lower in the local schemes of social types." In this perspective, the societal view of a person becomes significant in so far as it alters his face. Once a person is assigned to the status of the poor his role is changed, just as the career of the mental patient is changed by the very fact that he is defined as a mental patient. Let me give a few illustrative instances of what is at issue here.

Members of nearly all status groups in society can make use of a variety of legitimate mechanisms to shield their behavior from observability by others; society recognizes a right to privacy, that is, the right to conceal parts of his role behavior from public observation. But this right is denied to the poor. At least in principle, facets of his behavior which ordinarily are not public are in their case under public control and are open to scrutiny by social workers or other investigators. In order to be socially recognized as poor a person is obligated to make his private life open to public inspection. The protective veil which is available to other members of society is explicitly denied to them.

Whereas other recipients of social services may upon occasion be visited at home by investigators, most of their contact with the agency is likely to be in the agency rather than in their private homes. Generally, in modern society, the exercise of authority—except within the family—is separated from the home. With regard to the poor on relief, however, this not the case. Here their home is the place in which most contacts with the agency investigators are likely to take place. They are typically being investigated *in situ* and hence have much less of a chance to conceal their private affairs from the superordinate observers. Such an invasion of home territory, because it prevents the usual stage management for the visit of outsiders, is necessarily experienced as humiliating and degrading.

When money is allocated to members of any other status groups in society, they have the freedom to dispose of it in almost any way they see fit. Here again, the treatment of the poor differs sharply. When monies are allocated to them, they do not have free disposition over their use. They must account to the donors for their expenses and the donors decide whether the money is spent "wisely" or "foolishly." That is, the poor are treated in this respect much like children who have to account to parents for the wise use of their pocket money; the poor are infantilized through such procedures.

As the above examples make clear, in the very process of being helped and assisted, the poor are assigned to a special career that impairs their previous identity and becomes a stigma which marks their intercourse with others. Social workers, welfare investigators, welfare administrators and local volunteer workers seek out the poor in order to help them, and yet, paradoxically, they are the very agents of their degradation. Subjective intentions and institutional consequences diverge here. The help rendered may be given from the purest and most benevolent of motives, yet the very fact of being helped degrades.

Assistance can be given either by voluntary workers or by professionals. The former pattern prevailed till roughly World War I, the latter has come to predominate in our days. Such professionalization of assistance has had two divergent sets of consequences for the recipient. To be cared for by a professional who is paid for his work means that the recipient need not be grateful to him, he doesn't have to say thank you. In fact he can hate the person giving assistance and even display some of his antagonism without losing the institutionally provided aid. Professionalization removes the personal element in the relationship and marks it as an impersonal transaction thereby freeing the recipient both from personal embarassment and from personal obligation. When the poor is, so to speak, *"promoted"* to a case he may be spared certain personal humiliations. Yet this is not the whole story. The very manner of bureaucratic procedure used in dealing with a person on relief is different from that employed with respect to, say, an unemployed person. Receipt of unemployment insurance is seen as an unquestioned right which has been earned. Control by the donor agency over the recipient is minimal. Here it stands in contrast to control over the person on relief where control is a precondition for relief. Hence the professional in an agency dealing with the unemployed has little power over persons he serves, but the welfare investigator or the case worker has a great deal of power over the assisted poor. This power was considerably increased, it may be remarked in passing, when the giving of assistance shifted from so-called categorical assistance to granting case workers leeway to vary assistance according to the specific needs of the client. This change of policy was instituted for humanitarian and benevolent reasons, to be sure. But it stands to reason that it has greatly increased the discretionary power of the case worker over the client.

Prescribed impersonality has still other effects on the relationship between professionalized welfare workers and the recipients of aid. As long as volunteers or other non-professionals were the main dispensers of charity, condescension was likely to mark the relationship between donors and recipients of aid, but it was also likely to be characterized by a fairly high level of spontaneity. The relationship was so defined as to make a *reciprocal* flow of affect and emotion between the two actors possible, even if it did not always, or usually, occur. But professionalization by definition prevents the flow of affect. This is not due to happenstance but to the institutionalization of a structurally asymmetrical type of relationship. Those who render assistance have a job to do; the recipient is a case. As in every type of bureaucratic procedure, the impersonal aspects of the case must of need take precedence over distracting personal considerations. In fact, case workers or investigators would be incapacitated in the exercise of their tasks were they to indulge in "over-rapport," that is, in an undue consideration of the personal needs of the client. Excessive sympathy would impair role performance. The welfare worker, moreover, is not supposed to deserve esteem for his accomplishments from the recipient of aid but rather from professional peers and superiors. The client who is defined as "poor" has little if any possibility of controlling his behavior. Hence there exist built-in insulating mechanisms which insure that professional concern with the poor does not corrupt the professional into considering the poor as anything but an object of care and a recipient of aid. In this way the status discrepancy between them is continuously reaffirmed. This is accentuated, moreover, in those cases where welfare workers are of lower middle class origin and feel that close association with clients might endanger the respectable status they have but recently achieved.

The professionals and the poor do in fact belong to two basically different worlds. In Alexander Solzhenitsyn's fine novel about Russian concentration camps, *One Day in the Life of Ivan Denisovich,* occurs an episode in which the hero attempts to get some medical relief from the man in charge of the infirmary but is turned away with indifference. He thereupon reflects, "How can you expect a man who's warm to understand a man who's cold." This beautifully captures the gist of what I have been trying to say. As long as social workers and the poor belong to the opposite worlds of those who are warm and those who are cold, their relationship is necessarily an asymmetrical one. As in other aspects of case work, those who can relieve some of their wants as suppliants, and the asymmetry is not only one of feelings and attitudes, it is also an asymmetry of power. This is an extreme case of unilateral dependence. Peter Blau's formulation is helpful here: "By supplying services in demand to others, a person establishes power over them. If he regularly renders needed services they cannot readily obtain elsewhere, others become dependent on and obligated to him for these services, and unless they can furnish other benefits to him that produce interdependence by making him equally dependent on them, their unilateral dependence obligates them to comply with his requests lest he ceases to continue to meet their needs."

Blau stresses here that unilateral dependence comes into being when the receiver of benefits is not in a position to reciprocate with benefits that he can in turn bestow upon the crux of the matter. The poor, when receiving assistance, are assigned a low and degraded status by virtue of a determination that they cannot themselves contribute to society. Their inability to contribute in turn degrades them to the condition of unilateral receivers. Built into the system of relief is not only the definition of their being non-contributors, but the expectation that they are not even potential contributors. In an instrumentally oriented society, those who cannot give but only receive and who are not expected to give at a future time are naturally assigned the lowest status. They cannot engage in activities that establish interdependence and this is why they cannot be given social recognition. Poverty, therefore, can never be eliminated unless the poor are enabled to give as well as to receive. They can be fully integrated into the social fabric only if they are offered the opportunity to give.

In order to be able to serve, they must first be able to function at optimum capacity. Devices such as a guaranteed minimum income for every citizen, assuring him freedom from pressing want, may very well be a precondition for the abolition of dependency. But it is a precondition only. It needs to be considered not as an end in itself but only as a means which permits the poor to be free from anxiety while they train themselves for the rendering of such services to the community as will make them interdependent with others.

I showed earlier how the core category of the poor arises only when they come to be defined as recipients of assistance. We now see that correlatively the poor will be with us as long as we provide assistance so that the problem of poverty can be solved only through the abolition of unilateral relationship of dependence.

This is not the place to spell out in detail concrete measures which will "solve" the problem of poverty. I know of no such global solutions at the present moment. But I wish to indicate at least the direction in which, I believe, such solutions are to be looked for. I am impressed, for example, by the number of recent experiments, from Mobilization for Youth to Alcoholics Anonymous, in which "some people who do not seem to benefit from *receiving* help often profit indirectly when they are *giving* help." A number of such projects have of late used a variety of non-professionals recruited largely among the poor. The New York State Division for Youth and several other agencies for example employ former youthful offenders in interviewing and related tasks. Howard University's Community Apprentice Program trains delinquent youth to be recreation, child welfare, and research aides. Mobilization for Youth employs indigenous leaders as case aides, homework helpers, and the like. These jobs offer employment opportunities for the underprivileged and hence serve directly to reduce poverty by transforming dependent welfare cases into home-makers, and former delinquents into researchers. This indigenous non-professional, as Frank Riessman and Robert Reiff have written, "is a peer of the client and can more readily identify with him. He possesses no special body of knowledge which makes him an expert and can feel, therefore, that in reversed circumstances the client could do the same job just as easily. In the place of subtle patronage or *noblesse oblige* concepts, he is likely to feel that 'there but for the grace of God go I.' To the indigenous non-professional, 'helping others' is a reciprocal process. . . . "

These are only a few and still very feeble beginnings, but I believe that they point in the right direction. The task is to create valued status positions for those who were formerly passive recipients of assistance. Such valuable status positions can only be those in which they are required and enabled to make a social contribution and become active partners in a joint undertaking of mutual aid. This can be done through helping others with whom but recently they shared similar problems or through working in large-scale projects similar to a domestic Peace Corps or a replica of the New Deal's Civilian Conservation Corps. Yet another case in which the poor may themselves contribute to the abolition of the status they occupy arises when they cease "acting poor," i.e., when they reject the role behavior which is required by the status. When the poor begin to react actively, when they refuse to continue to be passive recipients of aid, they undermine the very status they occupy. This is why rent strikes, demonstrations, and other political activities by the poor should be seen as avenues of activization which tend to lead to a restructuring of their relationships in the community.

Simmel observes that though the notion of assistance necessarily implies taking from the rich and giving to the poor, it nevertheless was never aimed at an equalization of their positions in society. As distinct from socialist endeavors, it does not even have the tendency to reduce the differences between rich and poor but rather accepts and bolsters them. Or, as T. H. Marshall once put it, "The common purpose of statutory and voluntary effort was to abate the nuisance of poverty without disturbing the pattern of inequality of which poverty was the most obvious unpleasant consequence." This is why what I have suggested diverges sharply from most previous policies. It aims not at alleviating poverty but at abolishing it through the elimination of the despised status of the receiver of assistance. It is, to be sure, a Utopian proposal. But, as Max Weber, that supreme realist, has argued, "Certainly all political experience confirms the truth—that man would not have attained the possible unless time and again he had reached out for the impossible."

Bernard Beck

Welfare as
a moral category

Sociologists trying to account for social arrangements in the United States
today must carefully consider "welfare," both in itself and in its articulation
with virtually all other aspects of American life and social structure. Not only is
welfare extremely important today but its significance in the future will be even
greater. The role of welfare is even more impressive from the wider perspective
of industrial societies in general. There is reason to suppose that some form of
welfare activity characterizes all such societies, perhaps amounting to a structural requisite. One might argue that certain functional requisites satisfied by
various institutions in other societies can no longer be satisfied by them, because
advanced industrial societies place strict limits on their operations. This line of
reasoning is most familiar with regard to the family. As a result, it is argued,
requisites must be met by the peculiarly modern institutions of welfare.

All discussions of welfare which start from these intriguing points should
refer to a conceptualization or definition of welfare which would identify it as a
generalized structural category sociologists could use. In a comparative framework, one might attack the question by seeing how well any given notion of
welfare could be applied across societies.

Such a notion should show welfare as a sociological object of a certain type
and make it interestingly different from other sociological objects of the type. In
particular, in view of the increasing attention being paid to welfare by sociologists, we would want to know whether welfare is to be used as a technical term
of sociological discourse, like "ideology," or as the name of a specific event or
datum, such as "non-violence." One could ask how welfare would appear as a
property of social systems in general rather than merely of societies. The increasingly common use of terms like "welfare norms," "welfare institutions,"
"welfare organizations," and so on leads us to ask whether "welfare" designates
some sociologically distinctive form of the normative, institutional, organizational, or other realms.

Reprinted from Bernard Beck, "Welfare as a Moral Category," *Social Problems*, 1967,
14(3):258-277, with permission of The Society for the Study of Social Problems.
Footnotes omitted.

Attempts to satisfy these questions are frustrating, however. Outside the context of the advanced industrial societies with which we are familiar, the question of welfare seems hard to pose, let alone answer. How do you look for welfare in societies in which important activities are organized through the extended family and in which norms of mutual aid bind family members? Or in novel societies with a great many special categories of members, many of whom are supported in their needs even though they produce nothing our Western eyes can find valuable?

Even within Western societies, "welfare" is a label with political and ideological connotations, so that the term loads any discussions in which it appears. While "welfare" has been used in a variety of senses both ordinary and technical, at the present time it is of interest to us as a term which succeeds such older terms as "dole" and "relief," as a euphemism in the process of being discredited.

In this paper, I intend to show that there are serious difficulties involved in the unexamined extension of the Western folk usage of "welfare" into social scientific terminology. I will also suggest another direction of generalization from the historical experience of modern welfare societies; namely, the social definition of distinctions among human activities and ways of life, with reputational and moral overtones, and important consequences for the treatment accorded to different participants.

The first part will be a general discussion of a certain kind of discrepancy between specifications of social systems and the consequences of such a discrepancy on the differentiation of the systems. This process has several different exemplifications of interest, but in this paper I will focus on welfare as a special case. The second part will develop a view of welfare from the perspective of the general discussion. Finally, I will illustrate how this approach to welfare generates new lines of thought on specific issues which arise in the consideration of welfare as a matter of scholarly and of public concern. As an instance, the problem of "welfare dependency" will be discussed.

TWO VERSIONS OF THE "SYSTEM"

Social units can be specified in at least two main ways, by the boundary between the unit and the rest of the world, or by the distinctive patterns of operation within the unit. These can be called definitions by *boundary* and definitions by *structure*, respectively. Social units like societies, communities, and other "natural" systems, when defined by boundary, are seen to be located in a territory; the social system is specified by the membership included in this territory, or the *population*. The most familiar and conceptually comfortable kinds of societies, nation-states, have "sovereignty" over a territory. They include and are responsible for everything and everyone found inside its boundaries.

Definition by structure proceeds from the central features of a pattern of social arrangements and fixes the limits of a structure wherever discontinuities in a pattern appear. Such definitions ought to be of greater theoretical interest than those by boundary, since they refer directly to analytic features sociologists want to be able to discuss. But the expectation and devout wish revealed in most works is that boundaries and structures will be one-to-one; beginning with either kind of definition ought to lead unambiguously to the other. If we can construct a boundary for a social unit, we expect it is because things are a certain way within and otherwise without. If we can specify a connected set of patterns, we expect to be led ultimately to specifiable boundaries. We can see current disputes about the existence of value consensus in social systems, the character of variant subcultures, and so-called "problems of level" as all hanging on the question of the correspondence of these two kinds of definition.

The sociologist's situation is the exact counterpart of that confronting the actors in the system. They also face a social world which can be thought of either as the things they share with all those in the same place, or as the place where arrangements are of a certain kind. (Thus, what is "American" can be specified by what happens in "America" as a place, or by the occurence anywhere of an "American way of life.") When people accept a way of life, they understand that it is expected and that it is a good model of existence and of conduct in a certain place. Anyone within that territory ought ot be able to refer to it in constructing an adequate and well-ordered career for himself.

Ways of life are typically considered in sociology as systems of roles or alternatively as systems of institutionalized role requirements. Therefore, another way of stating this basic expectation and faith, both of members of the system and of sociological students of it, is to say that any member of a population can be "injected" into some reasonable place in the institutionalized role structure. The existence of a structure of institutionalized roles in a system implies that persons constructing careers find a set of positions ready to be occupied. The positions are present before the persons arrive on the scene. Whether persons actively compete for positions, drift into them painlessly, or are drawn in against their wills, we may speak of their assumption of such roles as an *injection* of the person into the role.

Participants in the system, like scientific observers of it, postulate the structural coherence of most, if not all, the institutionalized roles. Like scientists they have an interest in formulating a theory about the basic principles of this coherence. The folk thoery of the participants will be called the *Theory* and is distinct from the sociologist's account of the structural coherence of the system of institutionalized roles. In fact, one of the most interesting sources of latent patterns should be in the gap between the publicly accepted Theory and the actual structure found by an observer. The Theory generates as its main result an object of public definition which we have called a "way of life," but which might be called in a more abstract vein the Theoretical structure, or even the ideal structure. In this paper, it will be called the *Structure*. Another important result generated by the Theory is a model of conduct with respect to the Structure. The belief that the structure contributes to an orderly and predictable set of relationships among the persons who make up the population to a large degree explains its existence, according to the Theory. The implications of this notion are far-reaching and constitute the basic building blocks out of which is constructed a folk model of conforming behavior and of the significance, explanation, and necessary treatment of deviations from conformity.

But it is necessary only to raise the distinction between the territorial and structural definitions of social units to see that the faith of both sociologist and actor in the congruence between the two rests on a shaky foundation. In common with other natural phenomena, the Structure developed within a society can be more or less well-adapted, under some set of criteria, to the situation in which it is operating. Without advancing a theory of social chaos, one can imagine that many societies will, for relatively long periods of time, find themselves in situations in which the Theories to which most members are committed are not fully compatible with the conditions of the populations which are supposed to live under them. This result can come about in several ways, depending on the nature of the incompatibility. That is, the situation in which the Structure and the population available to fill it correspond is only one possible situation. It is also possible for the Structure to make demands of the population (for numbers of people, for example) which the population cannot fulfill. Or, the Structure may not provide suitable roles for all persons who are expected to be able to find them. Finally, to fill the inevitable fourth box, it is possible for a system simultaneously to have some roles which cannot be filled and some persons who cannot be injected into suitable roles. These problems may be complementary; for instance, if there is a shortage of females to be injected into waiting roles of wives or, otherwise defined, the absence of suitable roles into which a surplus of males can be injected, in a gerontocratic polygynous society.

Let us now consider the situation described by a surplus of individuals from the population over the possibilities provided by the Structure. This surplus constitutes a residuum, in the population but outside of the positions and careers specified by the Theory. This residuum will present a real problem to any social system, a problem which can be handled in one of several ways. In the first place, some form of compartmentalization, insulation, vicinal isolation may arise so that the apparent residuum is in fact organized with regard to some other Theory, and has a Structure of it own, so that there are actually two systems rather than a single one; they may have only negligible contact.

A second and quite drastic way of handling the problem of a residuum is to eliminate effectively from the population all members who cannot be injected into suitable roles as specified by the Structure. Such procedures include, for example, the practices of abortion, infanticide, contraception, forced migration, ostracism, banishment, and exile. In fact, as Coser has recently pointed out with respect to the poor, there is no requirement that the community agree or be willing to make any provision at all for these residual members.

However, in that subset of procedures for dealing with residua which includes active steps toward them but permits them to remain members of the population, a seemingly paradoxical situation is bound to occur. Those who are residual to the Structure will have to be provided with some defined place within it. They will have to be placed into some category created especially for them, in order to bring them back within the system and to allow the system to deal with them. What is paradoxical is that the role to which they are assigned is that of the roleless. In a sense, being outside the Structure is a structural position.

The dilemma raised by this paradox runs as a recurrent thread throughout the theory and treatment of deviance. By creating a special category of those whose role it is to be outside the role structure, one creates the situation of ostracism without exile. Those persons who accept the requirement of the Theory do so at a certain cost, and only on the understanding that all others are also committed to the Theory and with the faith and belief that all persons can find their places within the Structure. The very existence, however, of a set of roles which indicates the failure of the Theory to provide places for all potential members will pose a special problem to the moral organization and integration of "ordinary" members.

THE REPUTATION OF RESIDUALS

In the approach to deviance which concerns itself with labeling, attention is focused less on the differences between persons who engage in deviant acts and persons who engage in normal acts, and more on the question of how society attaches the label "deviant" to a person or to an act. Although the problems of the residuum we deal with here are not formally identical with the ordinary definition of deviance, the same labeling phenomenon is important. In both cases, an important constraint on the action of most ordinary people in society is their Theory of how society works and the model of conduct based on that Theory. Commitment to the Theory and to carrying out the conduct specified in the model are important to them. They therefore have a stake in validating the Theory and, as a consequence, the appropriateness of the model.

As we have seen, residual persons who are allowed to remain within the boundaries of the system and who are therefore injected into specially created roles pose a problem to persons who have committed themselves to the Theory, since it becomes apparent that it is possible to operate within the system in some sense without being committed to that Theory and without following that model. The very presence within the system of persons who are not similarly constrained embarrasses and creates moral distress to those who are committed in the ordinary way. Therefore, the process of attributing membership, either in the ordinary system or in the outside residual system, is a matter of concern to most people—they take the labeling seriously and treat people who have different labels differently. Just as in the case of the classical deviant, the existence of the deviance raises, in the Durkheimian sense, a threat to the conforming behavior of all (in that case, law-abiding persons and in this case, role-committed persons). The corresponding reinforcement of moral sentiments occurs whenever those in the deviant or residual category become the object of special attention and special condemnation.

Note that up to this point we have said nothing whatsoever about the characteristics of those who are residual or about the factors which lead to their being outside the Structure. In fact, we have even begun to depart from the question of whether any persons are outside of the available set of roles, and have become more concerned with the Theory as ordinary people see it. The question is no longer structural, but a question of the maintenance of commitment of persons to an idealized image of the structure, an image which they hope bears some relation to the structure.

At this point the sociologist parts company with the participant in the system, as far as their common problem of understanding the system is concerned. While the ordinary person, committed to a Theory, has a stake in the Structure and in the definition of categories of response to the Structure, the sociologist is not similarly constrained in his studies. Since the scientist does not take the Theory as a source of models for his own conduct, but wants only to understand it, his commitment is merely tentative, accompanied by no overwhelming costs. To the extent, of course, that his involvement in science is occasioned by his search for rational models of conduct, and the system under study is his own, he will have a stake in the outcome of research. But the ideal of a value-free social science requires that he declare this stake beforehand, rather than importing it into the analysis. In general, the sociologist cannot justify accepting the Theory of the ordinary or respectable segments of the population as an adequate scientific account of the structure of institutionalized roles, let alone investing its moral content with scientific legitimacy. From this point on, the actor must pursue his own theoretical career, while the sociologist looks on with interest.

THE ALLOCATION OF CREDENTIALS

One of the products of any role system is a set of *credentials*, a set of recognition signals which persons who occupy institutional roles can produce in public situations to certify that they occupy them. From the point of view of a role set, the credentials are the most immediate and most superficial aspects of any role vis-à-vis "society at large." Credentials are important because access to certain kinds of treatment, the granting of claims against the world at large, are dependent on them. If a person can certify himself as a morally acceptable person, he can command from those around him degrees of deference or other kinds of rewards which constitute valuable items within the system. This aspect of the participation of a person in the social system we can think of generally as *citizenship*: what he has access to, and the obligations that are laid on him by virtue of his participation in the system itself. While there is a great variation in any society in the degree of participation to which members can lay claim, even among those members who have acceptable places in the theoretical structure, there is in general a threshold. Below this threshold, one is thought not to be a participant at all or to be a qualitatively lesser participant in the system. In order to achieve the broad category of citizenly participation, one must qualify as an ordinary member, although many, if not most, of the ordinary members will be far below the maximum level of participation in the system and access to its possibilities that some members enjoy.

An aspect of the credential which is of particular interest is the reputational one. People, in the ordinary course of social life, have rather direct contacts with particular others. At the same time individuals and, more importantly, categories of persons are known by reputation only to others in the system. (This is a form of "interaction" which is much closer to the ecological sort than to the socio-logical sort.) Public reputation can itself have real consequences both for those judging and for those being judged, even though there is no role contact between them in the ordinary sense (e.g., theories as to the nature of criminals or spies). Thus, in addition to the particular claims which any person in a role can make on those who occupy complementary roles, and in addition to the general claims a person in a role can make on the public at large by use of his credentials, role incumbents have an interest in and devote some energy toward preserving the good repute of their role. This activity is directed toward people they may never see and who may never have any contact with them in the performance of that role.

These remarks regarding credentials are particularly pertinent to the situation of residual persons assigned to the role of the roleless. In association with that role, they have the credentials of persons who have no credentials. Furthermore, they have the reputation, among persons who are at great social distance from them, of not fitting into the system, although the reputation and distance themselves prove that they *are* within the system.

If such a category, set of credentials, and reputation could be established for residual persons without any kind of moral connotation being attached to the distinction, we would be dealing with a system in which persons committed to the prevailing Theory would have to recognize its failure to provide the adequate model they relied on. By placing moral condemnation upon those persons who must resort to the residual category or upon whom the residual category can be imposed even when not sought, those committed to the ordinary system preserve their belief in its efficacy. They transfer responsibility for the discrep-ancy to the motivations and character of the people found within the residual category. They propose a new Theory to support and further develop the original Structure.

The new Theory states those who have no role in the structure must some-how be faulty, principally in lack of motivation, of moral strength, and the like. It affirms that people who are found in non-ordinary positions, having their lives ordered by extraordinary sets of practices, have defaulted on the system rather than being the victims of an inadequately articulated system. By concerning ourselves with what is necessary to support the commitment of ordinary people to an idealized image of the role structure, rather than with the role structure itself, we see that the existence of separate categories with different moral con-notation can support commitment to a Theory even when there is no observable difference between those things labeled morally acceptable and those placed in the residual, morally suspect category.

THE "WELFARE" LANGUAGE

The main concrete application of these general remarks will be to the field of welfare. In the areas of public discourse and of scholarly investigation, a large and complex set of practices has arisen about the way welfare is to be discussed. These practices reflect the growing importance of welfare in the public life of modern societies and the commitment of social scientists to including an ade-quate account of welfare in their discussions of those societies, as well as societies in general. In both areas, there has been a good deal of confusion and disagreement. In the public sphere, there is a multiplicity of publics and perspec-tives on welfare, corresponding to diverse interests and commitments. In the scientific sphere there have been attempts to give the study of welfare a firm conceptual basis for inclusion into the general schemata which organize socio-logy and other disciplines, while preserving the unique character which most observers detect in the ordinary-language category of "welfare." To a great extent, the difficulties of scientific definition rest on the open texture of the folk usage.

In the realm of ordinary discourse, we would expect a high degree of disagree-ment about welfare. We have constant evidence of dissension in values about welfare, but it appears in the very meanings and beliefs about it also. There are several lines of differentiation in a social system which might produce different understandings about welfare: Those who identify with the label."welfare" as initiators or partisans of particular activities or programs; those who apply the label to activities or organizations in which they find themselves engaged; those who have dealings with persons or organizations which they call welfare; those who are not directly related to any activity they consider welfare, but who define themselves as having a stake in such operations; those who see themselves as unrelated to activities they think of as welfare.

Moreover, with regard to any of these categories, definitions of the label may be self-generated or adopted from the usage of others. Thus, in addition to those who are involved in something they call welfare, the term has meanings to a host of differentiated publics, in favor of, opposed to, or indifferent to welfare. Communication of divergent viewpoints can produce a modicum of consensus, but can also produce anomalous and apparently contradictory notions of welfare in the minds of particular persons or groups.

Furthermore, the very meaning of welfare is itself an important ideological factor, with implications for value arguments. Therefore, interested parties will attempt to manipulate the public definition of welfare in ways which will aid their respective positions. This process will introduce a further element of confusion and disagreement.

Nevertheless, the term has a specific origin and a specific history of use, so that it is reasonable to expect some core of consensus about the objects which are or are not welfare among all the differentiated segments of the system. The very agitation to have the public adopt a particular view indicates some understanding that public opinion holds a different view.

A full analysis of folk usages of welfare would contain separate accounts of each important differentiated understanding, as well as accounts of broad levels of consensus where they could be found. One of these accounts, which is related in particular to the broadest consensus, would be of the understandings of the large public not directly related to activities they define as welfare. This public is the audience for the various notions of special pleaders, and it is their tacit acceptance of some of those notions which set many of the conditions of operation of those who are directly involved. In particular, it is the public definition which constitutes the reputation of those who are involved. In the anatomy of moral entrepreneurship, such audiences are neither moral crusaders nor rule enforcers, but merely "rule consumers." Further work on the social use of the welfare category should consider the operations of both crusaders and enforcers in this setting.

Welfare is a categorization of a residual, morally suspect form of career. People consider some careers and some forms of activity in the welfare category and thereby set them apart from activities and careers in the ordinary category. The basis of the distinction is a difference in the relation of the activity (as perceived by those doing the labeling) to some ideal Theory of the way the system ought to work, and the consequences of that relation for the commitment of ordinary people to that Theory.

Welfare as a moral category is most closely related to that aspect of the Theory which concerns the nature of rewards and the ways one can deserve to be rewarded. In modern societies, the major scene in which rewards are defined and distributed is the world of work. It is not the only one, though; kinship ties, gambles and investments, voluntary associations, and even the passive receipt of good fortune are contexts in which people can get rewards more or less respectably. In welfare, however, there is a perception that the Structure has not generated rewards for certain people. By the terms of the Theory, they have not deserved rewards, since deservedness is defined in terms of participation in the

Structure sufficient to generate rewards. (This undeservedness does not apply in cases where a malfunction of the Structure is seen as the cause of the lack of rewards, but only where the lack of rewards is seen as associated with normal functioning of the Structure. The possibility of malfunction can itself cause upset to ordinary, committed people, so that it may be difficult for people to get themselves defined by others as innocent victims of it.)

Welfare is provided to people who have not participated in the system in such a way as to generate rewards for themselves automatically. It carries the stigma of being undeserved, because it attracts attention to the fact that it is extraordinary and unassociated with the institutions which confer the legitimacy of deservedness. When the generic term "welfare" is used, it denotes programs so regarded (even if there is neither awareness nor approval of the accompanying stigma); a program with this characteristic in the public mind is likely to be lumped under welfare, and a program which is reputationally free of such attribution is likely to be excused from consideration under the rubric. This striking consistency in usage, I suggest, will appear even though few public definitions of welfare would include such criteria in so many words. Below, I will suggest that the folk theory of deservedness, rather than any offered structural criteria, accounts for the choice of subject matter for scientific students of welfare, as well as for the participants.

The welfare language is only one of a range of possible folk usages which can work to differentiate suspect from ordinary careers and events. It is quite different in specifics from, for example, the rhetoric of racial inferiority. The institution of welfare in a Western society includes distinctive norms about the proper attitude with which benefits are to be provided to persons, the attitude recipients should show for the benefits, the kinds of treatment permitted to or required of participants in welfare activities, the self-image to which participants are entitled, and the nature of the Theory current in such a society. This analysis based on morally suspect categories, therefore, cannot claim to account for all the features of what we commonly call welfare nor to apply to all examples of what some parties might call welfare.

But, we can already see an advantage to this way of conceiving of welfare. The same definition encompasses the conceptions of welfare held both by its most ardent supporters and by its severest critics. To both groups the welfare system is extraordinary, provided for persons outside the purview of ordinary structures. Both groups would prefer welfare to come to a speedy end in the case of any particular individual, type of individual, or group. If possible, both groups devoutly hope, the ordinary system should work for everybody.

In fact, many people who are most intimately concerned with welfare must be seen as using welfare not to support the validity of some current Theory, but as a demonstration of the weakness of the Theory and its need for change. But in so doing they perpetuate the difference of welfare recipients from ordinary people and the differences in how they are to be treated. Whether the differential treatment is punitive or sympathetic, it reinforces a definition which sets the world of welfare apart from normal expectations.

Whether the welfare label is applied to a population of users, a program of activities, an organization, or a set of issues, it immediately signals an area of special phenomena, outside the normal scope of business. As such it generates reputational disadvantages for everything so labeled, in the eyes of ordinary committed people. These disadvantages need not arouse high feeling or even criticism. The mere attribution of doubt to the moral character of the labeled persons and programs can have far-reaching policy consequences.

Among welfare programs, those which have been called "residual" seem more vulnerable to such effects than those called "universal." The residual program is one used in case the recipient cannot provide for himself; in the universal programs, basic levels of convenience are available to all members of the system, irrespective of perceived need (e.g., guaranteed annual income). Residual welfare makes possible the separation of populations of persons who do and who do not use the programs, thus bringing the stigma of welfare use directly onto some people. Universal welfare, because it is provided to all members of the population, cannot differentiate users from non-users. However, as long as it is labeled welfare, and thereby distinguished from every other avenue through which people receive goods and services, the act of using, if not the user as a total person, can be reputationally disadvantaged. Thus, stages of the typical career can be suspect (e.g., periods of "dependency," like youth and old age, which are not deemed "productive"); typical decisions can be devalued (bearing children, buying TV sets); particular scenes of daily life can be sources of embarrassment (dealing with officials, filling out information questionnaires). Thus the reputational and ideological components of the welfare label can persist even if there is no concrete segment of the population excluded totally from the Structure throughout their lives.

The historical development and institutional arrangement of residual and universal welfare activities give them a similar place in the minds of most laymen and social scientists. However, on inspection they seem quite distinct structurally and functionally. They are bound by the similar labels and attitudes directed to both. Yet in order for universal welfare to fully avoid the reputational disadvantages of residual welfare, it ought to be removed from a category differentiating it from ordinary activity. Over time, if the label is dropped or changes occur in its implications for differentiation, these disadvantages can disappear. In particular, if people with self-evident respectability on other grounds participate in activities labeled "welfare." the activities and the label may become neutralized for everyone.

If the welfare label has important reputational and policy consequences, as suggested above, then its application to any object of social attention is a significant and real change in its status. Therefore, particular persons and groups will have vested interests in attaching or witholding, attracting or avoiding the label.

If the label is disadvantageous, then "bad guys" deserve it and "good guys" should be spared it. Ultimately, the distribution of things labeled welfare may be irrational and arbitrary, if seen in the light of the Theory of which welfare is a residual category.

While the resulting scenes are of great interest to sociology, from the perspectives of social differentiation and the effects of ideology, for example, versions of social theory will arise which may deviate from an objective sociological account in a double sense: First, the original Theory which generates the residual category may be incorrect; second, the distribution of labels may be an imperfect application of the Theory. Thus, we can say not only that welfare operates as a label with moral overtones, but that this use calls into question its validity as a term in other senses. In particular, the folk usage of the term is a very dangerous foundation for any project of scientific analysis, especially one that seeks a high level of generality.

In the case of the welfare language used by the public, much of the confusion and diversity can be attributed not to a multiplicity of contending versions, but to the divergence of actual practice from any public model in current use. Although the label is meaningful only with reference to some Theory, the application of labels is arbitrary with respect to any available Theory. In order to indicate the nature of the arbitrariness, I will consider some available public models of welfare and compare them with the actual collection of things usually labeled as "welfare" in modern societies.

Both the models I will propose and the assertions about what is and what is not welfare are derived from the remarks of people involved in the area of welfare either as practitioners, as trainers, as scholars, as policy planners, or as public commentators. These remarks come from textbooks in social welfare, interviews and public documents. They originate in several areas, mainly the Scandinavian countries and the United States, including Puerto Rico. These remarks were not about the personal views of the sources, but about their perceptions of common understandings in their respective societies. While legitimate objections can be raised about the possible bias of this segment of the population or biases in the sample of informants I interviewed or whose writings I surveyed, I believe my assertions will have considerable face validity. Even when exception is taken to a specific example, I think most knowledgeable students of welfare will be able to furnish comparable examples from their own experience and thereby serve as additional informants themselves.

Insofar as welfare is publicly seen as anything but an arbitrary grouping of activities and rules, without implications for any Theory, there is a public model of welfare as a distinct type of object on some objective basis. There are several possible forms of objective basis which I will discuss individually. Sometimes several of these models will be invoked simultaneously to form a more complex model. However, the remarks relevant to the individual models should also apply to mixed types in which they are included. The consideration of these models is not meant to exclude the existence or relevance of other appropriate models; I expect the same kinds of comments made here to be appropriate in the case of such other models.

Welfare is commonly understood under one of the following versions.

(1) Welfare is distinguished from other social activities, by virtue of the auspices under which it is carried out. It is considered to be one way people can receive benefits, support, help, or rewards, but it is distinct from the other ways in that these benefits are received from particular kinds of sources. The common feature is not easy to specify but among the suggested ones are formality, impersonality, or the absence of particularism; wide social or societal sponsorship; institutional and automatic mechanisms, as opposed to ad hoc programs or those based on good will. The most familiar version of this model specifies that welfare occurs under public auspices, the government or the state. This version is not satisfactory for most purposes, however, since the line between public and non-public areas is itself a difficult and ambiguous matter of folk usage. In fact, many programs of a quasi-public, pseudo-public, or would-be-public character are commonly included in the welfare category. As an example of the difficulties of definition, consider that Medicare and Old Age and Survivors Insurance—government programs—are almost universally considered welfare programs. The Danish system of health insurance under government-coordinated insurance societies is also firmly in the category. Yet similar health insurance schemes in the United States, such as Blue Cross or the Kaiser Plan in California, are in a category about which there is no consensus. Yet ordinary personal insurance programs of mutual insurance companies, such as life insurance or accidental death and dismemberment policies, are clearly out of consideration.

A far more serious form of ambiguity, however, lies in the differentiation of obviously public welfare programs from other kinds of public programs. This is an area where the welfare label has serious reputational consequences, because public programs are subject to influences through the political process. While governments are active in providing rewards to a variety of recipients under a wide variety of rationales, most of these are clearly unrelated to the collection of programs actually called welfare. The salaries of Congressmen, for example, are not considered a welfare benefit, except in jest. Wages, salaries, and payments for services rendered ought to be clearly excluded (except, perhaps, in the case of "make-work" public works projects). But consider the wide range of subsidies, allowances, price supports, tax credits, exemptions, advantageous financial opportunities, and so on through which governments distribute money, to say nothing of distribution of goods, services, and information. Without doubt, the criteria necessary to differentiate welfare out of this complex system must be contained in another model, if they can be specified at all. For the present, note that only unusual uses of the welfare language would apply to protective tariffs, farm price supports, or tax exemptions, while government programs in employment of lower-class people are characteristically included, even when no direct support payments are made. I suggest that this sort of anomaly will not be solvable under any model of welfare in public use.

(2) Another model, based on the occasion for welfare, is supposed to include programs which are activated to deal with particular situations. These situations are conceived either as crises in the normal, adequate conduct of life or as needs whose fulfillment would constitute an acceptable life. The former is heard as the notion that welfare deals with people who are "in trouble," "have problems," or "need help." The latter appears as the more general and sophisticated notions that welfare must operate to ensure that all members of the system enjoy minimum levels or optimum levels of living in various fields, which vary by time and place and are subject to considerable pressure and lobbying by interested parties.

Such a criterion should immediately draw our attention to the processes of defining needs and crises and of attributing a state of need or crisis in any particular case. These processes, however, may be invoked where there is in fact no occasion, or may fail to be invoked where there is (by the prevailing definition of need or crisis). There are likely to be many contending public views on these questions. Any way of noticing and responding to needs or crises which require help should lead us to a well-developed folk theory of necessity and possibility in social life and of the obligations of those who are "more fortunate." Note that the public need not accept the claim of need, but must believe only that the claim is the basis of a social response for that response to be considered welfare.

This view of welfare is persuasive until we consider that not every need or crisis will be called welfare. Only some of the cases will be so treated; according to this analysis, these will usually be the cases where an implicit characterization of the recipient or the means of giving is attached, specifically a stigma. There may be other stigmatized institutions of giving help, such as the treatment of mental illness or the "reform" of delinquents (if these are not included in the public definition of welfare). Yet many forms of aid given in cases of need are not stigmatized and are not labeled welfare. A good example is the institution of procedural due process in law. Due process is considered an elementary component of fair play and justice. The terminology of "giving" is rarely connected with it, except when, as in recent Supreme Court decisions, the primary beneficiaries are populations which are already stigmatized on other grounds. In general, the institutions which invoke aid for the needs and crises of respectable populations are far less likely to be called welfare than those dealing with typical welfare populations. Thus, the uses of terms like "need" and "crisis" in connection with welfare are far more restricted than the ordinary meaning of those terms. It is only certain kinds of needs and crises that bring the welfare language into play—those which pose a threat to the Theory of rewards in a modern society and which must be reputationally devalued. Many proponents of wider welfare programs are anxious to have welfare services viewed as a right of citizenship in society. Yet the welfare and need language itself seems to be associated with cases where ordinary people do not tacitly accept those rights. To call a program "welfare" is to suggest that it is not quite a right.

(3) Another version of welfare is more macroscopic. It focuses on welfare as an allocation of the scarce resources available in society, an allocation under special conditions. Two main variants of this version specify the nature of the special conditions. In the first, the allocation does not have productive results; that is, it does not result in the creation of value. In the second variant, the allocation is made in spite of its not being earned. It is apparent that some notion of distributive justice underlies a Theory which characterizes allocations of resources in terms of the value of the outcome or the deservingness of the recipient. Note that such allocations are not necessarily condemned on these grounds. Those who propose them may recognize the social fact that they have not been earned, in the popular view; they may support them in spite of it, for instance, on grounds of humanitarianism.

These criteria seem quite similar to the analysis of welfare I have already offered. The folk notions about productivity and deservedness are both aspects of the Theory in a modern society which deal with rewards and legitimate ways of getting them. The allocation of resources, which results in rewards to recipients, is made through structural amendments to the Structure. However, there is an important difference. Questions of productivity and deservedness are raised in the case of welfare allocations and are answered in the negative. Yet in the case of most other allocations, these questions are not even raised in the public mind. If one receives rewards, there is *prima facie* assumption that they have been obtained legitimately, for ordinary, respectable people. Yet if the criteria of productivity and deservedness were applied to all recipients of rewards, many uses would be considered wasteful and uneconomic, as in the case of drug addicts or drivers who have accidents; and many rewards would be considered unearned, such as gambling proceeds or money sponged from friends and relatives. In this area, once the question is raised, many different ideas would emerge as to who gets what he should not and who spends as he should not.

Moreover, there are many people who argue that welfare benefits are productive, because increased demand supports the general economy, or that they are deserved through past or future service to society. In general, it would be hard to show that recipients of so-called welfare benefits are actually in a more equivocal position regarding productivity and deservedness than other members of the system. What distinguishes welfare recipients from the others is not the facts asserted by this public model, but the questions that are raised in regard to them in the first place. I suggest that the best indication of whether such questions will be raised is whether rewards are provided in such a way as to cause a public scandal to the Structure.

Finally, the list of activites classified as welfare usually includes a number of programs based on insurance principles, which are regarded as fully legitimate means of receiving rewards in other spheres of social life. If Old Age and Survivors Insurance is considered welfare, it cannot be by any official theory of productivity or deservedness, but only by an implicit moral assessment of the program.

(4) A last, very interesting, version of welfare is one in which the public model follows the definitions of those officials and planners who are regarded as the proprietors of the welfare system. Since welfare is a term proposed and used by a somewhat self-conscious group who formulate and support programs, it may be seen as an established movement, whose own notions of what welfare is are accepted in some form by outsiders. A welfare program is thus one which is carried out under the management of welfare professionals, by their own definitions. This is very close to a situation in which welfare would have no public meaning aside from the particular list of diverse activities so named by their promulgators. This situation does not exist, though, as indicated by the difficulties which professionals committed to a welfare ideology experience in gaining public acceptance of the meaning they want for the concept. The resistance to extension is not merely a product of inertia. Whenever the scope of the concept is broadened to include areas which have been respectable parts of ordinary social life, there is resistance from the professionals and participants in those areas whose reputations would be penalized under the welfare label.

A thread runs through the foregoing comments which indicates how other possible versions of welfare would be addressed. Any version can be compared with the public classifications of activities and the resulting moral attributions which are supposed to be derived from that version. Often the process of application of a Theory to specific cases will result in some cases being overlooked and thus spared a pejorative label, while some cases which are already morally suspect will have an additional label applied, even though the Theory does not logically include them. There is good reason to suspect that public versions will be hard to reconcile with the differential labeling of actual cases, as indicated by the widespread dissatisfaction with definitions of welfare which is apparent in the literature of scholars and policy writers. Yet, in spite of this uneasiness about the state of conceptualization in the field of welfare studies, there is a rather good mutual understanding about the basic subject matter of the field. This is due, I suggest, to the common folk judgments which motivate most investigators. Rather than the perception of a common structural feature in welfare, this seems to be based on the common moral attributions made by ordinary people in defense of the Theories which underlie their social commitments.

These remarks on the public usage of the term welfare raise questions about its place in scientific usage. The phenomena in Western societies which are called welfare play an important part in those societies; thus, science must deal with it in the analysis of such societies. What status shall welfare have in the conceptual development of sociological analysis? Many students have implicitly or explicitly treated it as a general type of differentiated structure. I suggest, on the basis of the foregoing analysis, that lack of progress in the conceptualization of welfare is due to the acceptance by scientists of the folk notion of welfare as a special type of activity, leading to a lumping and confusion of the many diverse but sociologically legitimate questions posed by welfare. It is axiomatic that a folk theory has no validity as a scientific theory, per se; thus, we are not justified in importing any folk theory into a set of scientific criteria without independent scientific reasons. By reducing the preferred definitions of welfare to the level of folk theory, I do not mean to denigrate the study of welfare, but only to place it in the perspective of a folk theory which provides material for sociology, rather than conceptual structures.

By contrast with some other fields of social science investigation (family, religion), welfare studies have always been closely connected with policy issues; there have been contact and overlapping between students of welfare and welfare planners and administrators. The perspective of the stranger which has sometimes led to fruitful conceptualizations, based on ethnography and comparative study, has been largely absent in the field of welfare. Features which are offered as general characteristics of welfare might appear as ethnocentric and situation-specific if examined in such a light. While such a comparative test is not available, it is possible to achieve a similar result by treating any offered concept strictly at face value, deliberately refusing to make use of our implicit understanding of the societies most familiar to us. To the extent this is possible, we may inhibit ethnocentrism and judge the conceptual fertility of the definition.

"Welfare," as used recently by scholars like Zald and Wilensky, was not coined by scientists to denote a phenomenon observed in societies. Nor was it co-opted from lay discourse to apply to something under independent study by social scientists. Its origin is squarely in the world of policy planning, social participation, and public definition. Only afterward have scientists sought to generalize the term into a useful scientific one. Furthermore, "welfare" in its original uses derived from the situations and problems of specific societies; its meanings were built up in the context of the institutional structure of specific societies and spread across societies, most often by a conscious borrowing. It immediately acquired, in addition to its usage in planning circles, political and ideological importance to many groups and interests in those societies.

The scientists trying to abstract general features from the circumstances of this specific historical movement and activity in specific societies have understandably been constrained by two independent demands: the first for rigor, precision, and general applicability of technical terms; and the second for fruitfulness in the study of actual events which have caught the attention of observers. The usual result of this duality of demands has been a procedure of determining a concrete area of study and afterward specifying a set of concepts which will embrace that area. That is, scientists have not formulated a welfare concept and then discovered interesting examples of it in modern societies (which would be the expected, textbook, sequence of theory-building).

Instead, the process is reversed, and the choice of an area of study has preceded the process of definition which should indicate why that area is interesting to study. In short, conceptualization in this field runs the risk of being not the motivation, but the rationalization, of scientific interest in welfare. I propose that at this point students of welfare devote less attention to trying to specify the structural features of welfare directly accessible to the observer and spend more time investigating the definitions of the situation by participants which create such social objects as "welfare," for the definitions we have tried to build until now have largely been conceptually inelegant and, even more alarming, have not been an indicator of what students have been preoccupied with under the term "welfare." Furthermore, they implicitly require an account of the actors' definitions, although such an account is rarely forthcoming.

"WELFARE DEPENDENCY"

All these remarks are especially pertinent to the question, and in most minds the serious social problem, of welfare dependency. The term is not just a static assertion of the existence of different types of activity or of different types of persons, but a theory, a processual theory at that, of the development of certain kinds of conduct and certain separations within society, with causes and effects, preconditions, and implications built in. The theory not only distinguishes people who use welfare from others who do not, or activities which are welfare activities from others which are not, but also states that welfare tends to have certain effects upon persons who use it and that they can enter upon distinct sorts of careers under the protection of and using the resources of so-called welfare institutions. The theory which considers welfare dependency a problem envisages an ideal welfare career in which the welfare user experiences the need of special facilities, goes into a residual welfare institution to receive them, orients himself to a quick return into the ordinary activities specified in the Structure, and in fact leaves the aegis of the welfare world as quickly as he can.

By contrast with this ideal welfare career, those who see a problem see prolonged use of residual welfare facilities, turning them ultimately from a stopgap or a temporary expedient resorted to in a time of crisis into an ordinary institutionalized, ongoing, and continuous facility. The user depends upon welfare and he organizes a career indefinitely programmed into the future around it. The term "welfare dependency" indicates that persons become dependent upon the welfare system rather than using it in a relatively autonomous way and giving it up when it no longer serves any specific, immediate purpose. The term indicates that prolonged use of the welfare system is in some sense pathological and invites us to compare such use with other instances of dependency: the neurotic mama's-boy who refuses to grow up and leave home, or the neurotic patient who resists leaving psychoanalysis. It defines the welfare dependent as psychologically impaired, motivationally impoverished, and morally irresponsible.

All these notions depend upon the belief that things defined as welfare in nature (welfare institutions, welfare activities, and the rewards coming from the welfare system) are morally suspect, not part of what an ordinary man ought to think himself entitled to, or objectively accessible. Here we may note that what is considered a psychological problem, or even a problem of group organization, ceases to have that character. If the dependency itself is a matter of the definition of the *moral acceptability* of the career rather than of the *character* of the career, what is in question here is not whether the career considered is adult as opposed to infantile, authoritarian as opposed to democratic or any such set of issues applying to styles of conduct or levels of mental organization, but rather that certain careers are acceptable and expected in the Structure and other kinds of careers are not tolerated and in fact are suspected of being damaging and demoralizing.

This immediately leads us to recast our thinking about so-called welfare dependency as a process. If a welfare career is a career like any ordinary career, it becomes subject to the same theoretical and empirical interest that ordinary careers elicit from us. In other words, the study of welfare dependency becomes another interesting dimension of the sociology of occupations. Two kinds of questions emerge as a result.

First, how does it happen that the welfare career is evaluated and assigned to its particular category? Why is it called a welfare career as opposed to another kind of career? This is the kind of question that can be answered along much the same lines as the general discussion of welfare throughout this paper. Secondly, we can ask: Given that a definition of welfare exists as a morally suspect category of activity, including definitions of morally suspect types of persons, how do persons enter the career line? What extra steps must be considered in the typical career line because the person we consider enters a career which is subject to moral opprobrium, as opposed to an ordinary career permitted by the Structure? The theory held by the ordinary members of the system and by many social-problems-oriented sociologists points to certain peculiar characteristics of persons who react in an atypical way to the existence of the moral opprobrium. By contrast with most ordinary people, here is a set of persons inclined to enter a career either out of spite, since it is morally condemned, or as a gesture of indifference to the making of moral judgments on the part of the ordinary members of society. Either of these reasons is morally deficient from the point of the view of the Theory.

An entirely different, and more characteristically sociological, approach looks at persons who begin welfare careers as being insulated in some way or another from the force of the moral judgment which falls upon welfare activities. In the fields of deviance and criminology, for instance, such notions as differential association, opportunity structure, and the formation of delinquent subcultures, are all oriented toward this type of explanation of persons involved in careers the ordinary citizen condemns. To the extent that potential welfare careerists find themselves fully exposed to a Theory under which the welfare career is placed in a morally suspect category, the potentiality should not become actuality. In particular, in societies characterized by the prevalence of mass media, we would expect that the only places, other things being equal, that a welfare career could continue to be a likely line of development for persons, would be in isolated areas, or among groups which have clearly differentiated subcultures and are embedded within the community or society at large, but whose difference is recognized and attested to by symbols and signals both superficial and deep. In the extreme case such systems with variant cultures are surrounded by the larger system rather than embedded within it in any structural sense.

However, to the extent that we find "welfare dependency" a major problem with strategic sectors of the most modern and the most advanced, that is to say the most urbanized and industrialized, sectors of the system, some previously unmentioned and unconsidered factors must be at work to create an isolation from the moral judgment of what we have been calling society at large. The existence as a temporary phenomenon of such enclaves or variant culture as ethnic neighborhoods within cities would not give rise to such a concern over the structural problem of dependency associated with the welfare system, since it would seem to bring about its own termination after an appropriate interval (which comprises the transition from the subculture into full acceptance of dominant culture). To the extent that we see welfare dependency as an outgoing, increasingly serious, and increasingly magnified problem, which the dominant culture must take account of, it must be as a result of conditions which are built into the dominant culture itself. Welfare dependency in isolated rural pockets of a society is expectable and although it may trouble some, its conclusion can be foreseen in changes brought about by migration, industrialization, and the like. If large-scale dependency as a problem is found in the heart of urban and industrialized masses, then the structural arrangements which characterize the urban industrial society itself must contain the elements which give rise to the situation.

The single most interesting and most blatant arrangement which is likely to produce a subcultural isolation capable of reinforcing welfare dependency, in the sense of making it possible for people to enter welfare careers without feeling a moral burden in doing so, is found in the urban ghetto, or in neighborhoods bounded by impermeable social rules based typically on some particularistic criterion. We must look to the segregated ghetto as the primary mechanism by which persons who could consider welfare careers could find themselves mutually reinforcing one another and mutually legitimating the pursuit of such a career while at the same time inhibiting awareness of the moral judgment of the ordinary members. To some extent, this tendency for the dominant system to structure and permit the occurence of ghettos can be laid at the door of the labeling process once again, since part of the social distance and of the improbability of the moral judgments of dominant culture reaching those who become sub-culturally organized in ghettos is due to the withdrawal of ordinary people from contact with the welfare-prone. Thereby are established all the necessary conditions for a self-fulfilling prophecy.

It is important to keep in mind with respect to these processes that the likelihood of welfare careers arising is directly proportional to the rise within ghetto areas of the most desirable features of social organization. In the case of the welfare dependent, or the welfare careerist, there is a special poignancy to the suggestion. Considering the characteristics ordinarily ascribed to situations in which welfare is an appropriate and relatively accessible instrumentality, those conditions which foster welfare dependency represent, in some sense, the best and healthiest state of both the individual and his group, and are characteristically thought to be most lacking in the poor souls who need and use welfare: sense of community, common value system, mutual reinforcement, strong reference groups, and a clear and unambiguous notion of feasible conduct in society. But in those conditions where the most feared and inimical effects of the urban ghetto exist, we will find the least possibility of a stable and orderly welfare career arising. The stable welfare career requires the mutual reinforcement and legitimacy of one's colleagues, and the possibility of planning, order, and predictability in social circumstances. As in every other career, those who operate best in the welfare system are those who are least plagued by role strains or personality difficulties, those who are most outgoing, those with the most social contacts, those who represent the healthiest social persons rather than the most disorganized. Here again is a situation in which the dominant society defines what from their point of view are the worst effects of the ghetto as proceeding from disorganization. In fact, they proceed from quite the opposite. Rather than seeing the high welfare-use area as one in which great difficulties ought to be found, one can, if he wishes, be encouraged by the fact that high welfare use is as indicative as high activity of other kinds is in other neighborhoods of growing social activism and the ability to control one's social environment to one's own satisfaction and fulfillment of one's own ends. These are exactly the qualities most prized in advanced industrial societies, the qualities that tend to be rewarded by social arrangements in all areas and at all levels in advanced industrial societies, if not in all societies.

CONCLUSION

An attempt has been made in this paper to take an approach to welfare which is strictly neutral from the point of view of the elements of society under study and in which welfare is said to occur. In pursuit of this examination of welfare, it has been my aim to consider whether welfare exists as a legitimate category of sociological investigation at all. I conclude that it requires a refocusing of interest to avoid dependence on unvalidated folk theories. Welfare is an example of the labeling procedure which is generally interesting as a way of resolving the possible incongruities between an idealized Structure and the model of conduct which it implies, on the one hand, and the existence of a population contained within a territory to to which the Structure is supposed to apply and for which it is supposed to be appropriate, on the other. Seen in this perspective, welfare activities on the part of agencies and institutions of the society, welfare careers, and so on are in no structural way differentiable from agencies, institutions, careers, and uses in the non-welfare areas of the society. The distinction is one of labels and the moral judgments associated with the labels once applied by those persons for whom the labels are salient. The labeling process, by those for whom it is salient, creates the conditions which fulfill their worst fears. It is further suggested that although the results bear out the worst fears of such persons, the employed theory and the employed account of what states of society give rise to those results is in fact backwards and that is a high level of organization rather than disorganization that gives rise to the most morally opprobrious results. To the extent that a problem exists with regard to welfare, it can be seen more clearly as a problem of the allocation of moral approbation to different categories of activities and persons rather than as a problem of the failure of some persons or of the iniquity of some activities. It is to be hoped that future sociological treatment of welfare will not take for granted the position of particular elements within the population, and will not align itself with the needs for moral reassurance of those persons within the system that have been most in contact with and have given the greatest commitment to some idealized, characteristically official theory and model of conduct.

SELECTED BIBLIOGRAPHY

Abrams, Charles. *Man's Struggle for Shelter in an Urbanizing World.* Cambridge, Mass.: M.I.T. Press, 1964.

Ad Hoc Committee on Advocacy. "Social Worker as Advocate: Champion of Social Victims," *Social Work* (April 1969), 16-23.

Anderson, C. L. "Preliminary Study of Generational Economic Dependency," *Social Forces,* 45(June 1967), 516-520.

Anderson, M. "The Sophistry that Made Urban Renewal Possible," *Law and Contemporary Problems,* 30 (Winter 1965), 199-211.

Blau, Peter. "Orientation Towards Clients in a Public Welfare Agency," *Administrative Science Quarterly,* 3 (December 1960), 341-361.

Bowen, D. R., et al. "Deprivation, Mobility, and Orientation Toward Protest of the Urban Poor," *American Behavioral Scientist,* 11 (March 1968), 20-24.

Brager, George. "Organizing the Unaffiliated in a Low-Income Area," *Social Work,* 3 (April 1963), 34-40.

Brager, George. "Advocacy and Political Behavior," *Social Work,* 13 (April 1968), 5-15.

Brager, George, and Purcell, Francis (eds.). *Community Action Versus Poverty: Readings from the Mobilization Experience.* New Haven, Conn.: College and University Press, 1967.

Brehm, C. T., and Savino, T. R. "Demand for General Assistance Payments," *American Economic Review,* 54 (December 1964), 1002-1018.

Briggs, Asa. "Welfare State in Historical Perspective," *European Journal of Sociology,* 2 (1968), 221-258.

Burgess, Elaine. "Poverty and Dependency: Some Selected Characteristics," *Journal of Social Issues*, 21 (January 1965), 79-97.

Burns, Eveline. "Where Welfare Falls Short," *The Public Interest*, 1 (Fall 1965), 82-95.

Caplowitz, David. *The Poor Pay More: Consumer Practices of Low Income Families.* New York: Free Press, 1967.

Cloward, Richard, and Epstein, Irwin. "Private Social Welfare's Disengagement from the Poor: The Case of the Family Adjustment Agencies," *Proceedings of Annual Social Work Day Institute,* School of Social Welfare: State University of New York at Buffalo, May 1965.

Cohen, Albert K., and Hodges, Harold. "Characteristics of the Lower Blue-Collar Class," *Social Problems*, 10 (Spring 1963), 303-334.

Cohen, Nathan E. *Social Work in the American Tradition.* New York: Dryden, 1968.

Coser, Lewis, "The Sociology of Poverty," *Social Problems*, 13 (Fall 1965), 140-148.

Donovan, John C. *The Politics of Poverty.* New York: Western, 1967.

Ferman, Louis A., et al. (eds.). *Poverty in America.* Ann Arbor: University of Michigan Press, 1965.

Frieden, Bernard. *The Future of Old Neighborhoods: Rebuilding for a Changing Population.* Cambridge, Mass.: M.I.T. Press, 1964.

Frieden, Bernard. *Urban Planning and Social Policy.* New York: Basic Books, 1968.

Gans, Herbert. *The Urban Villagers.* New York: Free Press, 1962.

Gans, Herbert. *People and Plans.* New York: Basic Books, 1968.

Gilbert, G. E. "Policymaking in Public Welfare: the 1962 Amendments," *Political Science Quarterly*, 81 (June 1966), 196-224.

Glazer, Nathan, "A New Look at Social Welfare," *New Society*, 58 (November 7, 1968).

Glazer, Nona, and Creedon, Carol (eds.). *Children and Poverty.* Chicago: Rand McNally, 1968.

Gordon, Margaret S. (ed.). *Poverty in America.* San Francisco: Chandler, 1965.

Gordon, M. "Social Security and Welfare: Dynamic Stagnation," *Public Administration Review*, 27 (March 1967), 87-90.

Green, G. D. "The Professional Social Worker in the Bureaucracy," *Social Service Review*, 40 (March 1966), 71-83.

Haber, Alan. "The American Underclass," *Poverty and Human Resources Abstracts*, 2 (May-June 1967), 5-19.

Harrington, Michael. *The Other America.* New York: Penguin, 1962.

Hoshino, G. "Simplification of the Means Test and Its Consequences," *Social Service Review*, 41 (September 1967), 237-249.

Howard, Donald S. *Social Welfare: Values, Means, and Ends.* New York: Random House, 1969.

Irelan, Lola M., and Besner, Arthur. "Low Income Outlook on Life," *Welfare in Review*, 3 (September 1965), 13-19.

Jeffers, Camille. *Living Poor.* Ann Arbor: Ann Arbor Publishing, 1967.

Kahn, Gerald, and Perkins, Ellen. "Families Receiving A.F.D.C.: What Do They Have To Live On?" *Welfare in Review*, 2 (October 1964), 7-15.

Kaplan, S. S., and Delbecq, A. "Perceived Hindrance to Social Change in a Poverty Program," *Sociology and Social Research*, 52 (January 1968), 269-278.

Kellner, J., and Tadros, C. D. "Changes in Society and in the Professions—Issues in the Emergence of Professional Social Work," *Social Service Review*, 41 (March 1967), 44-54.

Kolack, Shirley. "Study of Status Inconsistency Among Social Work Professionals," *Social Problems*, 15 (Winter 1968), 365-376.

Law and Contemporary Problems, "Housing Perspective and Problems," 32 (Spring 1967), 191-370.

Law and Contemporary Problems, "Housing—The Federal Role." 32 (Summer 1967), 375-560.

Leacock, E. "Distortions of Working Class Reality in American Social Science," *Science and Society*, 31 (Winter 1967), 1-21; reply by Lee Rainwater, 32 (Winter 1968), 80-88.

LeBeaux, C. "Life on A.D.C.: Budget of Despair," *New University Thought*, 3 (1963), 26-35.

Liebow, Eliot. *Tally's Corner*. Boston: Little, Brown, 1967.

Lowe, Jeanne. *Cities in a Race with Time: Progress and Poverty in America's Renewing Cities*. New York: Random House, 1967.

Maas, Henry (ed.). *Five Fields of Social Service*. New York: National Association of Social Workers, 1964.

Marris, Peter, and Rein, Martin. *The Dilemmas of Social Reform*. New York: Atherton, 1967.

Marshall, Thomas H. *Class, Citizenship, and Social Development*. New York: Doubleday (Anchor), 1965.

Mayer, Martin. "The Idea of Justice and the Poor," *The Public Interest*, 8 (Summer 1967), 96-115.

Meissner, Hanna (ed.). *Poverty in the Affluent Society*. New York: Harper & Row, 1966.

Miller, Herman P. *Rich Man, Poor Man*. New York: New American Library, 1965.

Miller, S. M., and Rein, Martin. "Inequality and Policy." In Howard Becker (ed.), *Social Problems*. New York: Wiley, 1966, pp. 426-516.

Miller S. M., and Reissman, Frank. *Social Class and Social Policy*. New York: Basic Books, 1968.

Mooney, J. D. "Urban Poverty and Labor Force Participation," *American Economic Review*, 57 (March 1967), 104-119.

Moynihan, Daniel P. "The Professionalization of Reform," *The Public Interest*, 1 (Fall 1965), 6-16.

Moynihan, Daniel P. "The Crisis in Welfare." *The Public Interest*, 10 (Winter 1968), 3-29.

Moynihan, Daniel P. *Maximum Feasible Misunderstanding*. New York: Free Press, 1969.

Mugge, Robert H. "Aid to Families With Dependent Children: Initial Findings of the 1961 Report of the Characteristics of the Recipients," *Social Security Bulletin*, 26 (March 1965), 3-15.

Pauley, R. M. "Public Welfare Agency of the Future," *Social Casework*, 47 (May 1966), 286-292.

Rainwater, Lee. *And the Poor Get Children*. Chicago: Quadrangle, 1960.

Rainwater, Lee, and Yancey, William. *The Moynihan Report and the Politics of Controversy*. Cambridge, Mass.: M.I.T. Press, 1967.

Riessman, Frank, et al. *The Mental Health of the Poor*. New York: Free Press, 1964.

Rimlinger, G. V. "Welfare Policy and Educational Development: A Comparative Historical Perspective," *Journal of Economic History*, 26 (December 1966), 566-576.

Roach, Jack L., and Gursslin, O. R. "An Evaluation of the Concept Culture of Poverty," *Social Forces*, 45, (March 1967), 383-392.

Rodgers, Barbara, and Dixon, Julia. *Portrait of Social Work: A Study of Social Sciences in a Northern Town*. New York: Oxford, 1960.

Ross, Arthur (ed.). *Employment, Race, and Poverty*. New York: Harcourt Brace Jovanovich, 1967.

Schlesinger, Benjamin. *Poverty in Canada and the United States*. Toronto: University of Toronto Press, 1966.

Schneiderman, Leonard. "Value Orientation Preferences of Chronic Relief Recipients," *Social Work*, 9 (July 1964), 13-18.

Schorr, Alvin. "The Non-Culture of Poverty," *American Journal of Orthopsychiatry*, 34 (October 1964), 907-912.

Schorr, Alvin. *Slums and Social Insecurity*. Washington, D.C.: U.S. Government Printing Office, 1964.

Schorr, Alvin. *Poor Kids.* New York: Basic Books, 1966.

Schorr, Alvin. "Against a Negative Income Tax." *The Public Interest,* 5 (Fall 1966), 110-117.

Schorr, Alvin. *Explorations in Social Policy.* New York: Basic Books, 1968.

Schwartz, Jerome, and Chernin, Milton. "Participation of Recipients in Public Welfare Planning and Administration," *Social Service Review,* 41 (March 1967), 10-22.

Scott, R. A. "Selection of Clients by the Social Welfare Agencies: The Case of the Blind," *Social Problems,* 14 (Winter 1967), 248-257.

Shannon, Lyle W. "The Public's Perception of Social Welfare Agencies and Organizations in an Industrial Community," *Journal of Negro Education,* 32 (Summer 1963), 276-285.

Sharkansky, I. "Government Expenditures and Public Services in the American States," *American Political Science Review,* 61 (December 1967), 1066-1071.

Simmel, Georg. "The Poor," *Social Problems,* 13 (Fall 1965), 140-148.

Smelser, Neil J. and Lipset, Seymour Martin. *Social Structure and Social Mobility in Economic Growth.* Chicago: Aldine, 1966.

Steiner, Gilbert. *Social Insecurity: The Politics of Welfare.* Chicago: Rand-McNally, 1966.

Street, D. "Educators and Social Workers: Sibling Rivalry in the Inner City," *Social Service Review,* 41 (June 1967), 152-156.

Titmuss, Richard. *Essays in the Welfare State,* 2nd ed. London: Allen & Unwin, 1963.

Tobin, James. "The Case for an Income Guarantee," *The Public Interest,* 4 (Summer 1966).

Tobin, James. "Children's Allowances," *New Republic* (November 26, 1967), 16-18.

U.S. Riot Commission. *Report of the National Advisory Commission on Civil Disorders* (Kerner Commission Report). New York: Bantam, 1968.

Vadakin, James C. *Children, Poverty, and Family Allowances.* New York: Basic Books, 1968.

Vadakin, James C. "A Critique of the Guaranteed Annual Income," *The Public Interest,* 11 (Spring 1968), 53-66.

Waxman, Chaim (ed.). *Poverty: Power and Politics.* New York: Grosset & Dunlap, 1968.

Wilensky, Harold, and LeBeaux, Charles. *Industrial Society and Social Welfare.* New York: Free Press, 1965.

Will, Robert E., and Vatter, Harold (eds.). *Poverty in Affluence.* New York: Harcourt Brace Jovanovich, 1965.

Wilson, James Q. "The Bureaucracy Problem," *The Public Interest* 6 (Winter 1967), 3-9.

Zald, Mayer (ed.). *Social Welfare Institutions.* New York: Wiley, 1965.

Zander, Alvin, Cohen, Arthur, and Stotland, Ezra. *Role Relations in the Mental Health Professions.* Ann Arbor: University of Michigan Institute of Social Research, 1957.